BIZARRISM

VOLUME ONE

Also by Chris Mikul from Headpress

Bizarrism (1999)
The Eccentropedia
Bizarrism Vol 2 (coming 2017)

CONTENTS

3

INTRODUCTION

 was sitting in a lounge room at a party, some time in the early 1980s, getting nicely pissed. Reaching into the bookcase behind me I pulled out a volume at random and looked at the cover. It was called *The Strange Voyage of Donald Crowhurst*, but there was no writing on the dust jacket to indicate what the book was about.

Now at this time, I should explain, I was attempting to become a writer of short stories. In composing my little bits of fiction I found myself describing events which had supposedly really happened to someone, somewhere, at some time. Yet I knew that the conventions of fiction were causing me to shape my material constantly, to give it thematic unity and structure — a beginning, middle and an end, to throw in symbolism at every turn and eliminate the randomness which characterises real life.

I knew, of course, that the opposite was also true — that writers of non-fiction often use fictional narrative techniques to enliven their stories. And yet, who could ever mistake a work of fiction for one of fact (outright hoaxes excluded)? Were there, I wondered, any stories from real life which inherently followed these artificial, literary rules? In short, were there any non-fiction books that read like novels?

So I was looking at this book. I opened it to the photo section and saw a shot of a haunted looking man standing on a boat, the eponymous Crowhurst, and beneath it a quote from him. "I am going because I would have no peace if I stayed."

I began to read the book right there. I saw it was about a round-the-world voyage which had ended in a most unusual way, a news story at the time, now forgotten. And something told me I'd found the book I was looking for.

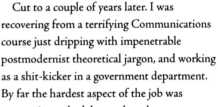

Cut to a couple of years later. I was recovering from a terrifying Communications course just dripping with impenetrable postmodernist theoretical jargon, and working as a shit-kicker in a government department. By far the hardest aspect of the job was attempting to look busy when there was virtually nothing to do. And in one corner of the office, a photocopier beckoned. It looked bored with copying government documents. Like thousands before and since, I had an idea.

Crowhurst went into the first *Bizarrism*, along with some of the street characters around Sydney at the time, Charles Fort, spontaneous combustion, a Mass Murderer Crossword Puzzle (these were the days before serial killers had been invented), and far too many clippings from newspapers. A hundred or so copies were collated on my lounge room floor in December 1986, ready in time to give

out as Christmas presents. It was only meant to be a one-off, but people kept asking me when the next one was coming out, and then I got curious to see it myself. After that it became a habit.

My basic formula remained much the same as the first issue — some strange ideas, cults (a pet subject as you'll see), a bit of true crime, an amiable eccentric or two, a scrap of folklore. My only criterion for including something was if it interested me. If someone else enjoyed it too, that was a bonus.

Along the way I collected others like Crowhurst. Some of them were artists, like Rosaleen Norton, or poets, like Harry Crosby or Arthur Cravan, or musicians, like Slim Gaillard or Joe Meek, but it seems to me that the greatest works of art they each produced were their own lives. Like Donald Crowhurst, they were the people who went overboard, the beacons of shining if erratic brilliance in a world of sensible conformity.

I'm enormously glad to have known them.

I first wrote the pieces, brought the stories up to date where necessary, and corrected some errors. I've also amended a few youthful infelicities of style. When I first started publishing *Bizarrism*, I was determined to write seriously about flippant subjects, and flippantly about serious ones. While I still adhere to that dictum to a large extent, I think that sometimes I went overboard.

The chief improvement in this new version of *Bizarrism*, however, is the addition of illustrations by my good friend Glenn Smith, who did such a sterling job on my previous book for Headpress, *The Eccentropedia*. Glenno can get a likeness on paper faster than I can make a cup of tea, and I continue to be in awe of his talents.

A NOTE ON THE REVISED AND EXPANDED EDITION

When the chance arose to publish the first edition of *Bizarrism* in 1999, I looked at it mainly as a way to get the contents of my flimsy, photocopied zine (which was up to issue 6 at the time) into a more permanent format.

Fifteen years later, I've taken the opportunity to revisit all this early material, and in some cases expand it considerably. I've added information that has come to light since

The Story of DONALD CROWHURST

OR, HOW TO BECOME A GOD

n 1968, in the wake of Francis Chichester's single-handed circumnavigation of the world in *Gypsy Moth IV* the previous year, the *Sunday Times* organised a non-stop, round-the-world yacht race. One of the first to announce his participation was Donald Crowhurst, a 36-year-old inventor and owner of a small electronics firm based in Somerset. Lately, his business had fallen heavily into debt, and this was one of the main reasons for someone who had previously only sailed for a hobby suddenly announcing he would be attempting to circumnavigate the globe — the publicity would ensure the sale of his inventions and the success of his business.

The other reason was that Crowhurst firmly believed himself to be destined for greatness, and he craved the sort of instant fame that Chichester had won. As this was to be the first non-stop single-handed circumnavigation (Chichester had made one stop on his trip) the adulation would likely be even greater.

Donald Crowhurst was born in India in 1932. His father, John Crowhurst, a railwayman, was a rather taciturn and distant figure, occasionally violent when he drank. Crowhurst was much closer to his mother, Alice, who was very religious. He did very well at school and was popular with the other boys who admired his fearlessness. After India gained independence, the family returned to England where they fell on hard times. John Crowhurst could only find work as a porter, and in 1948, when Donald was 16, he died suddenly from a heart attack. It was a heavy blow for the boy, who was forced to leave school.

Crowhurst joined the Royal Air Force where he studied electronic engineering, learned to fly and was commissioned. He was as popular with his peers as ever, always quick to order a round of drinks, issue a dare or suggest some outrageous escapade. He was in the air force for six years until one exploit — possibly riding a motorbike through a barracks full of sleeping airmen — was deemed to have gone too far, and he was asked to leave. He then joined the army, but was asked to leave it two years later after he was arrested trying to steal a car while drunk. Undaunted, Crowhurst made strenuous efforts to enter Cambridge, but failed.

On the bright side, Crowhurst met an Irish girl named Clare at a party early in 1957 and immediately announced that he was going to marry her. After exercising his considerable charm on her for several months, she agreed, and they were married within the year. They were living with Crowhurst's mother in Reading when their first child, James, was born. Later they moved to the village of Nether Stowey near Bridgwater in Somerset, where Clare gave birth to three more children, Simon, Roger and Rachel. Crowhurst adored his children, and they adored him.

Electronics was Crowhurst's true passion, and he was forever tinkering in his workshop, inventing gadgets that he hoped to market. After working for various electronics firms he decided to strike out on his own, using some of the proceeds from the sale of his mother's house to start a company called Electron Utilisation. He also became a keen amateur sailor, having purchased a 20-foot (six metres) sloop called *Pot of Gold* which he kept at Bridgwater. He combined his two loves, electronics and sailing, by inventing a hand-held navigational device called the 'Navicator', which became the first product sold by his company. And at first it all went well. With orders coming in, Crowhurst rented a factory and engaged six workers. The success he had long dreamed of finally seemed at hand.

Since he was a teenager, Crowhurst had been slowly putting together a philosophy of the world and his place in it. While he proclaimed himself an atheist and rationalist, his innate optimism made him open-minded about the possibilities the universe offered, and he was fascinated by the paranormal and the occult. In some ways, he thought like a magus who seeks to change reality though willpower and the harnessing of unseen powers. On a more mundane level, he saw life as a game which would be won by the most intelligent — and there was no doubt that Crowhurst was extremely intelligent. Yet his patchy education had left gaps. He could

solve technical problems brilliantly, but he also made basic mistakes.

And he was no businessman. Despite his enthusiasm and the long hours he put in, he could never get the marketing of his product right. He was thrown a lifeline for a while in the form of a £1,000 loan from a businessman named Stanley Best, but this eventually ran out. Crowhurst faced the prospect of Electron Utilisation folding, and there was something else affecting him as well. In the first flush of success with his business, he had gone out and bought a new Jaguar. In his usual reckless way he had driven it too fast and crashed it, receiving a head injury. Afterwards, his mood swings became more extreme and minor irritations could send him into a fury.

So this was Crowhurst's situation in May 1967 when Francis Chichester completed his circumnavigation, sailing into Plymouth to be greeted by a quarter of a million people, universal acclaim, endless sponsorship deals and a knighthood. Inevitably, a number of yachtsmen around the world began talking about going one better and achieving the first non-stop circumnavigation.

When faced with failure, Crowhurst's reaction had always been to redouble his efforts and throw himself into further challenges. What greater challenge could there be than this? So when the *Sunday Times*, which had reaped great rewards from sponsoring Chichester, announced its race in March 1968, Crowhurst soon declared himself in.

The rules of the race were simple. Any yacht which set out from any port in the world between June 1 and October 31 could be a part of the contest, and as the yachts would be starting at different times there were to be two prizes — one for the sailor who completed the voyage first, and another for the fastest time made. Crowhurst was convinced he could win both. His problem was that he had no boat suitable for the task, or money to build one. He therefore turned to his backer, Stanley Best, and somehow persuaded this hard-headed and extremely cautious businessman to put up the money for what could only be described as an uncertain venture. The catch in their agreement was that, should Crowhurst for some reason fail to complete the voyage, his company would have to buy the boat from Best, which would surely bankrupt it.

The October deadline for entering the race meant that Crowhurst only had seven months to have a yacht designed, built and tested. This was an impossibly short time, but he was used to achieving the difficult tasks he set himself. The craft he chose to have built was a three-hulled vessel — a trimaran. Crowhurst had never even sailed in one, but he had convinced himself that this was the ideal craft for the voyage. It was a risky choice. A trimaran is extremely stable, but once capsized it stays capsized. Crowhurst had invented a gadget to solve this problem, however — a rubber bag situated at the top of the mast which would be inflated automatically in the event of the vessel tipping over, thus bringing it upright again. This was only one of the devices Crowhurst planned to use in his boat.

Crowhurst acquired a press agent, Rodney Hallworth, a bluff former crime reporter who ran the Devon Press Agency. He also

looked after public relations for the town of Teignmouth, and told Crowhurst that if he started his voyage from there, the townspeople would rally to his support. Crowhurst agreed to this suggestion.

Crowhurst's boat builders managed to finish the trimaran's hulls in a very short time, but fitting it out proved far more problematic. Crowhurst, in a state of inventive elation, had

thought of innumerable electronic devices he wanted to incorporate in it, all of which required complicated wiring and machinery, but he kept changing his mind and coming up with new ideas. Sponsors proved hard to come by, and as the weeks went by the work fell increasingly behind schedule. One night in late September, after another serious problem had come to light, Clare confronted

worked frantically to gather the stores and equipment needed, but there was simply not enough time. Crowhurst himself was distracted and oddly subdued — seemingly overwhelmed by the number of things that needed to be done. When he said goodbye to Clare and the children and set off from Teignmouth on 31 October, the last possible day, his boat was about as badly equipped as it could be.

Things began to go wrong almost immediately. Screws worked themselves loose and someone had forgotten to put the spare ones on board. His generator had flooded, which meant he had no radio, and there were problems with the steering gear. One of the floats on either side of the central hull began to fill with water, and somehow it had been neglected to load the hose needed for the pump. The boat was a mass of wiring, intended to hook up Crowhurst's many electronic gadgets to a central computer, but he had not had the time to build either the computer or the gadgets. Even the device to bring the boat up should she capsize had not been completed.

Two weeks into his voyage, Crowhurst made a list of all the things wrong with his boat, evaluated their seriousness, and came to the conclusion that there was no way he could complete a round-the-world voyage. Returning home, however, would not only be humiliating, it would mean the bankruptcy of his firm. He considered the possibility of saving face by carrying on to somewhere like Australia, but the chances of doing even this were minimal.

It was now, faced with these unpleasant alternatives, that Crowhurst hit upon a plan.

her husband, urging him to admit he was unprepared and pull out of the race. He seemed to consider it, but then said, "I've got to go through with it, even if I have to build the boat myself on the way round."

Two days later the boat, now named the *Teignmouth Electron*, was launched at Brundall in Norfolk. Its maiden voyage from Brundall to Teignmouth proved disastrous. The trimaran was very fast with the wind behind it, but against the wind it slowed to a snail's pace. There were mishaps, and numerous design faults became apparent. Crowhurst was seasick almost the whole time, and burned his hand badly on an exhaust pipe. The trip took two weeks rather than the three days he had envisaged.

As the deadline for entering the race approached, Crowhurst's friends and sponsors

Instead of continuing his voyage — down through the Atlantic, around the Cape of Good Hope, past Australia, round Cape Horn and back up through the Atlantic to England again — he would simply remain in the Atlantic, out of the way of shipping lanes and hopefully unnoticed, and pretend he had sailed around the world. It was simple in theory, but would be enormously difficult to carry out in practice. He would have to make radio transmissions of false positions, fake the navigational record of his supposed voyage, even write a Chichester-like account of it. Crowhurst thought he could accomplish all this. There was no way he could win in this manner, for winning would mean his logbooks coming under close scrutiny and their inconsistencies being discovered, but he could make it appear that he had completed the voyage.

Crowhurst managed to fix his generator so was able to speak on the radio to his wife and Stanley Best, but he had given them no indication of his inner turmoil. Now that he had determined his course of action, he began to send telegrams giving false information about his position. In one of the first of these, he claimed to have sailed 243 miles in a single day, a record for a lone sailor, and the achievement was trumpeted by his PR man, Rodney Hallworth. Most commentators on the race had dismissed Crowhurst's chances prior to this, but now he was being talked about as a possible winner.

So Crowhurst spent the next few months sailing aimlessly around the Atlantic, listening carefully to the world weather reports so that he could record the conditions he would have been experiencing had he continued around the globe. After a while it would have become apparent that his radio signals were coming from the wrong part of the world, so he ceased communication in late January, giving a broken generator as his excuse. In his spare time he studied the few books he had brought with him, mainly books on mathematics and navigation. One of them, *Relativity, the Special and the General Theory* by Albert Einstein, began to increasingly obsess him. He also occupied himself by writing poetry and essays, and making tape recordings. (One of his sponsors, the BBC, had provided him with a tape recorder and a movie camera.)

There were, as always, innumerable repairs to be done on the boat, but he lacked the plywood and screws needed to fix the most serious problem, a split that had opened up

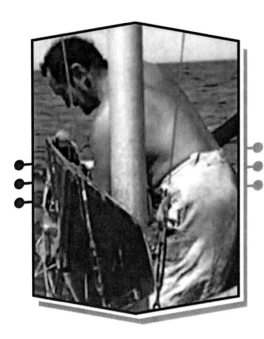

Cape Horn and re-enter the Atlantic. There were two other yachtsmen still in the race — Robin Knox-Johnston and Nigel Tetley. Knox-Johnston became the first to complete the race when he reached England on 22 April. As his overall time was slow, however, the prize for the fastest voyage remained for Crowhurst or Tetley to win, and a close finish was predicted. Crowhurst had only to follow in Tetley's wake, let him win, then sail home with honour but without too many people interested in the details of his voyage.

His elaborate plans would probably have succeeded had not something unforeseen occurred. In an effort to beat the times he believed Crowhurst to be making, Tetley began to sail more recklessly. On 21 May, while attempting to pass through a storm, Tetley's yacht, which was also a trimaran, capsized and he was out of the race. Crowhurst had only to reach England to win. He began to receive telegrams giving him the details of the welcome planned in Teignmouth, the boatloads of spectators, the helicopters filled with TV cameras and so on. His radio transmitter had really broken down now, so that he could no longer speak to anyone. He had entangled himself in a situation from which there seemed no escape.

It was at this point that Crowhurst had a revelation of such cosmic significance that it would inevitably change not only his own future but the future of all mankind. It was an idea that had been growing during the previous months, but only now did he realise the true importance of it. Its germ had come from a passage in the book in which Einstein,

in his starboard float. Crowhurst realised he would have to risk a landing. After considering several possible places, he headed for a small settlement by the Salado River on the coast of Argentina. He was greeted by a couple of bemused coastguard officers who knew nothing about a round-the-world yacht race, but after checking with a superior they were happy to provide Crowhurst with what he needed. He made the necessary repairs the next day, and dined with the coastguard officers that evening, communicating with them in sign language. He set sail the following morning, and as word of the strange Englishman's visit never reached Buenos Aires, the world remained ignorant of the secret landing.

Crowhurst broke radio silence on 9 April, when his false itinerary had him about to round while theorising about the way light travels, assumes a certain condition to be so. While he does this purely for the sake of argument, Crowhurst took it to mean that Einstein had changed the nature of the physical world by thought. He had therefore achieved what Crowhurst believed to be the next stage of human evolution — the freeing of the mind from the limitations of the body. And if Einstein could do this anybody could, it simply required an effort of will. Here was an idea so overwhelming that it rendered the problems Crowhurst was facing irrelevant. He could change his situation just by thinking about it. By becoming a god.

With his boat becalmed on the weed-strewn waters of the Sargasso Sea, Crowhurst banished mundane matters like navigation from his mind. He spent the next few days writing a philosophical essay in one of his logbooks. It eventually came to 25,000 words and veered from fairly cogent reasoning to complete incoherence, especially towards the end. He was convinced that writing about his revelation would in itself bring about the evolutionary leap he envisioned.

If I stipulate of my own free will that by learning to manipulate the space-time continuum Man will become God and disappear from the physical universe as we know it I am providing the system with an impulse. If my solution is rooted in the mathematical requirements of a solution it is "correct" and acceptable to a rapidly increasing body of men, then I am very close to God and

should, by the methods I claim are available, move at last to prophecy. Let's have a go!

He had one more decision to make — whether to conceal the evidence of his fake voyage or not. Revealing it would hurt his family, he knew, but in the end he concluded that his new status left him no choice, or as he put it, "Nature does not allow God to sin any sins except one — that's the sin of concealment." He therefore destroyed the fake logbook he had taken such pains to create, leaving behind the true record of his voyage.

On 1 July 1969, having put into words the most important discovery in history, Donald Crowhurst left his body by jumping into the sea.

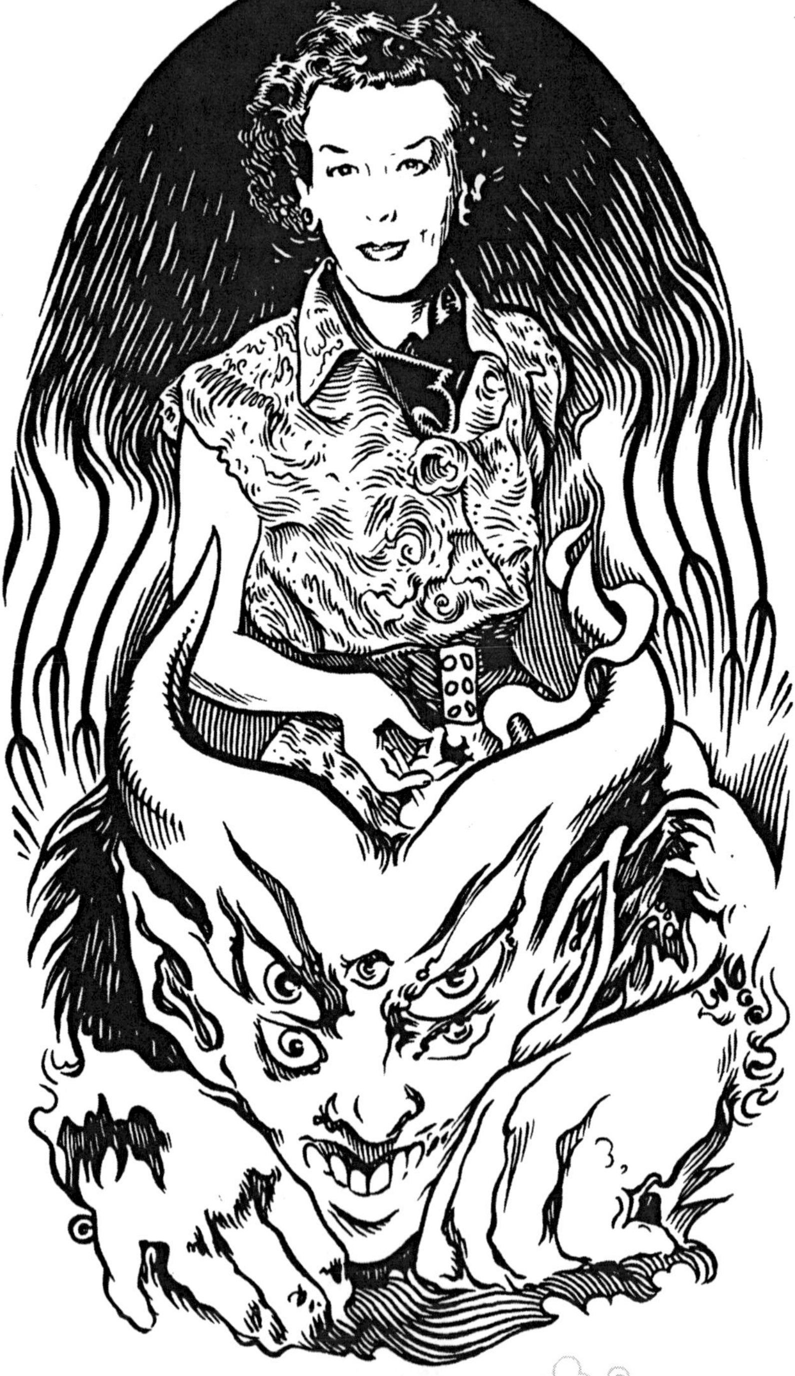

ROSALEEN NORTON

THE WITCH OF KINGS CROSS

osaleen Norton was unique in her time, and, sadly, she would still be unique today. She was a born mystic and visionary artist when to be such things meant being dismissed by most people as either possessed or insane. To the deadening forces of conservatism and conformity she was the epitome of wickedness, but despite the scandals which regularly erupted around her she carried herself with terrific style and a sense of humour. If she was the face of evil, she was a remarkably nice face of evil.

Rosaleen Norton, 'Roie' to her friends, made a suitably dramatic entrance to this world during a thunderstorm on the night of 2 October 1917, in Dunedin, New Zealand. She was born with a sinewy strip of flesh extending from her armpit to her waist, and later took this, along with other physical peculiarities such as pointed ears and two dark spots on her left knee, as signs that she was destined to be a witch.

She was the youngest of three daughters in a solidly Church of England family, her father being an affable merchant seaman named Albert Norton. When she was seven the family moved to Sydney, where they bought a house in Lindfield on the North Shore. Rosaleen grew up a solitary child, looking down her nose at other children, preferring the company of spiders and other non-human creatures. Night was her favourite time, when ghosts were about. She ate her evening meal alone on the roof of her house, and for years slept in a tent out in the garden. She liked drawing too, ghoulish stuff that got her into trouble with her teachers. When she was 14, the headmistress of her school, Chatswood Girls Grammar, became the first in a long line of people to identify Rosaleen as a corrupting influence on others, and she was expelled.

She studied art at East Sydney Technical College for two years, and in 1934 had three horror stories accepted by *Smith's Weekly*, a famously irreverent and lively newspaper which seems to have kept almost all of Sydney's bohemian community in gainful employment at one time or another. Its editor, Frank Marien, was so impressed with the literary skills of their 16-year-old author he offered her a job as a trainee journalist. When she told him she preferred to work as an artist, he stressed that he was looking for drawings which would amuse and entertain his readers. The cartoons that Norton delivered weren't quite what he was expecting (although the content of her stories should have warned him). In one of the three that he agreed to publish, a couple of stylishly-dressed 'flappers' stand in front of a cage in which an elegantly jacketed trainer puts three tigers through their paces. "Wouldn't it be a thrill," says one flapper to the other, "if one of the beasts devoured

him!" With Norton unable to produce anything conventional enough even for *Smith's*, Marien let her go after eight months.

Rosaleen's mother Beena had died, and she decided it was time to leave the family home. She took a room in the Ship and Mermaid Inn, a rambunctious establishment overlooking Circular Quay which was known colloquially as 'Buggery Barn'. Later she moved into a boarding house in Phillip Street run by a kindly old woman named Mrs Henderson. The other tenants included artists and a music student, Eileen Kramer, who would go on to become a well-known dancer. In her autobiography, *Walkabout Dancer*, Kramer captures Norton in a period of transition, the witch's persona of her later years only partially formed.

When I first saw Roie I thought she had a lovely figure, slim and shapely. But I was taken aback by the witches' eyebrows she pencilled on over her natural ones. "Are you pretending to be a witch?" I asked, thinking she'd been experimenting that day with her make-up. "Gee, Christ, Eileen, I am a witch," she said. She was pleased that I had commented on her eyebrows.

I wondered why her costume wasn't in keeping with the eyebrows. If I had wanted to be a witch I would have made a suitable costume of black crinkle cotton with wing-like sleeves and a cloak that would float in the wind when I walked through the Botanical Gardens searching for magic herbs and toadstools.

Roie expressed her witchiness with black cat brooches and jewelry like that pinned to the collars of conservative little dresses.

Norton scraped a living doing odd jobs — kitchen hand, waitress, postal messenger, pavement artist and artist's model for, among others, Norman Lindsay, whose work her own was often compared to (he called her "a grubby little girl with great skill who will not discipline herself".) At a party in 1935, she met another 17-year-old named Beresford Conroy, who aspired to be a playwright. They married in 1940 and spent some time hitchhiking around the country from Brisbane to Melbourne, but soon after this, Conroy joined the army.

In 1945, with Conroy still away in New Guinea fighting the Japanese, Norton met a young poet named Gavin Greenlees. He was a tall, dreamy, highly strung (years later he would be diagnosed with epilepsy) and, like Norton, bisexual. They met through a small and unconventional magazine named *Pertinent*, to which they had both contributed. Greenlees, who was influenced by surrealism, was a poet of some talent, and their interests meshed. They moved into a dingy flat at 7 Brougham Street, Kings Cross, Sydney's bohemian epicentre, and soon gathered a coterie of like-minded individuals around them. On the door Norton placed a sign reading "Welcome to the haunts of GHOSTS, GOBLINS, WEREWOLVES, VAMPIRES, WITCHES, WIZARDS and POLTERGEISTS."

She scored her first major exhibition in 1949, at the Rowden-White Gallery at Melbourne University. She had been

experimenting with self-hypnosis and
automatic drawing for years, devising rituals
which would put her into a trance state in
which she could explore other dimensions.
Her paintings and drawings were for the
most part depictions of the myriad gods,
demons and other entities with whom she
communicated — and caroused — on these
journeys. These beings — with the god Pan
being her personal god of choice — were as
real to her as the people around her, perhaps
more so. Rosaleen's swirling, flamboyant
compositions, full of grotesque detail and
writhing, interlocked forms, were at their
best extremely powerful. They were certainly
pretty strong meat for 1940s Australia, and
Constable Plod, turning up at the 1949
exhibition, predictably found them obscene.
The police seized four works. Various
academics came to Rosaleen's defence in the
ensuing trial and, perhaps surprisingly, the
obscenity charges were dropped and the police
ordered to pay costs. Rosaleen's comment on
the affair: "This figleaf morality expresses a
very unhealthy attitude."

A similar reaction greeted the publication
in 1952 of *The Art of Rosaleen Norton*, a
collection of her illustrations accompanied
by poems by Greenlees. The book's publisher,
Walter Glover, was charged with obscenity
and Rosaleen was back in court defending
her art in terms of Jungian archetypes. Such
arguments notwithstanding, the magistrate
fined Glover £5 and ordered that two
pictures, including one of 'Fohat', a cheeky
looking demon with a snake for a penis,
be obliterated from unsold copies of the
book. All of this, of course, generated huge

publicity, and the book became highly sought
after. Unfortunately, Glover could never get
distribution sorted out, and he eventually
went bankrupt.

Rosaleen was by now firmly ensconced as
one of the great characters of Kings Cross,
the stamping ground of Sydney's prostitutes,
criminals, artists and would-be cosmopolitans.
Her paintings adorned the walls of its cafés
and visitors to Sydney, whose first trip was
likely to be the Cross anyway, began to seek
her out. The press had by now come to label
her as a witch, and while the term never really
described what Rosaleen was all about, she
revelled in the attention, for a while at least.
She certainly looked the part, her eyebrows
plucked into high arches, her whole face,
framed with jet black hair, a pattern of striking
curves which resembled nothing so much as

one of her own paintings. She was now being called the leader of a witch cult, and while this 'cult' never seemed to amount to much more than a few friends gathering in her small flat for occult talk and the occasional friendly ritual, this was too good a story for the tabloids to let go. Here's a typical account of a night at Roie's, from the 1965 potboiler *Kings Cross Black Magic* by 'Attila Zohar'.

There were about eight or nine cult members present. They all wore hideous masks so were quite willing to be photographed, although they pointed out that there were certain rites which could not be performed before outsiders or cameras.

Later Rosaleen Norton changed into her witch's outfit. She was nude except for a black apron fore and aft from her waist and a black shawl over her shoulders. A cat mask covered her face but did not prevent her smoking with a long cigarette holder.

The reporter noticed that the witches did not seem to walk — but rather to 'drift silently' on bare feet. Later Rowie [sic] discarded the shawl, leaving herself bare from the waist up. 'Miss Norton has modelled in her time, and she was as unselfconscious with the shawl off as with it on,' observed the reporter.

All the witches denied a somewhat facetious suggestion that they were merely people who liked dressing up. They insisted they were serious-minded practitioners of the black arts. The reporter persisted and wanted to know what they got out of their cult.

Rosaleen Norton answered for all the witches when she said: 'I get a life that holds infinite possibilities and is entirely satisfactory to me on all planes of consciousness.'

Little outbreaks of scandal kept the legend of 'The Witch of Kings Cross' bubbling along nicely. In 1955, police picked up a homeless adolescent girl, Anna Hoffmann, who blamed her sorry state on her attendance at one of Rosaleen's black masses. She later admitted she made this all up and was sentenced to two months in jail, but not before the newspapers had taken the story and run with it. In the same year, the *Sun* was approached by two shady characters offering an undeveloped roll of film (which they had pilfered from Norton's flat). When the photographs were developed, they showed Gavin Greenlees and a naked Roie performing various unnatural — and rather silly — acts. The photos had been taken as a lark at one of her birthday parties, but the *Sun* deemed them too pornographic to publish and handed them over to police. Two days later Norton and Greenlees were arrested and charged with "making an obscene publication" and "the abominable crime of buggery". She made a memorable appearance at her first day in court, wearing a black top, red skirt and leopard-skin shoes. She and Greenlees were released on bail, and two years later were fined £25 each. Meanwhile, police had seized twenty-nine of Norton's artworks which had been on display in the Kashmir Café, and fined its owner. All of the artworks were eventually destroyed.

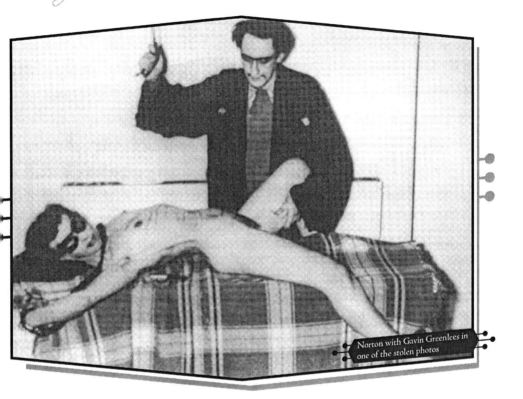

Norton with Gavin Greenlees in one of the stolen photos

And then came the sorry saga of Sir Eugene Goossens, the British-born conductor of the Sydney Symphony Orchestra and director of the NSW State Conservatorium. He earned more than the prime minister, conceived the idea of a Sydney Opera House, and has been called "the dominant figure in the Australian cultural landscape" of the time. The conductor, who arrived in Australia in 1947, had another side, though. As a young boy, he became fascinated by paganism, and did drawings full of gargoyles (which sound remarkably similar to Norton's youthful productions). Later, he became close friends with the composer and occultist Philip Henshaw, who was known as 'Peter Warlock'. It's little wonder,

then, that when he came across a copy of *The Art of Rosaleen Norton* in the early '50s, he recognised a kindred spirit. He wrote to Norton and she invited him to her Kings Cross flat for tea.

The rundown flat, crammed with occult paraphernalia including a makeshift altar, was only five minutes' walk from the room where Goossens rehearsed with the Sydney Symphony Orchestra, and he became a frequent visitor there. His much younger, glamorous wife Marjorie, who had had become a leading Sydney socialite, was often overseas, and his relationship with Norton soon became a sexual one. While away touring he wrote her torrid letters.

Contemplating your hermaphroditic organs in the picture nearly made me desert my evening's work and fly to you by first aerial coven. But, as promised, you came to me early this morning (about 1.45) and when a suddenly flapping window blind announced your arrival, I realised by a delicious oroficial tingling that you were about to make your presence felt…

I need your physical presence very much, for many reasons. We have many rituals and indulgences to undertake. And I want to take more photos.

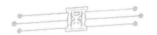

Photos, oroficial tinglings… oh, dear. Goossens urged Norton to destroy his letters after reading them; instead, she hid them behind her sofa. When she and Greenlees were arrested over the 'obscene' photos, he panicked and burned all his occult and pornographic gear. He didn't know that Joe Morris, a crime reporter from tabloid newspaper the *Sun*, had found the letters and some photos in Norton's flat and given them to police, who launched an investigation. By then, Goossens was on a five-month tour of Europe, where his schedule included collecting a knighthood at Buckingham Palace.

Detective Bert Trevenar, in charge of the investigation, was hampered by the NSW police department's lack of resources and turned to Joe Morris for help. If Morris could arrange for Goossens to be watched in Britain, the *Sun* would get a massive scoop.

Goossens was duly followed by reporters in London, and observed purchasing all sorts of goodies in seedy Soho bookshops. The newspaper relayed all this to the Sydney police, and let them know when he was due back in Sydney.

On 9 March 1956, a team of detectives and customs officers were at Mascot Airport to greet him. He arrived with a briefcase and six suitcases, expecting to sail through customs as usual, but this time he was asked to open them. As the first incriminating material was unwrapped from packages disguised as sheet music, he made a half-hearted attempt to blame his valet for putting it there, but as the extent of the haul became apparent, fell silent. The damning tally would eventually be 837 photographs which were deemed to be pornographic, a spool of film, some masks, a few mildly risqué books with titles like *Flossie and Nancy's Love Life* and some sticks of incense.

His ordeal was just beginning. Bringing prohibited material into the country was a Federal offence, but the salacious goings-on recorded in the letters and photos found in Norton's flat were a state matter, and Detective Trevenar asked Goossens to accompany him to vice squad headquarters. Already a broken man, not even thinking about getting a lawyer, Goossens was astonishingly open under questioning. Quizzed on the term 'SM' which recurred through his letters, short for 'sex magic', he volunteered that this entailed naked rituals with Norton and Greenlees, in which he indulged in cunnilingus with Rosaleen. "I placed my tongue on her," he told Trevenar, "and kept moving until I stimulated her."

Goossens was fined £100 pounds for bringing obscene material into the country, but to the frustration of the police, the NSW Attorney General dropped the charges relating to his 'salacious behaviour', possibly after the establishment had applied pressure. He was allowed to return to Britain, estranged from his wife and his glorious career in ruins, and died in 1962.

Because the investigation of Goossens was shut down so quickly, his association with Norton was not widely known, although there were rumours. Rosaleen never commented on the fate of this pillar of the establishment who had found spiritual enlightenment between her legs. But then the real world in which someone like Goossens operated was always a secondary concern for her.

Rosaleen Norton began to drop out of the public eye in the '60s. Suddenly her behaviour didn't seem so strange any more — who *wasn't* into the occult revival? All the notoriety had proved too much for Gavin Greenlees, it seems. He had been diagnosed as schizophrenic in 1957 and institutionalised. Rosaleen visited him, playing mother to him as she always had, but in 1964, given temporary release from Callan Park hospital, he turned up at the Brougham Street flat, threw her furniture into the street, and threatened to kill her. The police arrived to find him running a knife across his throat, and dragged him away, as Rosaleen sat inside praying at her altar.

Interviewed for a television documentary, *The Glittering Mile*, in the same year, Rosaleen told of the many teenagers who came to her wanting to become witches. "They're obviously just kids looking for a thrill," she laughed, and when asked if she ever missed the ordinary things in life, like getting married or having children, she said, "Oh, God no. I couldn't stand it. I'd go mad, or go sane. I don't know which."

In the 15 June 1967 issue of *Australasian Post*, journalist Dave Barnes gives an account of a visit to the increasingly reclusive witch. He describes how he and a colleague started their search for Rosaleen at the flat she had occupied at the height of her fame in the '50s, questioned a few less than helpful locals, and eventually located her front door through which they dropped a request for her to ring their office so an interview could be arranged. The following day they were invited into Rosaleen's dark, 10ft by 6ft room, adorned

with "giggling masks, a Satan statue, gongs and strikers, trinkets, snakes and growing creepers". They found her in an apparently cheerful mood, playing up her reputation for all it was worth. She then produced a little box and said, "Look, these are real bat's feet, there are not many of them about and I wear them for ear-rings, attractive aren't they?"

Politely ignoring their more flippant questions, she told them she enjoyed TV shows like *The Munsters*, *The Addams Family* and *Bewitched*, suggesting their makers knew a thing or two about how witches really operate. She was particularly interested in how the journos tracked her down, and at what time. Puzzled, they told her they had left their office just before 4 pm and dropped the message through her door at 4.45 pm. This made her laugh. Later, back in the office, they found that Rosaleen's call in answer to their message had been logged at 4 pm the previous day — before they had actually delivered it. Game, set and match to Rosaleen.

Rosaleen Norton's health began to fail in the '70s, and she became increasingly reclusive. She lived in a flat with her two cats and a tank of goldfish, in the same block as her eldest sister Cecilie, with whom she had always been close. In 1979, she was diagnosed with colon cancer and admitted to the Sacred Heart Hospice for the Dying. One of her friends during these last years was a young man named Richard Moir, who published a memoir about her in 1994. Moir drew a distinction between Roie, the private person he knew, and the Rosaleen Norton persona she created for the public, and painted a vivid picture of her final days.

When I arrived at the hospital I was ushered into the visitors lounge room, strange I thought, as Roie couldn't walk.

I waited in the lounge room for some time patiently, suddenly Rosaleen Norton appeared physically standing on both legs, welcoming me, escorted by two sisters. The vision I beheld was mind blowing.

Rosaleen Norton (not Roie) standing there in full garb, her hair flaming back, carefully arranged in her look. Her make-up had been very carefully applied, the face powder, the Rosaleen Norton full eye make-up and eye brows, the red lipstick. It was the Rosaleen Norton as I had always remembered her — but even more so

She stood there for only one minute... The last words Rosaleen Norton said to me were "Darling; I can't stay too long, I just came to say hello. Ah! I must go Darling." and with her head in a proud position Rosaleen Norton was escorted away out of my sight forever.

Rosaleen Norton died on 5 December 1979, surrounded by nuns but, needless to say, a dedicated pagan to the last.

HARRY CROSBY

"ive fast, die young and have a good looking corpse." It's been the promise of many would-be rebels down the years, but just how many of them have stuck to their guns? Enter, in a burst of light, Harry Crosby — poet, pilot, sun-worshipper, self-styled genius and the best-looking corpse of 1929.

Crosby was born on 4 June 1898 into a wealthy and ultra-respectable Boston family. He was the son of Stephen Van Renssaeller Crosby, an investment banker, and his wife Henrietta (neé Grew), a keen gardener, while his uncle was the millionaire financier J. Pierpont Morgan, Jr. Crosby's father was a fairly typical Bostonian 'stuffed shirt' (though he would go on to be surprisingly indulgent when it came to his son's excesses), and he was much closer to his mother, a kind and generous woman who passed her deep religious feelings on to her son. He was educated at St Mark's School, where he failed to excel academically and showed little interest in literature apart from falling under the hedonistic spell of *The Rubaiyat of Omar Khayyam*. After graduating in 1917, he and some school friends, keen to take part in the war, signed up with the American Ambulance Corps in France.

As an ambulance driver on the Western Front, Crosby witnessed much carnage

Crosby in 1919

which he related back to his parents in letters full of anatomical detail. On 22 November 1917 came his first 'death day', the most important day of his life. He had spent it transporting the wrecks of men to hospital from the front lines during the Second Battle of Verdun. The sun was setting and he had just taken on another load of casualties when a shell exploded near his Ford ambulance, 'vaporising' it. One of his childhood friends, 'Spud' Spaulding, driving an ambulance 10 yards behind, had his chest torn open by shrapnel, but Crosby was left completely and inexplicably unscathed. He had spent much of his spare time in France reading the Bible, and believed that God had spared him.

Having cheated death once, Crosby from this point seemed to lose all fear of it. Instead he became obsessed with the idea of choosing the time of his death, of dying at exactly the right moment. And he was someone who believed it was better to be too soon than too late.

On his return to the U.S., Crosby's path was clear. He would go to Harvard (more for the opportunity to join its elite clubs than acquire anything in the way of an education), marry a Boston girl and settle into a respectable business like banking. He went to Harvard alright, taking courses in English literature and French, but spent most of his two years there partying. Drinking was acceptable in Boston society, so long as it was done behind closed doors, but Harry was seen dead drunk at the best social functions. He also took to wearing almost exclusively black clothing, and painted his fingernails black.

Any hope that Harry Crosby was ever going to conform to Boston's rules went out the window when he met Polly Peabody, who had been born Mary Phelps Jacob in New York. When she and Harry met in 1920, at a party organised by his mother, she was 28 to his 21. She was also married — to an alcoholic ex-soldier named Richard Peabody, whose chief enthusiasm was watching buildings burn down — and had two children. Her main claim to fame was the invention of a wireless brassiere, which she had patented in 1914.

Harry was besotted by her from the beginning. Having somehow hung on to his

virginity in France, he soon lost it to Polly. If religion and death had been his two greatest passions until now, she became the third, and in his mind she was inextricably linked with the other two. Often separated from her while at Harvard, he took to praying in front of her photograph twice a day, and wrote her long letters in which he did not disguise his infatuation with death.

I promise you that whenever you want we shall die together and what's more I am perfectly ready now or will be anytime. With the absolute Faith that we shall be one in Heaven as soon as we die for ever and ever it is a great temptation to forsake this life… if worse should come to worse and you couldn't get a divorce I'll come down and kill you and then kill myself so that we can go right to Heaven together—and we can die in each other's arms and I'll take the blame so you don't have to worry, Dear…

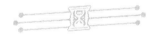

Polly was a dreamer, but she was also more conventional than Harry, and worried about what people would think of their relationship. At his urging she eventually told her husband about it, and being an amiable fellow, he agreed to a divorce immediately. His family was horrified by the news, however, as was just about everyone else in Boston, and Polly told Harry she would never be able to live in the city.

With Polly continuing to baulk at marrying him, Crosby grew depressed and quit the job he had taken in a bank, which he loathed.

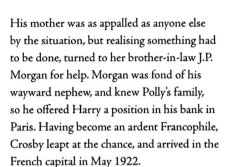

His mother was as appalled as anyone else by the situation, but realising something had to be done, turned to her brother-in-law J.P. Morgan for help. Morgan was fond of his wayward nephew, and knew Polly's family, so he offered Harry a position in his bank in Paris. Having become an ardent Francophile, Crosby leapt at the chance, and arrived in the French capital in May 1922.

He made resolutions to give up smoking, drinking and gambling, spent his days and nights smoking, drinking and gambling, and occasionally managed to drag himself to his desk at the bank. After a few months, missing Polly desperately, he made a snap decision and boarded a ship bound for the States. He arrived in New York on 9 September, and married Polly that afternoon. Crosby's mother was so upset she couldn't speak to him.

Crosby returned to Paris with Polly and her two children, Billy and Polleen (he could barely tolerate them at first but later became friends with them, and always insisted on treating them like adults). He threw in his bank job at the end of 1923, after he and Polly, whom he renamed Caresse, had decided they were going to be poets. They would not be starving poets, though, for he owned enough stock, courtesy of his father, to provide them with a comfortable living, servants and all. Not for Harry the smoke-filled Left Bank cafés frequented by the other American expatriates who flocked to Paris in the twenties — he dined at the Ritz.

He also had a useful ally in Paris in the form of his cousin, Walter Van Renssaeller Berry. A former international lawyer and contemporary of Crosby's father, Berry had a vast library and impeccable literary contacts, counting among his friends Henry James, Proust and Cocteau. He wholeheartedly supported Crosby's decision to become a poet, and steered him towards the French writers he admired the most. Crosby was particularly taken with Baudelaire and the other decadents, finding that their morbidity and love of artifice meshed with his own, and came to the conclusion, not unreasonable, that the only way he could transform himself from banker to genius was via the shortcut of madness. Taking to heart Lord Henry's dictum in *The Picture of Dorian Gray* that "The only way to get rid of a temptation is to give in to it", he embarked on a rigorous curriculum of smoking opium, gambling recklessly, going to parties and collecting mistresses — hard work but someone's got to do it. "PLEASE SELL $10,000 WORTH OF STOCK," read one of his cables to his increasingly despairing father, "WE HAVE DECIDED TO LEAD A MAD AND EXTRAVAGENT LIFE."

Crosby was completely open about his many lovers — he even wrote to his mother about them, telling her he wanted to have a harem. He might be dining at a restaurant with Caresse and a few friends when, spying a pretty girl at another table, he would approach her, chat to her then leave with her, without another word to the others. Caresse had little choice but to put up with this, although she could take comfort from the fact that the mistresses were rarely around for very long, and that her own exalted place in Crosby's heart was assured. Eventually she would take lovers, too, though never as many as her husband.

The highlight of their year, in terms of debauchery at least, was the Four Arts Ball,

thrown by Paris's art students every June. At the 1926 ball, Caresse won a prize after riding bare-breasted through the ballroom in the jaws of a papier mâché dragon, while Crosby's Incan prince costume consisted of a red loincloth, a coating of red ochre, and three dead pigeons strung around his neck. Next year, he upped the ante with seven pigeons and ten live snakes in a sack. Mornings after a Four Arts Ball usually saw Harry and Caresse waking up in their four-poster bed in their apartment in Rue de Lille, along with a few friends, their black whippet Narcisse Noir, and any other humans or creatures who happened to be about.

Amid all this carousing, Crosby was taking his vocation as a poet seriously. He made up for his patchy education by reading voraciously in all subjects, and set aside time every day for writing. Eager to see their work in print, he and Caresse decided to publish it themselves, and their first efforts, Caresse's *Crosses of Gold* and his *Sonnets for Caresse*, appeared in 1925. Their publishing venture, renamed the Black Sun Press in 1927, would go on to issue works by Oscar Wilde, James Joyce, D.H. Lawrence, Ezra Pound and other important writers. The books were exquisitely printed and bound, with many of the early titles featuring illustrations by an aristocrat of uncertain origins, the Baron Hans Henning von Voight, known as Alistair. He was a slight, effete, deathly pale character who wore white satin suits and lived in what Caresse described as "a *Fall of the House of Usher* house" attended by Negro servants, the very epitome of decadence. Yet Crosby himself was moving away from decadence as his artistic ideal. As

he got into his poetic stride, he looked to the modernists like T.S. Eliot and Joyce (who he worshipped) as his models. Most of Crosby's poems reflect the religion which he had devised for himself — an ecstatic worship of the sun. It doesn't make terribly much sense, but remember, one of Crosby's goals was to go mad. He took his praying to the sun seriously, and like any good magician, made up his own elaborate rituals.

Crosby was famed for his generosity. He would give expensive presents to people he had just met, or pay more than the asking price for items if he thought them worth more. When Walter Berry died in 1927, Harry inherited the bulk of his fabulous collection of rare books — 8,000 volumes in all. He was thrilled but, believing that "you can keep only those things that you give away", he began to systematically dispose of them, handing them to strangers or, better still, marking first editions with ridiculously low prices and secreting them on the shelves of secondhand bookstores. He handled his wealth in a similar fashion.

By mid-1928, Crosby and Caresse felt that city life was becoming too hectic. They decided to rent a derelict mill that adjoined the chateau of one of Caresse's lovers, Armand de la Rochefoucauld, in Ermenonville in the north of France. Crosby restored the mill, which had once been home to Rousseau, and named it the Maison du Soleil. He installed a swimming pool and circular track for donkey racing, and assembled a menagerie which included cockatoos, whippets, a cheetah and a macaw. If the plan had been to find a quiet spot where he and Caresse could concentrate

Crosby in the Sahara, with opium pipe and Berber girl

when allowed to fly solo for the first time on Armistice Day, and after that took to the skies up to twice a day. He flew recklessly, as he did everything, and was undeterred when one of his fellow flying students crashed and died. Flying was another way to get closer to the sun.

Crosby often referred to his death wish in his poems. "I shall cut out my heart and take it into my joined hands and walk towards the Sun without stopping until I drop down dead." Of course, whether poetry like this is crap or not depends on how serious the poet is, and Crosby was serious. Ideally he wanted to die with Caresse, and had set a date for their double suicide — 31 October 1942 — when the earth's orbit would bring it closest to the sun. He was impatient, though, and in the habit of asking her to jump from tall buildings with him, but she was always putting him off. So did his various mistresses when he brought the subject up. It wasn't until Josephine Rotch that Crosby met his match in obsessiveness.

She was another Boston girl with a reputation for being 'fast' and saying things to shock. When he first met her in Venice, in July 1928, she was engaged to a Harvard hockey star and architecture student named Herbert Bigelow. "She was mad and madness is very appealing especially to me who is mad," he wrote excitedly to his mother, who must have been thrilled. Crosby always gave nicknames to his mistresses (there was the Sorceress, Nubile, the Dark Princess). Josephine was the Fire Princess, and their lovemaking was violent, even by his standards (Crosby had once shocked D.H. Lawrence by extolling the erotic virtues of biting). As always, he made no secret of the affair. He pasted Josephine's

on their literary pursuits, it was a dismal failure, for the mill became the scene of almost endless parties. The guests included a roll-call of 1920s notables including Salvador Dalì, Douglas Fairbanks and Mary Pickford, Prince George of England, Max Ernst and Aldous Huxley. The American poet Hart Crane spent months at the mill, ostensibly writing poetry for the Black Sun Press to publish, but mostly being drunk and belligerent. (In 1932, Crane would jump overboard from a steamship en route from Cuba to the U.S. after shouting, "Goodbye, everybody!")

Crosby had been dreaming about flying planes since watching dogfights during the war. He and Caresse witnessed Lindbergh's triumphant landing in France at the end of his transatlantic flight, and he began taking flying lessons in mid-1929. He was ecstatic

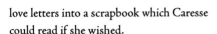

love letters into a scrapbook which Caresse could read if she wished.

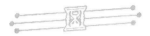

On 22 November 1929, Crosby and Caresse arrived in New York on a steamship, then caught a train to Boston. A letter from Josephine, who had married Bigelow six months earlier, was waiting for Harry at his parents' house. They contrived to meet regularly over the next few days, then spent some time in Detroit, away from the prying eyes of society. They returned to New York on 7 December and Crosby was reunited with Caresse. Josephine had agreed to return to her husband (immersed in his studies, he was oblivious to her affair), but instead she stayed in New York, and two nights later delivered an envelope addressed to Harry to the Crosbys' hotel. It contained a poem entitled 'Two Fires that Make One Fire', in which she listed all the things that she and Harry both liked, from caviar to the number 13, and ended with the line "Death is our marriage."

The following morning, 10 December, Crosby bought two steamship tickets for his and Caresse's return journey to France, then went to an art exhibition. In the early afternoon, he arrived at the studio apartment of his friend, the painter Stanley Mortimer, in the Hotel des Artistes, with Josephine in tow. Mortimer let Crosby use the studio for romantic trysts, and at Harry's signal, he left the two lovers alone.

Crosby had made an appointment to meet Caresse and his mother (the two women had long ago patched up their differences and become friends) at J.P. Morgan's townhouse at 5 pm. Crosby had intended to present his uncle with a copy of his latest collection of poems, *Sleeping Together*, which was dedicated to Caresse. Five pm came and went, with no Harry, and as he was famous for his punctuality, Caresse grew worried. She and her mother-in-law went to dinner, but Caresse could not eat, and managed to get a phone call through to Mortimer. He agreed to go to his studio to see what was up.

He found the door to it bolted from the inside. Receiving no response to his knocking, he summoned the manager who broke the door down with an axe.

He found Harry and Josephine on the bed. They were lying beneath the coverlet, fully clothed but with their feet bare. They were facing each other, holding hands, a bullet hole in his right temple and one in her left. In his right hand, Crosby grasped the .25 automatic pistol he had bought a year before, which had a sun symbol engraved on it. He was 31-years-old, she was 21.

It was estimated that Josephine had died first, and Crosby had waited two hours before shooting himself. At some point he had removed his gold sun ring, which Caresse had bought for him in Cairo, believing it to have come from Tutankhamen's tomb, and which he had told her he would never take off, and stomped on it.

The newspapers made much of the 'decadent poet slays young bride' angle. Back in Paris, the artists considered Crosby's death almost as a practical joke. Everyone was amazed that a compulsive writer like Crosby had left no suicide note, but in his case that would have simply been overdoing it.

Tales of the
HOLLOW EARTH

John Cleves Symmes

Cyrus Teed

'm all for commonsense — in certain situations, but I've always got time for a bit of wild, uninformed speculation. And what better to speculate wildly about, from the comfort of your armchair, than the vast, unexplored interior of our own planet? Sure, those boring old scientists tell us that the earth is solid, that there's nothing down there but rock and a lot of rather frightening red-hot magma, but then, to borrow the immortal words of Mandy Rice-Davies, "They would, wouldn't they?"

Such was not always the case. Cosmological theories involving a hollow earth were part of orthodox science until the late 18th century. In 1692, British astronomer Edmund Halley — he of comet fame — in an attempt to explain variations in the measurements of the North Magnetic Pole, proposed a world made up of four concentric spheres, one inside the other, each separated by an atmosphere, and

all turning about a common axis but at slightly different speeds. In a speculative mood, Halley went on to wonder whether each of these spheres might support life, just as the outer sphere supports us. For Halley, as for many of the early hollow earthers, one of the reasons for such speculation was a simple one if somewhat puzzling to us today — economy. God, they reasoned, would surely not waste the vast interior of a planet by filling it up with rock. (This reminds me of the doddering old Christian Brother I once had as a history teacher, who solemnly told us that the pyramids were so big the Egyptians would not have wasted them on just one pharaoh each.)

Advances in physics and geology soon made theories like Halley's untenable. That left the business of promoting a hollow earth to enthusiastic amateurs, the first and most enthusiastic of them all being an American named John Cleves Symmes. An ex-soldier and frontier trader, Symmes retained Halley's concentric spheres separated by an 'aerial elastic fluid' but added his own idea of twin openings at the poles (the one at the North Pole being 4,000 miles in diameter). These holes were joined so that the earth was in effect shaped like a doughnut, and it was possible to sail into the openings and reach the inner world.

In 1818, Symmes distributed a circular throughout America outlining his ideas and requesting funds to mount an expedition — to be led by him — into the northern opening. Undeterred by the ridicule with which this was generally met, the single-minded Symmes spent the next few years lecturing and hectoring, picking up some

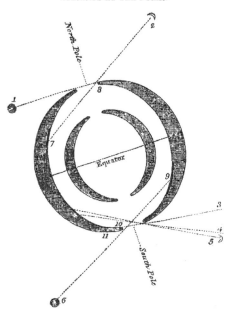

SECTIONAL VIEW OF THE EARTH.
SHOWING THE
OPENINGS AT THE POLES.

prominent supporters along the way (no less than nine petitions advocating Symmes's expedition were debated by Congress). After his death his work was carried on by his son, Americus, who was big on the idea that the interior world was inhabited by the Lost Tribes of Israel.

Other hollow earthers followed in Symmes's wake. One of the more indefatigable was Marshall Gardner, a sewing machine manufacturer whose masterpiece, *A Journey to the Earth's Interior; or, Have the Poles Really Been Reached?* appeared in 1913. Gardner kept Symmes's polar openings but jettisoned the system of concentric spheres, believing instead in the earth as a hollow bubble equipped with an interior sun. Gardner, in Jules Verne mode, wrote vividly of an internal world bursting with lush vegetation and roamed by animals such as mastodons which were thought to be extinct. As with many of the early hollow earthers, one of Gardner's main themes was that here was a vast amount of land ripe for colonisation by the United States.

Gardner lived long enough to see both north and south poles reached — in 1911 and 1913 respectively — but went to his grave believing that instead of reaching the poles (which of course he did not believe in), the explorers had simply wandered aimlessly around the rims of his vaunted polar openings.

Meanwhile the theory of a hollow earth had been given a novel twist by the social visionary Dr Cyrus Teed. He too postulated a hollow earth warmed by a central sun, but then went on to suggest that we are actually living *inside* such a globe. This is what is known in Hollywood as a 'high concept'.

Teed, who was born in 1839, was a doctor of what would now be called alternative medicine and a dabbler in 'electro-alchemy'. One night he was sitting in his alchemical laboratory in New York, pondering the mysteries of the universe, when he had a strange and erotic vision. A beautiful, golden-haired, purple-robed woman appeared who told him he had been reincarnated many times — once as Jesus Christ — and revealed to him the secrets of the cosmos. Teed (as Vernon Howell of the Branch Davidians would do many years later) adopted the name of Koresh (Hebrew for Cyrus), and

began preaching his revelation to his patients, most of whom thought him unhinged. Undaunted, he moved to Chicago and during the 1880s acquired a large number of — mostly female — followers, attracted by the man's magnetic personality.

There was a lot more to Teed's ideas than an eccentric cosmology. Like many 19th century idealists he dreamed of setting up a utopian community, a New Jerusalem, the capital of the world. His opportunity came in 1890 when a German settler in Florida was persuaded to sign over 320 acres on Estero Bay to the Koreshans. Teed moved about a hundred of his followers there and set up the Koreshan Co-operative and Communistic Society, run, as its name suggests, on communist lines. Alcohol and tobacco were forbidden and celibacy was recommended for the community's upper echelons. Women occupied an exalted position in Koreshanity. The community was ruled by Teed, his long-time companion Anna Ordway, whom he had renamed Victoria Gratia, and a council of seven women representing the seven planets. (The fact that the majority of Teed's followers were women led, not surprisingly, to allegations of sexual impropriety on his part, but for once these seem to have been unfounded.) Teed's community prospered, with its population reaching 200 by the turn of the century.

According to Teed's cosmology, the sun, moon, stars, indeed everything we can see is inside the earth and outside there is — nothing. It was all quite literally a return to the womb — that of the earth goddess, the beautiful girl of his vision. Teed nevertheless

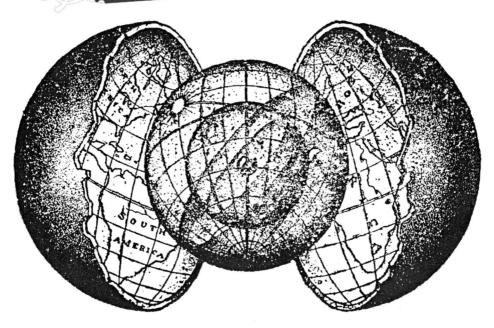

continued to think of himself as a scientist, and cast about for some proof. To this end, a device called the Rectilineator was constructed out of large T-squares, and over several months in 1897 experiments were carried out with it which proved that the earth was indeed, as Teed's theory required, concave. A large sign above the entrance to the Koreshan community proudly proclaimed "WE LIVE ON THE INSIDE".

Teed's mistake was to go into politics. Growing dissatisfied with the Democrats, for whom he had previously instructed his followers to vote, he formed the Progressive Liberty Party, which began to look like it might do well in the 1904 election. The tensions this caused led to a public brawl between Koreshans and some locals, during which Teed was beaten about the head. He never fully recovered from his injuries and died three years later. His followers, expecting

his body to undergo 'Theocrisis' (i.e. disappear in a flash of electro-alchemical light), laid it in state and watched, only to see it decompose. Eventually the health authorities forced them to bury it, and the community Teed had founded went into a slow decline.

While soon forgotten in America, Teed's ideas had a second lease of life in Germany when several issues of a Koreshan magazine fell into the hands of an ex-WWI pilot, Peter Bender, who was so taken with them he came to believe that he too was a reincarnation of Koresh. He began to promote the 'Hollow Earth Doctrine' or 'Hohlweltlehre' vigorously, aided by the fact that he was friends with several high-level Nazis including Herman Göring. In 1933, an engineer named Mengering, who lived in the city of Magdeburg in Prussia, conceived an experiment to test the theory. His idea was a simple one. If we indeed live inside a hollow sphere, then a rocket launched vertically from

results of these experiments proved less than promising, the Nazis apparently lost patience with Bender, and soon afterwards he and his family were carted off to a concentration camp where they perished.

In 1959, Ray Palmer, who had made quite a stir in the '40s by publishing Richard Shaver's stories about an underground race of evil, hypnotising dwarfs called deros, began to promote the idea that flying saucers came not from outer space, but from the interior of the earth. His chief piece of evidence for the existence of polar openings — from which UFOs emerged — was the claim that famed polar explorer Admiral Richard E. Byrd, in expeditions in 1947 and 1956, had flown over the north and south poles and found lands 'beyond' them, facts which Palmer claimed the government had suppressed. Byrd had indeed been on expeditions in these years (although they had in fact both been to the south pole) but the tale of polar openings seems to have been made up by one F. Amadeo Giannini, who wrote about it in his book *Worlds Beyond the Poles*. This tale has proved to be an extremely tenacious one. What was purported to be Byrd's uncensored log of the North Pole trip was published as a book in 1990, and excerpts from it continue to pop up in alternative and conspiracy magazines and on the internet. In the log, Byrd describes flying over rolling green hills and spotting what looks like a mammoth. Suddenly, flying saucers appear, emblazoned with swastikas! Byrd's plane is forced to land and he is met

Germany would, if it travelled far enough, eventually land in somewhere like Australia. Mengering obtained financial assistance from the city council and the help of several rocket experts from Berlin. Unfortunately rocket technology in 1933 wasn't quite up to this experiment and when, after several test flights, a projectile was launched on 29 June it travelled vertically rather than horizontally (it must have provided a good day out for the locals, though). The Hollow Earth Doctrine was put to the test at least once more 10 years later. With Germany desperate for new weapons to win the war, the Naval Research Institute financed a study into the theory's naval applications (the idea here being that, if the surface of the earth is concave, objects at a distance — including enemy ships — might be detected by pointing a sufficiently powerful telescope at the sky). When the

by several blond, German-speaking men who take him to a glowing 'crystal city'. Here he meets the 'Master', who says that they have been observing 'our race' and warns Byrd that we are on a path to atomic destruction. (Byrd had obviously wandered into a variation of the idea that a group of Nazis — usually including Hitler — had escaped Germany in secretly developed flying saucers or 'flügelrads' and were hiding out beneath the Antarctic.)

The Nazis are also linked to the hollow earth via a cluster of stories about Agharti, a legendary underground city somewhere in Central Asia which is said to be the home of a race of superior beings. Basically a corruption of certain Buddhist ideas (in particular the story of Shamballah, a hidden city which is sometimes thought of as a real place), the legend originated in the writings of a 19th century French political philosopher, Joseph-Alexandre Saint Yves, who advocated an authoritarian system called 'synarchy' — as opposed to anarchy. As an example of a society run along such lines, Saint Yves wrote about 'Agharta' (which he claimed to have learned about through telepathic communication with the Dalai Lama). With the spelling changed to Agharti, the city was popularised by a Polish scientist and explorer, Ferdinand Ossendowski, in his 1922 blockbuster *Beasts, Men and Gods*. According to Ossendowski's colourful account, he was travelling through Mongolia when a succession of monks and lamas all told him the same strange story. In 1890, they said, a personage with the grand title of the 'King of the World' had appeared to them to deliver a great prophecy, a tale of coming wars and tribulations which would only end when the

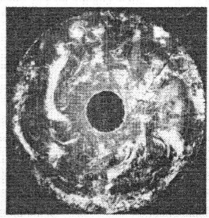

FIRST PHOTOS OF THE HOLE AT THE POLE! Satellites ESSA-3 and ESSA-7 Penetrate Cloud Cover! Mariners Also Photograph Martian Polar Opening!

King and his subjects emerged from Agharti to bring about peace. Variations of this story have been kicking round for years. In the Nazi version, the city becomes the home of evil Tibetan monks who helped Hitler in his rise to power in the thirties.

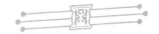

The supposed polar discoveries of Admiral Byrd figure largely in Dr Raymond Bernard's *The Hollow Earth* (1963), which is the best-known book on the subject. Bernard — a pseudonym for Walter Stieglitz — was a health food crank and confirmed celibate who had been warning people of a coming nuclear holocaust since the '50s (he lived on an island off Brazil which he claimed was outside fallout range). He also dreamed of a super race of females who reproduced parthogenetically,

and came to believe they lived inside the earth. Bernard's attempts to sell land on his island were seen by some as little more than a real estate scam, but it seems that he genuinely believed in the interior world, and himself suffered at the hands of conmen who claimed they could show him a way into it.

The hollow earth's biggest booster in recent years has been Rodney M. Cluff, the author of *World Top Secret: Our Earth IS Hollow!* Born in the Mormon enclave of Colonia Juarez in Mexico, Cluff first heard about the hollow earth when he was 16 and working on a farm in New Mexico. "What an ideal place for the Lord to hide the Lost Tribes of Israel!" he thought. Later, he read Bernard's book, and became so convinced about the idea that he moved his family from Arizona to Alaska in 1981. One day, he and a number of other hollow earthers set off on a mission to find the fabled opening. "We started on the road to Point Barrow," he recalled. "We saw a sign, at one point, saying 'This is a Private Road, Don't Go Any Further'. So we didn't go any further."

After the failure of this mission, Cluff and his family returned to Arizona, but the dream of the hollow earth remained alive. In 2003, he was contacted by Steve Currey, who had inherited a travel business in Utah called the Expedition Company. Currey asked Cluff for his help in planning an exhibition. The first step, they decided, would be to fly a plane over the pole and find the opening. A chartered Russian nuclear icebreaker, the *Yamal*, would then make its way there. Forty people paid $26,000 to take part in the voyage, but in 2006, three months before the plane was due to go on its reconnaissance mission, Currey

was diagnosed with six brain tumours and died shortly afterwards.

Another expedition member, Dr Brooks Agnew, was appointed as leader, more funds were raised, and summer 2014 was pencilled in for the Voyage to Our Hollow Earth Expedition. Alas, in September 2013, Dr Agnew was forced to pull out after a major shareholder in his electric car company heard about his involvement with the expedition and withdrew his funds. When another expedition member was killed in a plane crash, Cluff lamented, "There seems to be some force that's trying to stop this happening. I think it's the international bankers. They don't want the Inner Earth people messing around with their slaves, here on the outer world." At the time of writing, he was still accepting applications for a new expedition leader.

Whatever science may say about it, the hollow earth is such a neat and satisfying concept it's unlikely to ever disappear. According to a story that has been doing the rounds of the New Age media for years, in 1991 a Danish scientist named Edmund Bork led an international expedition to the North Pole, which passed through a polar opening and found a land of tropical vegetation, lit by its own sun, with a warm shallow sea and a peaceful population of humans — the ideal holiday destination in fact. Let's face it, we live on the skin of a large rock hurtling at unimaginable speeds through a vast, cold, mysterious and potentially dangerous universe. Wouldn't it be nice to go inside?

LESBIAN VAMPIRES

t had been a pleasant night for Eddie Baldock, a night of good conversation and perhaps a few too many soothing ales. Now the pot-bellied, 47-year-old Brisbane council worker and father of five was on his way home and finding the going a little rough. He was leaning against a lamp post, having a breather, when the metallic green Commodore drove up and the four nice young women offered him a lift…

Tracey Wigginton's friends believed she was a vampire. The tall, heavily built 24-year-old constantly wore dark glasses, avoided mirrors and seemed to go out only at night. Sometimes she defrosted meat and drank the blood, or bought it fresh from the butcher. Her lover, Lisa Ptaschinski, would cut her hand and let Tracey drink from it. Like two of Tracey's other friends, Kim Jervis and Tracey Waugh, she believed that Tracey was unable to eat solid food and needed blood to survive. Lisa had a heart condition and was reluctant to keep providing Tracey with sustenance, so the four women began to discuss finding a victim for her.

They met on Friday, 20 October 1989, at a lesbian club in Brisbane's sleaze district, Fortitude Valley. After sharing a couple of bottles of champagne they went for a drive, first to the city's Botanic Gardens, then to a nearby park where they found Eddie Baldock. Having enticed him into the car they drove to another park where Tracey led him down to the bank of the Brisbane River, while the others stayed in the car. After a while, Tracey returned, saying, "This guy is too strong, I'll need help." Lisa accompanied her back to the river where Eddie was sitting near a rowing clubhouse, naked except for his socks. Lisa was supposed to stab him first, but couldn't bring herself to. She watched as Tracey stabbed Eddie 15 times with two knives, almost severing his head from his body. "Have you ever seen a shark frenzy, a feeding frenzy?" asked Lisa at her trial. "That's what it was like." When Tracey was finished she washed herself in the river before returning to the car, looking, according to Kim, like someone who had just eaten a three-course meal.

The next day Kim, Lisa and Tracey Waugh all went voluntarily to the police, but Tracey Wigginton would have been caught soon enough anyway — her Commonwealth Bank key card was found in Eddie Baldock's shoe. In a trial which lasted just nine minutes, Tracey pleaded guilty and was sentenced to life imprisonment.

At their trial, held in February 1991, Tracey's accomplices described her as having an almost hypnotic hold over them. Tracey

Waugh called her a devil worshipper who could read minds and disappear, leaving only her "cat's eyes" visible. Like all good vampires she feared crosses. Kim had worn one around her neck, but on the Monday before the murder it had broken and, said Waugh, "once that cross came off she didn't have any protection". Tracey Waugh said she had not wanted to take part in the killing, but when Tracey walked up to her on the Friday night and said, "Come with me," she had felt compelled to go.

"When Tracey wasn't there we knew it was [wrong]. As soon as we saw Tracey on Friday night… as if she just sort of, I don't know, mind control. She used her mind to make us think it was all right."

Tracey's Waugh's counsel claimed his client had been a 'reserve victim' whose blood would have been drunk had they not found Eddie Baldock.

Kim Jervis said that Tracey had told her, "I want to scare you, to frighten the living hell out of you." Kim said she thought all the talk of killing had been a joke, but this hadn't stopped her buying one of the knives Tracey used on Eddie Baldock. It was probably this act which led to her being convicted of manslaughter and sentenced to 18 years, even though she remained in the car while the killing took place. Lisa Ptaschinski was convicted of murder and sentenced to life imprisonment.

It's a pity that Tracey Wigginton pleaded guilty, for her trial would have been a fascinating one. The compulsion to drink blood from which she suffered is not as uncommon as some might imagine. American folklorist Norine Dresser has collected many cases of people who believe themselves to be vampires. Some think of themselves as blood fetishists, and there is an undeniably sexual component to most blood drinking rituals. Others identify more heavily with the romantic image of the fictional vampire, and adopt the trappings that go with it — black clothing, sunglasses, avoiding mirrors and garlic. Some believe they have inherited their condition, and can pass it on to those whose blood they drink. Most of them can carry on normal lives, and seem to have little difficulty in finding people willing to donate their blood. Among the reasons given by these modern day vampires for their compulsion are the romance of the image, the life-giving properties of blood, and the feeling of power which the act of blood drinking provides.

But did Tracey Wigginton really believe she was a vampire? The case is not as straightforward as the headlines suggested.

Tracey Wigginton was raised by her grandparents, George and Avril Wigginton. George was the millionaire owner of a transport company and a pillar of Rockhampton society. Unable to have children, George and Avril adopted two girls, Rhonda in 1942 and Dorrell in 1950, and later took in a part-Indian girl named Michelle. Avril, a domineering woman who, it has been alleged, was sexually abused as a child, treated her adopted daughters

mercilessly, frequently flogging them with electrical cords and a hose with a chain in it. She had a pathological hatred of men, telling them, "When you grow up men will do horrible things to you. All they want is sex." The girls were rarely let out of the house.

Rhonda was 21 when she married and gave birth to a daughter — Tracey — in 1965. The marriage soon failed and she moved back to George and Avril's. When she later married a Townsville man and moved there to be with him, Tracey, aged four, was left with her grandparents. Three years later they formally adopted her. In contrast to their treatment of the other girls, George and Avril spoilt Tracey, sending her to the best schools and paying for her to have expensive music, dancing and elocution lessons. Meanwhile Michelle, whom Tracey thought of as a sister, was given the usual treatment. Once, Avril tied her to a post and whipped her, then locked her in a kennel overnight. She was even punished for things which Tracey did. When Michelle was 16 she ran away.

The young Tracey Wigginton was a mass of contradictions. A devout churchgoer, she also developed an interest in the occult, attending séances and learning to read tarot cards (later she was said to belong to a satanist group which practised animal sacrifice, although the details of this are predictably sketchy). A generally pleasant and generous girl, she had a violent temper, too. Shortly after Avril's death in 1981, an event which left her devastated (George had died two years previously) she trashed her aunt Dorrell's house, daubing the walls with swastikas and obscenities. She had boyfriends, but began

The Young Tracey Wigginton

to live openly as a lesbian, acquiring cropped hair, tattoos and a very big black bike. After squandering $75,000, the first instalment of her inheritance from George, she moved to Brisbane where she was known in the gay community as Bobby.

Shortly after her arrest, Tracey Wigginton was examined by a psychiatrist, Dr Jim Quinn. Noting that she had lapses in memory, he began to suspect Tracey was suffering from multiple personality disorder, and persuaded her to participate in a course of hypnotism. After many hours of hypnosis, five personalities were identified: Bobby, who was aggressive and spoke in a deep voice; Little Tracey, a frightened eight-year-old; Big Tracey, who was depressed; the Observer, who watched over the others; and Avril, who was, according to Dr Quinn, "the most terrifying of all", the one who controlled

Bobby. As with most cases of multiple personality, the cause of Tracey's mental fragmentation was said to be childhood sexual abuse. Tracey claimed that her grandfather George had been abusing her since she was nine. (This latter allegation was not, it should be pointed out, an example of a 'recovered memory' surfacing during hypnotism. When Tracey was only 10-years-old she had told a friend that she was being abused.)

"I didn't kill Edward," Tracey later told Dorrell. "I killed George. All I could see was George." "I just hope she does not want to kill Avril as well," commented Dorrell.

The concept of multiple personality is an extremely controversial one. Cases of it have proliferated in the wake of popular films like *The Three Faces of Eve* and *Sybil*, but some psychiatrists flatly reject the concept, or maintain that if it exists it is extremely rare. Instead, they claim it is created during the therapy which is supposedly treating it. It is now generally accepted that patients can lie under hypnosis, and will say what they believe the person hypnotising them wants to hear. This was the view taken by the Queensland Mental Health Tribunal, which rejected Dr Quinn's diagnosis and ruled Tracey fit for the trial that ended so quickly with her guilty plea.

In his 1992 study of the case, *The Vampire Killer*, Ron Hicks argued that Quinn's diagnosis of multiple personalities was correct, and that this was the only possible explanation for the inconsistencies in Tracey's character and behaviour over the years. (Interestingly, he was inclined to dismiss Tracey's accusations about her grandfather,

as did the rest of Tracey's family, at least initially. George certainly did not molest any of his other daughters.) Hicks also disputed the idea that Tracey Wigginton thought she was a vampire, as Tracey herself has denied since her arrest. Vampires were Kim Jervis's fantasy, he maintained, not Tracey's. After the murder, the three accomplices latched onto the concept of a vampire Tracey to demonise her and diminish their own responsibility. (It must be said, though, that their stories seem remarkably consistent.) Instead, Hicks believed the murder of Eddie Baldock was a satanic ritual. When he interviewed Tracey in Brisbane's Boggo Road Jail, however, she flatly denied any connection with the occult, while the other three women refused to speak to him.

So, was Tracey Wigginton a multiple personality, a victim of childhood abuse, a satanist and a crazed blood-drinker, some of the above, or none of the above? On the available evidence, it's impossible to say.

There was an interesting postscript to the case, which demonstrated the degree to which the vampire has become the stuff of erotic fantasy. Eddie Baldock's widow, Elaine, who claimed to have suffered abuse and harassment from lesbians since the trial of Tracey's accomplices, drew attention to a Telecom phone sex service called 'Lesbian Vampires'. The recording portrayed two lesbians (one of them named Lisa) who, after dancing together at a nightclub, picked up a man and took him to a spot by a river. They ordered him to strip to his "jocks", tied him up to a tree and performed lesbian acts in front of him before one of them bit him on the neck. Elaine

Friday, February 1, 1991

Trial told of blood drinking frenzy

BRISBANE: A woman who alleged a victim and drank his blood like a shark in a fee Brisban trial w

Vampire controlled my mind, court told

BRISBANE: A woman fell under the control of a lesbian vampire after breaking a neck chain bearing a "protective" crucifix, a Supreme Court murder trial was told yesterday.

In a video-taped interview played to the court, one of three accused women said she and her

Vampire killer set out to scare

BRISBANE: A vampire woman wanted to "frighten the living hell" out of one of her alleged accomplices during a killing for blood, a Supreme Court jury heard yesterday.

In a video-taped police interview, one of the murder accused, Kim Aileen Jervis, said she was told by "vampire" Tracey Avril 'Wigginton: "I want to scare you."

Wigginton has already pleaded guilty to the murder, alleged to have been committed to satisfy her craving for human blood.

Jervis and tw 'order on trial

Vampire's 2nd victim theory

said his client had been manipulated by ...inton and may drank his blood.
...ter Peter Feeney, for

Clayfield, Tracey Ann Waugh, unemployed secretary, also aged 24, of Clayfield, and Lisa Maree Ptaschinski, 25, of Leichhardt, west of Brisbane.

In the tape played to the court yesterday, Jervis said she thought plans made for the killing were a "joke".

Wigginton urday, February 16, 1991 to scare you, hell out of ;

She said tl killing the drive after nightclub i Valley.

Woman gets life term for vampire murder

After pl who had a staggering drove out went wit Jervis Baldoc clubhou been sl ping o

BRISBANE: One woman was jailed for life yesterday and another for 18 years after being found guilty of the 1989 vampire Court style killing of a drunken man in a Wi park mor on four trial in Brisbane's Supreme sho Tracey Ann

(Clockwise from top left) Wigginton and alleged accomplices Jervis, Waugh and Ptaschinski. But instead, Wigginton' killed dward Clyde Baldock, of subur. n West End in a park near the she stabbed his along

Baldock called the recording "disgusting". A couple of days later it was disconnected.

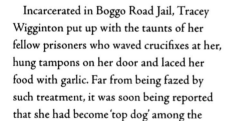

Incarcerated in Boggo Road Jail, Tracey Wigginton put up with the taunts of her fellow prisoners who waved crucifixes at her, hung tampons on her door and laced her food with garlic. Far from being fazed by such treatment, it was soon being reported that she had become 'top dog' among the female prisoners.

Wigginton had plenty of fans outside jail, too, with the most obsessive being a Melbourne woman named Tina Joy Dillon. In 1995, having sent Wigginton numerous letters, Dillon arrived in Brisbane determined to meet her idol. After spending a night out drinking, she hailed a taxi and asked to be taken to the nearest police station. When the driver pulled up outside Brisbane's police headquarters, Dillon handed him a note demanding money, then slashed his neck with a piece of broken glass. She was quickly arrested, and charged with aggravated assault and intent to steal. At the hearing, the public defender argued that she should be sent back to Melbourne for psychiatric treatment. Dillon strenuously objected to this — she wanted to go to jail to meet Tracey — but when told she might not end up in the same jail, she relented.

In 1996, a journalist named Ella Riggert managed to enter the jail posing as a lawyer and interview Wigginton, whom she described as a 'model prisoner'. Wigginton expressed remorse for the killing of Eddie Baldock, but denied drinking his blood. "I have always hated the sight of blood. It physically makes

me ill — even a little cut on my finger." She explained the killing as the result of pent-up rage caused by the traumas of her childhood. "I was off the planet when I killed. I wasn't even my usual doormat self — I was an animal." Wigginton told Riggert she was studying philosophy and anthropology by correspondence, and all she wanted to do now was "help people". The prison authorities were furious when the interview appeared in the *Courier Mail*, and made sure their notorious prisoner received no further publicity.

Wigginton became eligible for parole after 15 years, but her first applications for it were rejected. Parole was finally granted in January 2012, despite the objections of Queensland's attorney general and other politicians. She emerged from prison grey-haired and hobbling on crutches. She was said to be suffering from a back complaint, a knee injury and hepatitis C, and the *Courier Mail* published an article bemoaning the fact that her poor health would make her eligible for up to $928 in fortnightly welfare payments. It was reported she intended to change her name, and perhaps she has, for she has managed to stay out of the headlines since then.

VAMPIRES
A HISTORICAL NOTE

Vampires are part of the folklore of many countries, from most of Europe to China, Indonesia and the Philippines, and many theories have been put forward to account for this. In one of the more ingenious theories, an American chemist, David Dolphin, linked vampirism with the rare, degenerative genetic disease porphyria. One of the treatments for porphyria is the injection of heme, the pigmented part of haemoglobin. Medieval sufferers of the disease, argued Dolphin, unable to benefit from such injections, might have resorted to drinking blood in order to absorb heme. Moreover, victims of porphyria may suffer from photosensitivity (which would account for the vampire's famed aversion to sunlight), while other symptoms include discolouration of the skin and an abnormal lengthening of the teeth. Dolphin also suggested that the vampire's dislike of garlic may stem from the fact that one of garlic's main constituents destroys heme, and might therefore be expected to worsen a porphyria attack.

Dolphin's theory gained wide publicity when he announced it in 1985 (to the consternation of modern sufferers of porphyria). At first glance it looks persuasive, but upon examination quickly collapses. For a start, heme cannot be absorbed through the stomach lining, so even if a porphyria sufferer had conceived the idea of drinking blood, it would have done them no good whatsoever. As for the other correspondences, porphyria is not one disease but several, and it's only in the rarest form (only 60 cases of which have ever been identified) that the symptoms of photosensitivity and lengthening of teeth are found. It is highly unlikely that such a rare condition could have led to such a widespread belief. (In any case, long, sharp teeth are not a characteristic of the vampire of folklore.)

A much more coherent and convincing theory was put forward by folklorist Paul Barber in his book *Vampires, Burial and Death* (1988). Barber returned to the original accounts of the detection and destruction of vampires, and found the root of the myth in a basic misunderstanding of what happens to the human body after death. In order to appreciate this we must first put aside the conventional image of the vampire — a gaunt, pale, long-fanged, sophisticated sort of gent in evening dress and long cape, who was largely a product of the imagination of Bram Stoker. He bears little resemblance to the vampire of folklore, usually described as plump, florid or ruddy of face, evil-smelling, long-fingernailed and hairy.

A typical vampire scare went something like this. Misfortune would befall a village; a series of unusual deaths perhaps, or an outbreak of property damage. The villagers, searching for a cause, would cast their minds back to someone who had died recently in mysterious circumstances. A person who had died young, for example, or been murdered, or committed suicide (all of which, it was believed, could turn you into a vampire). Having fixed on a suspect, off they would go to the cemetery (torches optional), tear open the grave and uncover the body. And what would they see?

Most people, if they think about the subject at all, would imagine that a dead body decomposes fairly rapidly. In fact, the rate of decomposition varies wildly, with factors such as temperature and the moisture content and composition of the soil playing a part. Far from being dead, a corpse is actually a riot of microorganisms, and a great many changes may take place within it after interment. It changes colour; the skin may shrivel, making it appear that hair, teeth and fingernails have grown (something which does not actually happen); alternatively the skin may slough off, revealing a layer of pink skin underneath; a build-up of gases such as methane may cause the body to bloat, or even burst, and move the limbs about; blood and other fluids may be forced through the mouth; or very little change may take place, so that the body appears not to have decomposed at all.

Our Medieval villagers, having uncovered their corpse, would thus have seen a variety of things, all of which would have confirmed their belief that they had found a vampire. Bloating would have been perceived as plumpness, blood around the mouth a sign that the vampire had been feeding, while sloughing of the skin showed that new skin was growing. A powerful stench was a sign of a vampire (which is why garlic and other strong-smelling substances were good for warding them off — the practice of fighting like with like) but the absence of odour could mean the same thing. Indeed, in the hundreds of accounts which Barber studied, he found only two where villagers, having uncovered their corpse, were persuaded by its appearance that they had not found a vampire. Of course once identification had been made, they could get down to the important business of disposing of the vampire using whatever method was customary in the region — dismembering, beheading, burning, or the tried and trusted stake.

WILLIAM CHIDLEY
EMPEROR OF AUSTRALIAN ECCENTRICS

illiam James Chidley, visionary, reformer, and a man who realised that, when it comes to sex, we are all making a simple yet terrible mistake, was born in Melbourne around 1860. He was one of five orphans adopted by John James Chidley, a toy shop owner and later a photographer with a mobile studio drawn by horses, and his wife Maria, whom he met on the boat which brought him to Australia from England. The elder Chidley was a somewhat eccentric character in his own right who raised his family as vegetarians, experimented in communal living, and once constructed a flying machine of bamboo. His adopted son grew up tormented by sexual guilt and masturbatory fears extreme even by the standards of his day, all of which he documented in painful detail in his autobiography, *The Confessions*. From the beginning, Chidley found in his body an enemy. A typical incident:

It must have been about this time that my penis became erect and stiff and would not go down, so that a doctor had to be called in. I stood in the corner by the fireplace, face to the wall, refusing to let him see 'it'. I remember my rage and shame, and Mother's kind words—even

the amused look in the young doctor's eyes as he dabbed at 'it' with a sponge, which increased my rage so that I kicked at him.

Chidley left school at 13, and was briefly apprenticed to a solicitor. His parents, noticing that he had artistic talents, then placed him with an architect who was usually absent from his office, leaving the boy to his own devices. "So for five years," he wrote, "when Mother and Father thought I was learning a good profession, I was reading novels, drawing caricatures—and self-abusing." Chidley had no doubts about the toll the latter activity was taking on him. His temper was bad and he was cruel to his mother; he was eating too much meat; he was red around the eyes and a strange ridge had developed on the back of his head. His mother, who had found one of the 'indecent cards' he carried around with him, told him that her favourite brother had killed himself with self-abuse, which had led to a heart attack (she heard the doctor say so). Even his friends noticed the telltale physical signs, although it seems they may have been teasing him. (He recalled one friend saying to him, "Why, Willy, your head is getting smaller.")

Chidley lost his virginity to a middle-aged prostitute ("a miserable experience", he called it). Despite his own fears about his

appearance, he was a good looking fellow, 6ft 2in (1.9 metres) tall, and afterwards had sexual liaisons with many women. For a while he was the partner of a Melbourne photographer, and managed to seduce some of the female customers who came to his shop (the resulting scandal saw the photographer evicted). He also made a little money painting portraits, but for most of these years he was unemployed and living hand to mouth. He spent much of his time in public libraries reading books on philosophy and metaphysics, and decided he would one day like to write a book.

When he did get a little money, he usually spent it on drink, and in 1882 that almost got him into very great trouble indeed. He and his friend Arthur were in Adelaide, heading back to their hotel after a day's drinking, when they passed a young man who was hitting a woman. When they confronted him, he threw a stone which struck Chidley on the head. He and Arthur punched the man and left him lying unconscious on the pavement. A few days later, they heard he had died. Chidley and Arthur were arrested, charged with manslaughter and spent time in jail, but the charges were eventually dismissed. Chidley felt great remorse about the man's death, and resolved to give up the grog, which he did briefly.

In his early 20s, Chidley took up acting, joining an amateur travelling company based in Adelaide. The performers included a pretty young actress named Ada who was on the run from her husband, a violent criminal named Thoms. They entered into a volatile, poverty stricken and ultimately doomed relationship that lasted over two decades, living in a succession of dingy rooms and cottages in Melbourne, Adelaide and Sydney, with many separations, followed by tearful reunions.

Ada clearly adored Chidley, but he was a troubled, moody and difficult man, and his anxieties only increased when in the mid-1880s a doctor told him he was suffering from a disease of the lungs which would kill him in two years. He pored over medical books, searching for the causes of his misery and the misery he saw in those around him. He strove to lead an abstemious life, avoiding meat, alcohol, tobacco, tea and coffee. All of these, he was sure, contributed to humanity's lamentable state, but he was convinced the real problem lay with sex. The physical effects of sexual intercourse on the body he could see clearly in himself and others.

Another thing that occupied my thoughts at this time was the look of convergence of my brows, and indeed of my whole figure. I was still consumptive and thin, but sometimes, especially after coition, I seemed to be and to feel converging. I don't know how else to say it.

He was sure, too, that sex was the cause of Ada's epilepsy, having noticed that her fits were less frequent after periods of abstinence.

For a while, Chidley reasoned that 'excessive coition' was the culprit. Yet he had noticed that even a single instance of sexual intercourse resulted in adverse physical effects — furrowed brows, injured eyes and

The ANSWER.

surprising them both. ("It must be because I love you," he had said.) He thought little of it at the time, only gradually realising the extraordinary significance of what had occurred.

The problem was not 'excessive coition' but 'unnatural coition'. The male erection and the shocks on the body its use entailed — the 'crowbar method' — was, he now realised, the main cause of illness, ageing and disease. Erections had caused him enough trouble throughout his life — now he would declare war on them. In the natural act that he envisaged, it was the woman who had a sort of reverse erection, her vagina distending and creating a vacuum which drew in the penis. He gave the proviso, though, that such intercourse could only occur during spring, between two people who were in love. That Chidley himself never again achieved intercourse in this manner did not deter him at all.

Ada was distinctly unimpressed when Chidley told her of his discovery. "What, do you mean that what people have been doing for thousands of years — is unnatural? You have discovered that?"

The third element which came to define Chidley's philosophy, after vegetarianism and 'natural coition', was dress reform and the benefits of fresh air. Heavy clothing was unhealthy, led to unwanted erections in men, and was the reason why people craved meat. He took to wearing light clothing, even in winter, and slept naked with the bedroom window wide open.

In the early 1890s, Ada left Chidley again, returning to her hometown of Adelaide and taking up with a man name Madigan, another violent fellow who beat her. This time, the

thickened joints. How could an act that was so natural cause such 'shocks' to the body? Could it be that the act itself was *not* natural?

He recalled a night when an extraordinary thing had happened. He had been lying beside Ada in bed when his unerect penis had somehow found its way into her vagina,

separation lasted for several years. When she eventually rejoined Chidley, she had a little boy named Donald with her. According to Chidley, the boy had been born nine months after their separation, and resembled him, so he believed he was the father. In 1900, Chidley took him to New Zealand, where they were later joined by Ada. It was only then that she revealed to him the truth about Donald — she had adopted him in a hospital after the woman in the next bed had died giving birth to him, and after her own baby (presumably Chidley's) had been stillborn. When Chidley and Ada returned to Australia, Donald stayed in New Zealand, and died there in 1926.

Chidley and Ada fell back into their usual pattern of brief periods of happiness punctuated by quarrels and separations. Chidley's greatest problem was that he could never stick to his own principles for happiness, and Ada bore the brunt of it. He would refrain from having sex with her for long periods but then, overcome by lust, force himself on her. He tried to limit himself to a diet of fruit and brown bread, and make her do the same, until the craving for meat returned. His efforts at abstaining from alcohol had never been very successful, and during these years they both appear to have been drinking more than ever. Ada's health went into a steep decline. They were living in rooms in Melbourne in December 1908 when she had a particularly bad fit and became delirious. Chidley accompanied her in the ambulance to the Poor Hospital, where she died several hours later. She was 48.

Chidley was distraught, blaming himself for Ada's death. As he looked back on their life together, he saw so many points at which he could have turned over a new page, lived a natural life, and saved both of them. But it seems that her death also galvanised him. He had told a few of his drinking companions about his theory of unnatural coition over the years, and most had simply laughed at him. Now he would do whatever he could to take it to the world.

Chidley had poured a lifetime of reading, experience and observation into a book which he called *The Answer*, or *The World as Joy*. He sent the manuscript to numerous doctors, scientists, publishers and other eminent persons. It had been returned to him with polite notes, even a few words of encouragement, but never an outright endorsement or offer of publication.

The only intellectual to take him at all seriously was the British sexologist Havelock Ellis. Chidley initiated a correspondence with him in 1899, and later sent him the manuscript of his *Confessions*. Ellis was deeply impressed by the forcefulness of the writing, calling it "by far the most remarkable thing — indeed the only thing — that has come out of Australia". While he couldn't subscribe to Chidley's sexual theories, he included extracts from the *Confessions* among the case studies in his *Psychology of Sex*, which upset Chidley. He had not intended his autobiography to be published before his death, and while Ellis had not named him, he still worried that Australians who read the extracts might recognise him.

In 1911, with no one willing to publish his book, Chidley paid for a short version of it to be printed as a booklet, also called *The Answer*. He began to peddle it on the streets

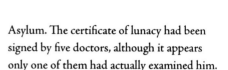

of Melbourne, but it seems that he launched his campaign in earnest one hot Sunday in Sydney. He wore a flimsy, sleeveless Roman-style tunic of white cotton, was barefooted, and carried a Gladstone bag full of copies of *The Answer*. He headed towards the Domain, the large park which was the home of the city's soapbox orators. People turned their heads in amazement, ruffians jeered, children giggled. A crowd gathered and the head of the gardens appeared and told him to move on. Attaching placards to himself, front and back, he walked down George Street where he was stopped by a policeman who asked him what he was doing "hustling women and children". He was arrested and fined 10 shillings. The template for the last few years of Chidley's life was set.

In Melbourne, copies of *The Answer* were seized by police, and while following the advice in them would have effectively led to celibacy, they were declared obscene and burned. Chidley returned to Sydney where the arrests continued, and police put pressure on the halls he tried to book for lectures. The strapping, sun-bronzed, tunic-clad figure of Chidley became a familiar sight on the streets of Sydney, and he gained some supporters who, if not exactly won over by his sex theories, could at least see that his dress was hardly crazy compared to the three-piece suits in which most Australian men still sweated through the summer months. A Chidley Defence Committee was even formed, whose members paid his fines so he could get out of jail.

In August 1912, apparently after pressure from higher authorities, the police tried a new tack. Chidley was arrested, charged with being insane and committed to Callan Park Mental Asylum. The certificate of lunacy had been signed by five doctors, although it appears only one of them had actually examined him.

To Sydney's eternal credit, the news was greeted by a wave of outrage. Many letters supporting Chidley were published in newspapers, and there was a long debate about him in the NSW Legislative Assembly on 20 August. One MP declared, "It does seem to be a most peculiar thing that because the police find some difficulty in bringing Chidley within any section of the criminal law dealing with indecent behaviour or conduct they should resort to what I call this cowardly expedient of arresting him on a charge of lunacy in the hope of getting rid of him in that way." While the debate was inconclusive, Chidley was quietly released from Callan Park on 1 October, after giving an undertaking that he would wear normal clothes and refrain from speaking about his beliefs in public. He would give numerous such assurances over the next few years, but once on the streets again the sight of his fellow humans, their faces etched with the shocks of 'unnatural coition', always demanded that he resume his crusade.

The endless series of arrests and incarcerations inevitably wore Chidley down. In September 1916, after being once again committed to the asylum, he wrote his last letter to the public.

You have looked on for five years and seen me done to death by fools, quacks and rogues (including unjust "judges"). Well, listen: —Every word of my book The Answer *is true, which*

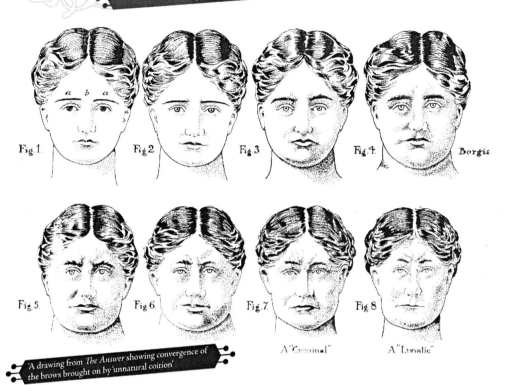

Fig 1. Fig 2. Fig 3. Fig 4. Borgia

Fig 5. Fig 6. Fig 7. Fig 8.

A "Criminal" A "Lunatic"

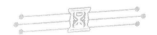

'A drawing from *The Answer* showing convergence of the brows brought on by 'unnatural coition'

you will find if you read it without prejudice. It is what I claim for it: the only solution of our troubles — of the misery and suffering of the world; the only Hope for Humanity.

The slightest investigation or observation will verify what I (and Gilruth) say of the animals. Our coitus is plainly false — a secondary mode, the result of tampering and ignorance.

There never has been such a grave miscarriage of justice as my conviction for lunacy.

Those who have crushed me out will try to crush out my book, The Answer. Don't let them! I ask Australians, with all the solemnity of a sacred message: Don't let them! I give Australians this mission in the world: —shepherd my Book! Oh! Shepherd my book! Remember, it is the One hope for Humanity! Let those read it who want it; its truth will become apparent in time…

Mine has been an unhappy life, but it contains a moral, namely, that all my misery comes from that "erection" in boys and men. Farewell!

A few days after writing this, Chidley doused his clothes with kerosene and set his troublesome body on fire. The flames were quickly extinguished and he wasn't badly burned, but friends who saw him after this said that all the spirit had gone out of him. On 21 December 1916, Chidley was chatting to another patient in Callan Park when he collapsed suddenly and died, probably from a heart attack. His lasting achievement is his vivid and heartfelt autobiography, which was finally published in 1977.

THE FAMILY WAY

THE DELIGHTFUL STORY OF ANNE HAMILTON-BYRNE

The woman who calls herself Anne Hamilton-Byrne was one very successful cult leader. In four decades of breathtaking self-aggrandisement she suffered only one setback, when police raided a Victorian property in 1987 and freed the brood of purpose-built Aryan children she had been raising and torturing for two decades. Apart from this minor hitch, it was all smooth sailing for a woman who loved cats, hated wrinkles and proclaimed herself to be the reincarnation of Jesus Christ.

Anne Hamilton-Byrne, 'the Teacher' to her followers, claimed descent from French royalty, but was born plain Evelyn Edwards in Sale, Victoria, on 30 December 1921. Her father, Ralph, was a railway cleaner, her mother, Florence, went mad and died in an asylum, and the young Evelyn was confined to an orphanage for a time. The details of Anne's early life are extremely sketchy. It is known that she married when she was 20 and had a daughter. In the 1950s she studied yoga, and somewhere along the line she picked up a smattering of Eastern mysticism which came in very handy indeed. Her big break came in the early '60s when her second husband, Michael Riley (her first died in a car accident) was working as a gardener for the respected academic Dr Raynor C. Johnson. A physicist and former head of Queen's College,

University of Melbourne, Johnson was the author of several books, such as *Nurslings of Immortality*, which dealt with spirituality, the paranormal and the question of life after death.

Anne turned up at Johnson's house one Sunday and was invited into his study. We will never know what she said in there, but it must have been quite a spiel. Johnson, by all accounts a kindly and intelligent man, emerged convinced that his gardener's wife was his spiritual master. He was keen to introduce her to others, telling them she was "a divine being who was going incognito in the world". The pair formed a partnership, attracting their first followers from Johnson's circle, and the cult which became known as the Family had begun.

The elderly professor provided the fledgling cult leader with a most valuable commodity — respectability. From the beginning Anne Hamilton-Byrne set her sights on professional people — doctors, lawyers, nurses, academics — people whose knowledge and connections would prove invaluable over the years. She recruited the owner of the Newhaven Psychiatric Hospital and several of its staff, and was made a director. (She met her third husband, Bill Byrne, in 1968, after his son was admitted to Newhaven.) Anne's medical contacts ensured a ready supply of prescription — and other — drugs,

which would become an integral part of life in the Family. Even more useful was the inside knowledge she gained. The health professionals who became her disciples had no compunction about sharing the case histories of their patients with her — after all, Anne had told them that joining her had freed them from the constraints of conventional morality. She therefore had a host of troubled individuals to pick and choose from. Introduced to them, she could appear to miraculously know all about their problems — and have solutions.

Once a person had pledged their allegiance to Anne, they were subjected to a ritual she called 'going through', which involved being locked in a darkened room and given repeated doses of LSD. As they hallucinated, initiates had to work at uncovering all the bad aspects of their personality, so that these could later be overcome. Anne or one of her lieutenants would check on them regularly, noting the personal demons that emerged. After the trauma of 'going through', many followers seemed content to hand over control of their lives to Anne.

A hall was built next to Raynor Johnson's house and named Santiniketan Lodge. When Anne was in Australia, twice-weekly services were held there which all followers were expected to attend. Sitting on a throne, bathed in bluish light, Anne delivered long, rambling sermons, full of sentences that trailed off to nothing and could have meant anything. They were punctuated by readings from other gurus she approved of, including Sai Baba, Bhagwan Shree Rajneesh and especially Swami Muktananda, the founder

of Siddha Yoga in America, and a personal friend of hers.

Anne was a woman of striking appearance who kept herself looking years younger than her age with regular bouts of plastic surgery and liposuction, and her receding hairline — the sign of a powerful mind, she said — was hidden under flowing blonde wigs.

While the Family, or the Great White Brotherhood as it was also known, never seems to have numbered more than a few hundred at a time, Anne milked them so well that her wealth at its height was estimated at over $150 million dollars, and included properties in Australia, England and the United States. Anne's grip on her followers remained firm, and it is in fact highly likely that she would today be unknown outside the small circle of her devotees had she not embarked on the scheme which made her infamous.

In the late '60s, Anne conceived the idea of raising a group of children in supposedly ideal circumstances, isolated from the outside world, indoctrinated with her ideas and convinced of her divinity. Once again, her medical contacts came in handy. Most of the children were the offspring of young, unmarried mothers from Australia and New Zealand who had been vetted for racial purity and soundness of stock. They were persuaded by Anne's followers to give up their children for adoption, sometimes moments after they had given birth. Anne acquired her first child in 1969, and adopted 13 more during the next few years. All were given the name Hamilton-Byrne, and grew up believing they were the biological offspring of Anne and Bill. Initially

kept at a property in the Dandenongs, they were later moved to a house named Kai Lama, on the shores of Lake Eildon.

The life the children led at Kai Lama has been described by one of them, Sarah Hamilton-Byrne, in a book called *Unseen, Unheard, Unknown* (which was Anne's motto for the cult). Their existence was known only to the cult's upper echelons, and as far as possible they were kept totally ignorant of the outside world, banned from TV and newspapers, and forbidden to leave the property or even swim in the lake it adjoined.

They were taught to hide in the cellar whenever strangers approached, and to particularly fear the police who, they were told, would kill them. The children's lives followed a mind-numbingly strict routine which hardly varied day after day, year after year. Much of their day, which began at 6:30 each morning, was taken up by yoga, meditation and listening to tapes of Anne's rambling and largely incomprehensible sermons. They were given rudimentary schooling, chiefly languages and mathematics taught by a cult member who was a teacher. (Later, in the '80s, the cult was able to con some officials from the education department into registering Kai Lama as a school.) The children were kept on a grossly inadequate and monotonous vegetarian diet, and grew up constantly hungry, even malnourished. At the same time they were given massive doses of vitamins, tranquillisers and other prescription drugs.

Anne Hamilton-Byrne was only infrequently at Kai Lama, spending most of the year at her other Australian properties or

in England, but her presence was everywhere in the house, in photos and in her recorded voice. The children believed that she possessed psychic powers, could see when they misbehaved even when she wasn't there, and could kill them if they tried to escape. They were actually raised by a gang of middle-aged women known as the 'aunties'. These were trusted cult members, mostly trained nurses who, under Anne's tutelage, became reasonable facsimiles of Nazi concentration camp guards. When it came to the raising of children, Anne's ideas about karma seemed to translate into the belief that the harder their lives were the better for their souls, and the aunties were happy to oblige. They rigidly enforced the ridiculously long list of rules that Anne had drawn up and was continually adding to, punishing the children when they infringed them by beating them, ducking their heads into buckets of water, or withholding their already meagre rations of food.

It is common for cult leaders to mess around with the identities of their followers, changing their names and cutting them off from their families. Anne raised this to a fine art. She renamed the children regularly, and even changed their birthdays on a whim (she also had multiple passports for each child under different names, presumably so they could be moved easily around the world in an emergency). They were given identical clothes to wear and most had their hair dyed blond. Some of them, unaware that the substance regularly applied to their hair was dye, had no idea they weren't really blond until they had been freed.

Anne Hamilton-Byrne moved through the world she created behind a fragrant persona of sweetness and love. It can be seen at its most cloying in a home video, shot in England and sent back as a message to the children, which later fell into the hands of Channel 9 (whose *A Current Affair* programme waged a long campaign against the Family). Anne and Bill are seen frolicking in a garden on a lovely summer's day.

ANNE: *Can I talk to the children? We'd just love you to be here, children. We don't often get days like these. You can count them on one hand…*
BILL: *Oh, the reason I'm going home — to see the children… I'm going to spend a month with them. Just a month with those babies of ours…*
ANNE: *Lovely.*
BILL: *…who were so tiny and they're all growing up.*
ANNE: *You love them don't you, Daddy?*
BILL: *I do love them, darling, I do.*
ANNE: *And I love you, darling.*
BILL: *I love you, Annie.*

Sure Bill loved the children. He loved in particular to beat the crap out of them. Whenever Anne and Bill returned to Kai Lama from their travels it was retribution time, with the aunties recounting how each child had broken the rules. If the children were scared of the beatings inflicted by Anne, they were terrified of the normally ineffectual Bill, who would go into a frenzy, striking them repeatedly and throwing them against walls.

Now, what was going on here? What did Anne Hamilton-Byrne think she was doing?

She used to tell her followers that these children of hers would survive a nuclear holocaust and go on to repopulate the earth, but that sounds far-fetched even by her standards. Had she become addicted to worship and, no longer satisfied with what she received from her adult followers, craved something stronger, from individuals who had grown up believing their mother to be a god? If that is what she wanted, she achieved it — for a while at least — for Sarah Hamilton-Byrne makes it clear that, in the absence of anything else to focus their affections on, they did love their glamorous and distant 'mother'. But it is clear that the cult underestimated the money and resources needed to raise 14 children, as well as the impossibility of cutting them off from the world. As they entered their teens they became, not surprisingly,

more difficult for the aunties to control, while the aunties, despite the fleeting pleasures of beating small children senseless, clearly loathed their job. The experiment had gotten out of hand. Perhaps it was a relief all round when the police stepped in to end it.

While a number of journalists began to investigate the Family in the '80s, no official action was taken against the cult until Sarah Hamilton-Byrne, who had been expelled from it after an argument with Anne, went to the police in 1987. The Lake Eildon property was raided in August of that year and the remaining children taken into care.

Eighteen months after the raid, a police task force codenamed Operation Forest was formed to investigate the Family. In June 1993, police and FBI agents arrived at a property in the Catskill Mountains, outside New York

Anne Hamilton-Byrne with husband William in 1993.

City, where Anne and Bill were living with about 30 dogs and 70 cats (cats had always had a much better time in the Family than humans). They had a warrant for the couple's arrest for perjury and conspiracy to defraud. Anne asked if she could take some wigs with her but was told she could not, and had to suffer the ignominy of having her receding, reddish-grey hair filmed by TV cameras. (Anne's internationally televised bad hair day was, it would turn out, the worst punishment she ever received.) Extradited to Australia, the couple were charged with defrauding the New Zealand registry of births by falsely claiming that three of the children they had adopted were triplets and their biological children. This charge was dropped when it was ruled that the Victorian Supreme Court had no jurisdiction in the matter, and the pair

were eventually convicted on a lesser charge and fined $5,000. Some of the aunties were convicted of falsely securing social security payments and given short prison sentences.

Many people were surprised that, after a police operation lasting four years and costing thousands of dollars, no child abuse charges were laid, but the police had problems here. Many of the incidents of abuse were subject to the statute of limitations, while the children, brought up without holidays or newspapers to mark the passage of time, were unable to assign dates to specific incidents. Nevertheless, when you consider the number of influential people under Anne's spell, the suspicion lingers that someone may have been pulling strings for her.

Today, some of the children who grew up in the dark rooms of Kai Lama are dead, while the others continue to struggle with the after-effects of their upbringing. In 2004, after a change in laws made it possible, one of them, Anouree Crawford, commenced a civil action against Anne Hamilton-Byrne. She claimed that the treatment she had received as a child had caused her to suffer from depression, obsessive compulsive disorder, an eating disorder and an inability to socialise. Interviewed on television, she said, "I think maybe when I was younger I thought everything was going to be alright and I am going to manage quite well, this is just a short period of time, this is going to stop, this is going to go away. Now that I'm 34, I think it's time to actually accept that it is not going to go away." In 2009, Crawford and Anne's granddaughter Rebecca Cook-Hamilton, who had sued her in 2007, also claiming psychological damage from her upbringing, received out-of-court settlements of $250,000 each.

Meanwhile, one person who has managed to forgive Anne is Sarah Hamilton-Byrne (now Sarah Moore). In a 2009 blog post, she wrote of her visits to Anne, which began shortly before Bill Hamilton-Byrne died in 2001. She described how much of a wrench it was for her to leave the cult, and said that her actions were motivated by her desire to ensure the safety of the other children rather than any serious disagreement with Anne's teachings. She believes that Anne's adoption of the children was a misguided overcompensation for her own awful childhood. Anne, for her part, had acknowledged the sufferings of the children, but blamed it all on the aunties.

Anne Hamilton-Byrne is spending her last

days on earth in a Melbourne nursing home. In May 2014, Sarah told a reporter "She's very demented, rocking back and forth. Her only connection seems to be a plastic baby doll that she talks to and dresses… You can see the child she was and perhaps see how it all ended up in her grand but disastrous illusion."

Many of her followers have remained loyal, and while the group's wealth is well down from its glory days, it is still estimated at over $10 million. A number of people are said to be jockeying to take over once 'The Teacher' finally passes on.

CIRCUS FREAKS

The Nightmare of WILLIAM LINDSAY GRESHAM

There was no head — it was joined to its big brother's body by a thick cord of flesh where the neck should be. This was no gaff; the man was a genuine freak, one of the top human-oddity acts in the business. The inside talker in his lecture introduced the gentleman and announced that he was the father of five children, all normal. At this point my mother looked as if she was going to be sick. I figured it was something she had eaten for to me there was nothing about the man with an extra little body hanging out of him to sicken anybody. He had a noble face, and a calm, poised manner. Besides, he had winked at me. I thought it would be wonderful to have a vestigial twin. I wouldn't have to work as hard as my father did, bossing people in a factory all day, and I wouldn't be plagued by "money worries" like Mother. Bitterly I realised that it was too late for me to be gifted like the Italian gentleman, but hope surged up within me that someday I might get tattooed all over and so qualify.

So went William Lindsay Gresham's first encounter with a sideshow freak.

Today Gresham is remembered as the author of the novel that grew out of this experience, *Nightmare Alley*, made in 1947 into one of the bleakest movies ever released by a major Hollywood studio.

Gresham's life was in many ways just as bleak. He was a tormented individual for much of it, but he managed to channel some of that torment into a fascinating body of work.

Gresham was born on 20 August 1909 in Baltimore, Maryland, into a family he described as "flotsam of the Old South". They moved to New York in 1917, and it was while wandering through Long Island with his parents one day that he encountered the dignified looking Italian and his vestigial twin.

At the age of 16, Gresham had a sort of spiritual awakening where he suddenly found himself inspired by poetry and the physical beauty of the world, but shortly afterwards his parents separated, an event which upset him badly. He blamed a terrible outbreak of acne, which he felt made him repulsive to others, on the stress he suffered from their divorce. After graduating from Erasmus Hall High School in Brooklyn in 1926, Gresham embarked on a series of jobs. He worked as a reviewer for the *New York Evening Post*, and for an advertising agency. He contributed a few stories to pulp magazines. At night he played guitar and sang folk songs in Greenwich Village cafés, but as he was some three decades too early for the folk boom he didn't get very far with this, or with singing cowboy songs on the radio.

Despite his family's move to the North, Gresham retained much of the Southerner about him, and was known for his impression

of a fiery Baptist preacher, which he could turn on at will. He did this to amuse his friends, but there was something about the performance which indicated the spirituality hidden beneath his cynical exterior. At one stage he considered becoming a Unitarian minister.

He spent a couple of years with the Civilian Conservation Corps, one of Roosevelt's New Deal job creation initiatives. It was around this time that he married Jean Karsavarina, a free-spirited communist and aspiring pulp writer from a wealthy Polish-Jewish family. Gresham joined the Communist Party in 1937, and, inspired by the example of a friend who had died fighting on the Republican side in the Spanish Civil War, went to Spain where he served as a medic with the Abraham Lincoln Brigade. During his two years in Spain, he never fired a shot, but returned home alcoholic, sick with tuberculosis and close to a nervous breakdown. His marriage to Karsavarina, shaky prior to his departure for Spain, was basically over, although they would not divorce until 1942. He began seeing what would be the first of a long line of psychiatrists. At one point, he tried to hang himself with a leather belt fastened to a hook, but the hook broke and he came to on the floor.

In 1942, Gresham married a talented young poet named Joy Davidman whom he had met at a Communist Party meeting, and they moved into a tiny flat on the East Side. Joy edited a communist literary magazine and Gresham continued with his freelance writing, but neither of them made much money. Soon they had two sons, David and Douglas, to feed as well. Still in therapy, Gresham spent much of his time drinking

with carnies at a hotel called the Dixie, and having affairs with women. To remove him from the temptations of the city, Joy organised a move to Westchester County, 20 miles north of New York. Gresham maintained an office in the city, and one night in 1946 rang Joy from it to say he felt his mind was going and couldn't come home. She spent the rest of the day making frantic phone calls in an unsuccessful attempt to track him down. That night, as their sons slept, Joy, who had been brought up an atheist, had a religious epiphany. She became as committed a Christian as she had once been a communist.

Eventually Gresham came home, and then their luck changed. *Nightmare Alley* was published, and shortly afterwards Twentieth Century Fox paid him $60,000 for the film rights.

As Gresham told it in *Monster Midway*, the seed for his first novel was sown during his time in Spain, in a village outside Valencia in 1938. His superior officer, a man named Clem Faraday, also happened to be a carny veteran. One evening, as they shared a bottle of brandy, Clem told Gresham about the geeks who occupied the lowest rung on the carny ladder. These were the fellows who entertained the crowd by biting the heads off snakes and chickens. Gresham wondered how they ever found anyone who would do it. "Kid," Clem told him, "you don't find a geek, you make a geek."

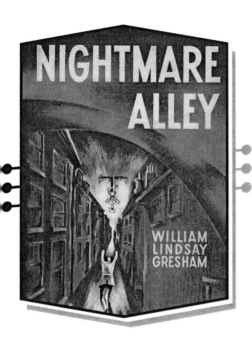

"When you get hold of one of them fellows, he ain't a geek — he's a drunk. Or he's on the morph. He comes begging you for a job. You tell him, 'Well, I ain't got anything regular, but I got a temporary job. My wild man quit on me, and I got to get another to fill in. Meanwhile you can put on the wild man outfit and sit in the pit and make believe you're biting the heads off chickens and drinking the blood.' [...]

"Well you let him go on, faking the geek for a few days, and you see he gets his bottle regular. Or his deck of 'M' so he can bang himself night and morning and keep the horrors away. Then you say one night after the show closes, 'You better turn in the stuff and hit the road after we close tomorrow night. I got to get me a real geek. You can't draw no crowd, faking it that way.' You slip him the bottle and you tell him, 'This is the last one you

get.' You tell him that. He has all that night and the next day to think it over. And the next night when you throw in the chicken, he'll geek."

I was stone cold sober.

Nightmare Alley opens with ambitious, 21-year-old Stanton Carlyle working as a talker for a travelling show. Watching the resident geek doing his stuff, he is sickened, but as the crowd files out of the show Stan has a smile on his face, "the smile of a prisoner who has found a file in a pie".

Stan begins an affair with Zeena who does a mind-reading act, but Pete, her alcoholic husband, is in the way. One night Stan slips him a bottle of wood alcohol, killing him. Stan takes his place in the act, learning the code that Zeena and Pete had developed to communicate while she was on stage.

Tiring of Zeena, Stan takes up with Molly, the show's 'electric girl'. He teaches her the code and she becomes his assistant. But he has his eyes on greater pickings than can be made in a carnival. As his fame grows he is invited into the homes of the rich. He moves into the spiritualist racket, donning a clerical collar and calling himself The Reverend Stanton Carlyle of the Church of the Heavenly Message. A woman whose daughter he has materialised gives him a house, which he fills with hidden devices for the faking of spiritualist phenomena.

Despite his success, Stan is haunted by memories of his childhood, and in particular the time he found his mother in the woods with her lover. And there is a recurring nightmare, too.

Ever since he was a kid Stan had had the dream. He was running down a dark alley, the buildings vacant and black and menacing on either side. Far down at the end of it a light burned; but there was something behind him, close behind him, getting closer until he woke up trembling and never reached the light.

Stan consults a female psychiatrist, Dr Ritter, and they soon become lovers. Dr Ritter, predictably enough, finds the source of Stan's nightmare in the 'Oedipus complex'. But Stan realises she has more to offer him than therapy. She has the case histories of her patients.

"You've got enough stuff in that bastard tin file cabinet to blow 'em all up. I know what you've got in there — society dames with the clap, bankers that take it up the ass, actresses that live on the hop, people with idiot kids. You've got it all down. If I had that stuff I'd give 'em cold readings that would have 'em crawling on their knees to me…"

Dr Ritter tells Stan about Ezra Grindle, a fabulously rich industrialist. After winning the sceptical Grindle over with an display of psychic power, he goes for the old man's weak point — when young he had forced his girlfriend, Dorrie, to have an abortion which killed her. Grindle agrees to donate a small fortune to the City of Spiritual Light which Stan proposes to build, in return for his materialising Dorrie. Stan has Molly play the part, but when Grindle grabs his long-dead girlfriend, apparently with less than spiritual motives, Molly panics and gives the game away. Stan knocks Grindle unconscious and escapes, leaving her behind. He's about to board a train and make good his escape when he discovers that the money he swindled from Grindle has been swindled from him by Dr Ritter, and he is penniless.

On the run, Stan grows increasingly paranoid that Grindle's agents are closing in. Drinking heavily, hitching rides on freight trains, he finds himself one night in an alley like the one in his nightmare. But this time he's being chased by a policeman whom he manages to kill in a struggle (using a remarkable strangling technique which Gresham describes in precise detail).

Stan has one last shot at a comeback. He approaches a carny manager and begs for a job as a palm reader. The boss looks at Stan, his yellow hair dyed black, his shirt filthy. He doesn't need a palm reader, but he has another job…

Matinee idol Tyrone Power, in a brave career move, took on the role of Stan in the movie version of *Nightmare Alley*. He gives a thoroughly convincing portrayal of Stan's descent into degradation, and it's now considered his best performance. While the

ending was softened somewhat, with Molly coming to Stan's rescue, this remains a faithful and powerful version of Gresham's novel.

Gresham used the money from the movie to buy an imposing, if somewhat decaying, 14-roomed, white-columned mansion, set amid lush pine forests and fields in Staatsburg, 75 miles (120 km) north of New York. Into this the Greshams moved thousands of books, innumerable cats and dogs, two horses and various other animals. Gresham played the part of the Southern gent to the hilt, riding around his estate on horseback wearing jewelled cowboy boots (until a fall from the horse and a broken arm put an end to equestrian activities).

Gresham's Communism dried up at about the same time as Joy's, and like her he turned to Christianity. He joined Alcoholics Anonymous and gave up drinking for a while. His new-found faith colours his second novel, *Limbo Tower* (1949), which is set in the tuberculosis ward of a large city hospital. The diverse group gathered here includes an Arab, a passionate young communist, an ex-boxer and an itinerant preacher. Over the course of three days, two of them die and there is much discussion of philosophical issues and the relative merits of Marxism and capitalism. Compared to the nihilism of *Nightmare Alley*, the book's tone is one of almost unreasonable optimism. In fact, its conclusion, uttered by the wise and elderly Judge Stone, that the truth lies with "the Carpenter; rabbi of Nazareth; prophet of the New Jerusalem; Jesus the Christ" seems to come out of nowhere. It's not surprising that Gresham's own enthusiasm for Christianity did not last long, and he later wrote to his son David that

he could never be a Christian "since I cannot understand the basic concepts nor accept them". He spent the rest of his life clutching at various beliefs — the I Ching, Buddhism, tarot cards and L. Ron Hubbard's Dianetics.

With the success of *Nightmare Alley* and *Limbo Tower*, Gresham must have felt himself established as a writer, but the idyll at Staatsburg was not to last. The Inland Revenue was demanding a hefty sum in back taxes, and Gresham was hitting the bottle again. "One of the most destructive experiences a writer can have," he remarks in his biography of Houdini, "is to sell a novel to the movies after years of a grinding, hand to mouth existence. Like a deep-sea fish, accustomed to the pressures of the deep, when brought to the surface suddenly by a net, he often explodes when the pressure is removed."

Gresham was a gentle man when sober, but he changed when he drank. Douglas Gresham recounts the slow deterioration of their family life in his autobiography, *Lenten Lands*.

When Dad drank. He drank heavily. He became volatile, his temper explosive; he would roar around the house, uncontrollable and at times dangerously violent. Once he broke a bottle over my head; he smashed to matchwood a good guitar when he repeatedly failed to master a difficult run. I can remember the porch chairs being reduced to small pieces against the pillars at the front of the house. For me, the house became slowly but inevitably a place of tension; the dusty, interesting attics changed from places for exploration and adventure to rooms of forbidden aspect…

In early 1952, Joy's cousin, Renée Rodriguez, fleeing from her own violent and alcoholic husband and accompanied by her two children, took refuge in the Greshams house. Joy and Renée got on well together, and Renée took over many of the household chores (which Joy had never had the slightest interest in doing). Renée's presence provided an opportunity for Joy to make a long-planned trip to England. She had been ill and her doctor had advised her to take a break, but her main reason for going was to meet a man with whom she had been exchanging letters. This was C.S. Lewis, an Oxford don, writer on Christianity and author of the 'Narnia' series of children's books which began with *The Lion, the Witch and the Wardrobe*. Joy met Lewis in Oxford and they got on well, although her brash New York manner horrified some of Lewis's more conservative friends, such as JRR Tolkien. She stayed for a while in the cottage Lewis shared with his brother in Oxford. A few days before she was due to leave she received a letter from Gresham saying he had fallen in love with Renée and wanted a divorce.

Joy went home and, after some wrestling with her conscience for religious reasons, agreed to the divorce. She returned to England, taking Donald and Douglas with her, and married C.S. Lewis, but only a few years later died of cancer. The story of their love affair has inspired several books and a movie, *Shadowlands* (1993), in which Lewis and Joy were played by Anthony Hopkins and Deborah Winger.

Paying his tax bill but losing his mansion in the process, Gresham took Renée and her children to Florida, where they were married.

His third marriage was a happy one. He churned out fact and fiction for a host of magazines, including the *Saturday Evening Post*, *True*, *Fantasy and Science Fiction*, *Ellery Queen's Mystery Magazine*, *Argosy* and *The Gent*. Many of his articles dealt with show people, and these formed the basis for *Monster Midway* (1953), a book notable for the empathy Gresham had with his subjects, and his curiosity about the nuts and bolts of carny life. Gresham was the sort of man who, once shown a particular skill, is not happy until he has mastered it himself. Over the years he became adept at many of the carnival arts, from conjuring tricks to knife throwing (although he could never conquer his gag reflex sufficiently to become a sword swallower). When lecturing on carny acts, he liked to liven up proceedings with demonstrations of fire-eating (with the show-stopper being the act he called 'the Human Volcano').

As a teenager, Gresham had seen Houdini perform, and his biography of the illusionist, *Houdini: The Man Who Walked Through Walls*, appeared in 1960. After completing the manuscript, Gresham wanted an expert to check it for errors. His publisher put him in touch with James Randi, the stage magician who performed as the 'The Amazing Randi', and they became friends. Gresham was planning a book on Mina Crandon, the spiritualist medium known as 'Margery', who had been investigated by Houdini in the 1920s. Fascinated by the mechanics of fraudulent séances, he enlisted Randi's help in staging one in a house in New Jersey. Randi played the part of the medium, and at one point the sitters were startled to see him and his chair levitating. (The effect had been achieved by a weightlifter

friend of Randi's who had quietly entered the darkened room.) In later years, Randi became well known as a scourge of pseudoscientists and fraudsters, and the man who offered a million dollars to anyone who could prove they had paranormal abilities.

Gresham also had ambitions to write a book on the celebrated Scottish medium Daniel Dunglas Home. He was able to examine some of Home's possessions in the library of the Society for Psychical Research in London, and was excited when he found a harmonica which was small enough to be played inside the mouth. He was sure he had solved one of the mysteries about Home — how he had produced the sound of accordions during his séances.

Neither the Margery or Home books ever saw the light of day. Instead, Gresham's last book was *The Book of Strength* (1961), a guide to weight-training, which he had been practising since his teens. In describing the mindset required to be a successful body builder, Gresham suggests adopting the '12 Steps' of Alcoholics Anonymous, which must have bemused some of the younger readers of his book who were just after muscles.

In 1960, after Joy's death, Gresham visited his sons in England. Douglas records that the visit was not a complete success. They got on well enough, but they had grown apart ("I was an English schoolboy by then"). This was the last time Douglas saw his father.

Gresham's health had been deteriorating for some time. He developed cataracts which left him unable to read a newspaper, and an operation on them was only partially successful. Then, shortly after his return from England, he was diagnosed with cancer of the tongue (caused, it is said, by one of the chemicals in the lighter fluid he used during his fire breathing act). The treatment for this was going to be expensive, and he didn't have the money for it. He had an appointment with a cancer specialist in New York on 12 September 1962, but instead checked into the Dixie Hotel, where he used to drink with his carny buddies. He signed in as "Asa Kimball, of Baltimore", and committed suicide in his room.

A self-described "eclectic grabber of the truth", William Lindsey Gresham spent his life picking up one belief system after another, holding it up to the light, and seeing right through it.

There is no doubt that he failed to live up to his early promise as a writer, and that alcohol was probably a major factor in this. He wrote no more novels after *Limbo Tower*, and most of his output in the last decade of his life was hack work — much of it interesting, but hack work nevertheless. Yet it seems that *Nightmare Alley*, which is still regularly reprinted, will live on as one of the most compelling works of noir fiction, while Gresham's other writings remain a treasure trove for anyone interested in the gaudy, now almost vanished world of carnies, freaks and geeks.

DRUGS VIRUS GERMS

DRUGS

VIRUS

GERMS

How to defend the nation, the family and the children

The INTERNAL DEFENCE OF THE NATION

he price of liberty is eternal vigilance! No one understood this better than a certain Mr Reginal W. Levgiac, author of the remarkable pamphlet *Drugs Virus Germs*, a little gem of paranoia which deserves a place in every thinking person's library alongside the Bible and those little booklets the government used to circulate advising on what to do in the event of a nuclear war.

Levgiac's pamphlet is 16 pages long, printed in green ink on yellow paper, and was published in South Australia in 1988. Chapter one, 'Hypnotic Control Drugs', begins by introducing us to Levgiac's chief area of concern.

The development to a point of perfection of a tasteless drug which would allow a person to gain control of another person's mind would surely be the greatest achievement in the drug world of medical or chemical science.

What would happen if this were to be established as being a reality? A drug of this nature could be used in education, business, religion, politics and civil conflict.

The following has been suggested. If such a thing is possible, science has reached such a stage of brilliance that if it's possible it can be done. Based on this statement, let us seriously consider the tasteless drug problem.

As you will note, the distinction in Mr Levgiac's mind between 'what could be' and 'what is' seems a tenuous one, but having established the existence of the tasteless drug problem, let us move on to its effects. Children, of course, are particularly at risk.

To apply a drug of this nature to education would mean that the mind of the child would develop towards the greatest influence dominating at that time, even if it were based on lies and trickery. Mass mental control would be possible if a combination of two drugs were perfected.

Business people could be made to sign contracts against their will or leave jobs for no reason. Preachers would find themselves preaching someone else's words. The whole political process could be subverted.

A politician under hypnotic control drugs would find that he or she would have to repeat statements in parliament and would have great difficulty in not doing so. Government authorities could be tricked into making wrong decisions. Mass drugging of the voting public. Habitual voting would take place rather than policy. They would be unable to adjust their voting to meet the new problems until their country is destroyed and their democratic rights are lost permanently.

(Come to think of it, this seems like a pretty accurate description of the current Australian political scene, but I digress.) Tasteless drugs may be used to create all manner of mischief.

A drug which causes excessive body odour to develop causing serious embarrassment to the person concerned…

A drug which weakens the nerve system of the spine to such a point that if a sudden jerk in the wrong direction could cause the victim to become a paraplegic…

A drug which causes excessive gases to develop while sleeping, a special problem for double bed

sleeping. A drug which causes a man to throw his arms around dangerously while sleeping endangering his wife.

Drugs can be used to cause accidents and chaos on the roads.

A drug which would cause sudden dizziness, which would be very dangerous for night drivers the car would get out of control and crash.

A drug which could draw a driver towards an oncoming light similar to a moth to a light, resulting in a head on crash. A drug which causes a sudden black out day or night, the driver would crash at high speed.

In fact, engineering car accidents seems to be one of the favourite pastimes of these enemies of society (Levgiac provides diagrams to show how it's done). They don't even need to resort to drugs for this.

Criminals can drive out in front of you at a cross road causing you to crash.

Criminals can get you to follow a truck or some other vehicle until you become accustomed to it being there, without warning the criminal stops suddenly causing you to crash.

Divorces may be incited to further the destruction of the family.

Divorce seldom occurs without disagreement or argument. The drug would play an important part in perpetuating the argument base. Arguments would become habitual…

In addition to the repeater drugs two other drugs would also be devastating to the lives of a married couple. Sex stimulant and sex retardant drugs. To drug one with excessive doses of sex stimulant drugs, and the other with sex retardant drugs would drive one against the other, causing a serious base for disagreement and dissatisfaction. Most of the drugs can be tasteless.

Families may be undermined by drugs causing cot deaths. Alternatively, babies may be secretly switched at birth.

Later in life the child now in its early teens is secretly told that the people he or she is living with are not their parents, leaving the youngster confused and an easy target for political or drug agents.

Pornography is just another weapon in their arsenal.

How some pornographic films are made.

A battery operated alarm clock placed in a private bedroom, hotel, guest house, caravan, motel, inside the battery operated alarm clock is a secret infra-red movie camera, which can use one of the letters on the face of the clock as the eye of the camera.

Warn your daughters. When the criminals want the alarm clock movie camera back again they place another one exactly the same type and colour in its place. The victim does not know she has had a movie camera in her bedroom. The film can be sold for pornographic viewing possibly in some other part of the country to prevent identification of the person concerned.

Locking your door does no good, as there exists a 'duplicate key service system' which enables the enemy to enter your home at

any time to plant hidden cameras and lace your food with tasteless drugs. No one can be trusted.

Those near you would never commit a crime while in your company. They would feed a request for some type of action into the crime network. A different section of the underground movement would then be organised to carry out the attack, be it a drug virus or germ attack through your food or drink supply or an organised accident or something similar.

Clearly what is needed is a coordinated national defence system, with the compulsory teaching in schools of *Drugs Virus Germs* being the first step.

Democracy as it is known today may depend on the results of such an educational programme.

Now, you may be wondering just who might be responsible for all this planting of tasteless drugs, car accidents, baby switching and destruction of families. This is a subject on which Mr Levgiac is quite remarkably vague. They are simply 'criminals', or 'political agents', or even organisations "that try to cause as much sorrow as possible to other people". They could be anyone, and they are clearly capable of *anything. Drugs Virus Germs* represents paranoia in its purest form. The world it describes fearfully, with people having car accidents and getting divorced and all sorts of other unfortunate things happening to them, is simply the world as it's always been. But there must be someone to blame for it all, mustn't there?

Who was the mysteriously spelt Reginal Levgiac? It's something I've wondered about for years, but recently I've discovered a few facts about him.

His real name was Eric. E Gerlach, and he was a member of the Lutheran Church. *Drugs Virus Germs* is billed as volume five in the 'Knowledge Wisdom Liberty' series, and what I presume was the first in the series — because it is simply called *Knowledge Wisdom Liberty* — was published in Gawler, South Australia, in 1957. Fortunately the State Library of NSW has a copy. It begins, "This book has been compiled for the purpose of assisting any individual who may be disturbed in some way by the so-called 'Modern Scientific Discoveries' and claims of some of the scientists in the various fields of research and education today." It's basically a spirited attack on atheism and the teaching of evolution in schools — which is turning children into criminals — combined with much praise for the British Monarchy.

There is a great deal of pondering about the origins of the universe, and puzzling things like gravity. ("Consider how mysterious it is that, no matter on which side of the earth you stand on, you always stand upright.") He considers various scientific advances — electricity, cars, agricultural techniques — but his point is that all these things were designed and created by humans, as the universe must have been designed and created by God. The thing is, Levgiac knows full well that scientists are just as much in the dark about the way the universe works as he is. Gravity "has all science baffled up to this stage", while "If you ask a scientist what electricity is he will say, if he's honest, 'I do not know', apart from the fact that it is connected with the atomic field." As for radio, "Just what it is remains a mystery, but it plays a big part in our modern world, but it is an invisible power." Levgiac's reasoning is at times ingenious. On the subject of dates, he notes that if you count back from 1955, you eventually get to the year one, and then the dates start to go backwards. "Something must have happened here which was the basic reason for this world's existence, for during this period of time history was altered as far as the dates were concerned…" Of course the answer to this mystery is that Jesus Christ was born in the year one, which proves this was "the Greatest Event in the World". All of this is illustrated with photos of agricultural equipment, koalas and camels, Aborigines and many — some would say too many — vintage cars.

I have also managed to obtain a copy of volume four in Levgiac's series, which is entitled *Research Truth Confidence*. This is partly a re-run of the first book, but with a lot more Biblical interpretation. It's firmly aimed at young people, and Levgiac assumes amazing ignorance on their part — he's forever explaining the meaning and pronunciation of common words ("Create — say kree-ate"). There are chapters on planetary rotation, the ice age, fossils and atomic energy (which he warns will cause earthquakes and alter the climate). There's a hint of paranoia, with Levgiac warning that you should never trust what your friends tell you, and

there's a brief mention of the tasteless drug problem, although this has not assumed the proportions it later will.

Tucked into my copy of *Research Truth Confidence* is a form letter dated 19 June 1982 and signed by E.E. Gerlach. It begins "Dear Friend" and asks the recipient to "permit the youth of your church, especially the 14–16 year olds to read this small book". At the bottom of the letter Gerlach has scribbled, "All Lutheran pastors in Australia have received a copy of this book to be used by them as they think fit."

While *Knowledge Wisdom Liberty* is an entertaining work, *Research Truth Confidence* is dull and repetitive. Neither of them comes anywhere near the bravura performance of *Drugs Virus Germs*, where Levgiac managed to encompass his strange, paranoid worldview in a form so concentrated it becomes almost hypnotic.

What happened to Gerlach/Levgiac after he wrote *Drugs Virus Germs*? Well, strangely, he may have gone to America. I say this because the National Library of Australia has a reprint of *Research Truth Confidence* which was published in New York in 1990. Of course, Gerlach may have arranged for its publication from Australia, but that seems unlikely.

My investigations continue…

OFF WITH THE MASTERS

MADAME BLAVATSKY & THE BIRTH OF THE NEW AGE

The Mystic East, land of unexplored deserts, hidden valleys, sacred rivers and, above all, gurus.

Since the rise of materialism and industrialism in the 19th century, Westerners dissatisfied with Christianity have looked east for spiritual sustenance, eagerly seizing on concepts like reincarnation, karma, auras and astral travel. Instrumental in this process was perhaps the most entertaining religious leader in history, an immensely fat, coarse, chain-smoking, tale-spinning Russian woman with steel-wool hair and the face of a determined bullfrog. Madame Blavatsky may be almost forgotten today, but the Theosophical Society that she founded was the cauldron in which the so-called New Age was brewed.

She was born Helena von Hahn in 1831. Her father was a Russian army officer, her mother a popular romantic novelist. At 17 she married Nikifor Blavatsky, a vice-governor in the Caucasus who was considerably older than her (although he was nowhere near 23, as she later claimed) but soon ran away from him. The next few years were extremely busy ones, if even a fraction of the stories she later told is true. She claimed to have ridden bareback in equestrian shows, fought with Garibaldi in Italy, redecorated Princess Eugenie's rooms in Paris, consorted with red Indians in America, survived a shipwreck off the coast of Greece,

and found spiritual enlightenment in Tibet. What is certain is, shortly after being exposed as a fraudulent medium in Cairo, she travelled to the United States in 1873. Soon after her arrival she read an account of spiritualist phenomena in the home of the Eddy family in Chittenden, Vermont, and went there to meet its author. This was the magnificently bearded Henry Steel Olcott, who had been a farmer, soldier, and lawyer, but had lately turned his attention to investigating the claims of mediums. Blavatsky joined in the séances at the Eddys home and soon convinced Olcott of her mediumistic powers. The two became inseparable.

A year later they were set up in New York, with HPB (to use one of Blavatsky's many nicknames) living in an Addams Family-style apartment filled with oriental oddities and stuffed animals, and Olcott promoting his new book, *People From the Other World*, with little success, as spiritualism was going through a slump. Blavatsky was no ordinary medium however. Since her arrival in America she had been regaling people with tales of the Masters, or Mahatmas, of the Great White Brotherhood, whom she claimed to have studied under in Tibet. Vague ideas about secret brotherhoods and hidden bodies of wisdom had been floating around in the west for centuries, but Blavatsky was the first person to give them names, personalities

and an address. They were, she explained, semi-corporeal beings who communicated telepathically, could appear anywhere at will, and lived in a vast underground complex somewhere in the Himalayas. Their number included Morya and his assistant Koot Hoomi, who were Blavatsky's chief contacts, religious leaders like Jesus Christ, Buddha and Lao-Tze, and historical figures like Plato and Saint Germain.

In March 1875, Olcott received a letter from one of the more obscure Masters, Tuitit Bey. Sent from Luxor, Egypt, this letter, like many of the hundreds from the Masters which would follow, had not been posted but 'precipitated', meaning that it had fallen from the ceiling or in some other way mysteriously appeared. In his letter, Tuitit Bey sang Madame Blavatsky's praises and invited Olcott to become a disciple of the Masters. Despite Blavatsky's warnings of the arduous work ahead of him, Olcott readily agreed.

Blavatsky and Olcott attracted a circle of like-minded individuals who met regularly in her apartment. At one of these meetings, on 7 September 1875, they decided to form a society dedicated to the study of occult knowledge, with Olcott as president. Later they settled on 'theosophy', meaning divine knowledge, as a label for their beliefs, which Blavatsky set out in a book, *Isis Unveiled*, published in 1877. A 13,000-page regurgitation of Blavatsky's readings in science and religion, it was partly, she claimed, the work of the Masters writing through her (while she had not even had to put pen to paper for some passages, these having appeared spontaneously as she slept). *Isis*

Unveiled is Blavatsky's bare-knuckled assault on materialism and in particular Darwinism, which she replaces with a theory of spiritual evolution. The beliefs of Theosophy were eventually formulated as three aims — to promote Universal Brotherhood, to study comparative religion, science and philosophy, and to investigate unexplored laws of nature and psychic powers. As admirable as these aims might be, they were a little vague. Was it necessary, for example, for a Theosophist to believe in the physical existence of the Masters? Such ambiguities, coupled with the ambitious people the society attracted, would ensure that this society dedicated to Universal Brotherhood had a turbulent history.

Isis Unveiled sold well and the society gained considerable publicity for its support for the then shocking (to Westerners) practice of cremation (an early member, an impoverished European aristocrat named Baron de Palm, was given America's first public cremation after Olcott himself constructed an oven for the purpose) but Blavatsky and Olcott found few people eager to join their society. They decided on the radical step of moving to India (on the Master's instructions, they said). Arriving in Bombay in February 1879, they eventually located to a spot by the Adyar River near Madras, which remains the society's headquarters to this day. Transplanted to its spiritual home in the East, Theosophy proved much more successful. Blavatsky soon attracted attention among the Anglo-Indian community with her psychic phenomena — producing objects out of thin air, causing unseen bells to ring and so on — while the society's novel opposition to Christian missionaries and

support of nationalist causes proved popular with the Indians. Olcott, who began to dress like a native soon after arrival, became a national hero in Ceylon after establishing a number of Buddhist schools there.

Over the next decade membership increased steadily and lodges were set up in many countries. The first tensions appeared. In 1884, Blavatsky and Olcott travelled to England to deal with a rebel group of Christian Theosophists, upset by the society's increasing preoccupation with Buddhism. In their absence, their housekeeper at Adyar, Madame Coulomb, was stirring up far more serious trouble. Blavatsky had originally met Coulomb in Cairo and invited her to India. Apparently frustrated by her domestic position, Coulomb claimed that she had helped Blavatsky to stage some of her phenomena, and had letters to prove it. When the board of trustees refused to buy these letters she sold them to a local clergyman who published them. Back in London, the recently formed Society for Psychical Research, which had taken an interest in Blavatsky's claims, dispatched a researcher, Richard Hodgson, to India. Hodgson examined the 'shrine room' where Blavatsky had worked some of her wonders, and found that the shrine, a wooden cabinet in which things had miraculously appeared, had an opening to HPB's bedroom. Hodgson produced a damning (albeit with a hint of admiration) report in which he labelled Blavatsky "one of the most accomplished, ingenious and interesting imposters in history". Its publication caused much mirth in London and the society had its first wave of resignations. Blavatsky was outraged, as she

always was when her powers were questioned, but she was also known to show copies of the report to prospective Theosophists to see how they would react. According to a Russian journalist, V.S. Solovyov, who made an attempt to get to the bottom of Blavatsky's character, she once made a candid confession of her frauds to him, saying that such phenomena were necessary if she was to interest people in her ideas. "If you only knew what lions and eagles in all the countries of the world have turned themselves to asses at my whistling and obediently clapped me in time with their huge ears," she is alleged to have said.

To the relief of Olcott, Blavatsky spent most of her remaining years in Europe, producing another huge book, *The Secret Doctrine* (1888). This purports to be a commentary on the 'Book of Dzyan', the oldest book in the world, a copy of which she had perused during her time in Tibet. Blavatsky explains the origins of the cosmos, constructing an elaborate framework into which she manages to squeeze just about every occult and pseudoscientific notion thought of before or since. She writes that life on earth is destined to run through a cycle of seven 'root races' and various sub-races. The First Root Race were astral beings who lived in 'The Impenetrable Sacred Land', wherever that might have been. The Second Root Race, also astral, lived in Hyperborea near the North Pole. The Third Root Race, becoming more material now, lived in Lemuria, evolved into anthropoids and developed for the first time consciousness and the ability to reproduce sexually. Despite some help from superior beings from Venus they fell, to be succeeded by the Fourth Root Race,

which lived in Atlantis. We are part of the Fifth Root Race, the Aryans, who will soon be replaced by the Sixth Root Race, which will emerge in America. They will be rolled by the Seventh Root Race, who will again be astral. And then the cycle will come to an end.

One of the more enthusiastic reviews of *The Secret Doctrine* was written by a freethinker and social reformer named Annie Besant. A friend of George Bernard Shaw, she was famous for her support of causes such as birth control and home rule for Ireland, and was one of the most powerful orators of her day. Blavatsky, sought out by Besant, invited the younger woman to join. Besant, who had begun as the wife of a clergyman before converting to freethought, had found a new career.

Blavatsky had been engaged in a struggle with Olcott over control of the society. In order to bolster her position in Europe she had founded the Esoteric Section, a circle within it. When Madame Blavatsky finally succumbed to enough illnesses to kill several people and died in 1891, Besant became leader of the Esoteric Section. Meanwhile, another bitter struggle was being fought between Olcott, still in India, and the society's original secretary, William Quan Judge, who now headed the powerful American section. Letters from the Masters were being precipitated all over the place, some supporting Judge, others Olcott. Judge eventually left the society, taking most of the American section with him. After his death in 1896 its leadership was taken over by Katherine Tingley, also known as the 'Purple Mother', who steered the group in a typically American direction, founding an alternative city at Point Loma, California. Built on a lavish scale, with fantastic architecture, it eventually folded due to financial mismanagement.

Besant proved as zealous a Theosophist as she had been a social reformer. She found a spiritual mentor in the absurd and scandalous figure of Charles Webster Leadbetter. While he would eventually invent an early life as eventful as HPB's, the massively bearded Leadbetter was a lowly country curate when he joined the society in 1883. A letter from Master Koot Hoomi, precipitated through Blavatsky, prompted him to go to India, where he remained several years. Back in England, he met Besant, who was impressed by his almost daily visions of the Masters and absolute self-assurance in matters psychic. Leadbetter rose through the Theosophist ranks and was put in charge of the society's youth section which, given that his predilection for young boys was already widely suspected, was like putting a kid in charge of a candy shop. In 1906 he was accused of teaching the boys in his care to masturbate and forced to resign. When Besant, who was elected president after Olcott's death the following year, managed to have him reinstated, another wave of resignations followed.

If Madame Blavatsky despised organised religion, Besant and Leadbetter did their best to turn Theosophy into one. Orders, rituals, titles and costumes proliferated. But the most dramatic development came when the pair began to talk of the imminent coming of a new World Teacher who would rival Jesus. One day in 1909 Leadbetter, who had been keeping his eyes peeled, noticed a young boy on the beach at Adyar with a particularly strong aura. This was Jiddu

Leadbetter and Krishnamurti

Krishnamurti, whose father worked at the society's headquarters. The stage was set for a fascinating psychological experiment as Krishnamurti, considered by those around him a backward child, suddenly found he was to be the physical receptacle for the Master Maitreya. Leadbetter began to supervise his spiritual education, overseeing everything from his diet to his bathing habits (uh-oh), and Krishnamurti was soon paying nightly visits to Master Koot Hoomi. Besant founded another order within the society, the Order of the Star in the East, to prepare the world for Krishnamurti. In 1911, accompanied by

his brother Nityananda, he went to England, where he spent the next 10 years being alternatively fussed over and bossed around by a gaggle of rich Theosophist women.

Scandal continued to surround Leadbetter who, in 1914, moved to Australia where he spent the rest of his life in self-imposed exile. Theosophy enjoyed considerable success in Australia. Its most visible achievement was a huge amphitheatre built on Balmoral Beach in Sydney, which was completed in 1924 (the fact that it overlooked a boys' bathing shed can't have displeased Leadbetter). Designed as a venue for the World Teacher to speak in, the impressive structure was the source of much amusement, it being popularly believed to have been built for the return of Jesus Christ, who would walk across the water between Sydney Heads to reach it. In Australia, Leadbetter joined the Liberal Catholic Church, an odd group of disaffected Catholics associated with Theosophy, and could henceforth be seen swanning about in the purple robes of a bishop.

Whatever one thinks of the flamboyant Leadbetter, he certainly made a remarkable choice when he picked out Krishnamurti, although he would not get the sort of guru he was expecting. Dragged around the world by Besant and forced to address countless meetings, the naturally introverted boy gradually became an effective speaker, not so much for what he said as for his ability to seem to be saying what each member of his audience wanted to hear. It took him a while to accept the role forced on him, but in a 1925 speech he finally referred to the World Teacher in the first person,

causing much ecstasy among Theosophists. Krishnamurti proved an attractive figure to young people, and many flocked to join the society. The 1920s were probably the high point of Theosophy, its principles of pacifism and internationalism fitting in well with the prevailing mood of the decade. At the same time, the society was wracked by constant in-fighting among its leaders, with an ageing Annie Besant no longer able to keep everyone in line. Krishnamurti became increasingly disillusioned. In 1926 he disbanded the Order of the Star in the East and resigned from the society the following year. He ended up rejecting not just Theosophy and its Masters, but the whole idea that religion or spiritual leaders could lead anyone to enlightenment, which could only come from within. He became, in effect, an anti-guru guru.

The Theosophical Society never recovered from the blow of Krishnamurti's defection. Annie Besant was succeeded as president by George Arundale who reorganised it, doing away with many of the costumes and ceremonies thought up by Besant and Leadbetter, but membership steadily declined. Madame Blavatsky's society may today be a mere shadow of its former self, but her Masters are alive and well, appearing in slightly different guises in many systems of belief. They are the space brothers yearned for by UFO contactee groups, the higher intelligences dispensing wisdom through Californian channelers, the Aryan supreme beings of various mystical white supremacist cults. Unfortunately, since Madame Blavatsky's passing, one thing these superior beings have conspicuously lacked is a sense of humour.

A conversation with
MR PONNUSWAMY

live in the Sydney suburb of Newtown, which has always been a haven for eccentrics, and during the 1980s and '90s it boasted a particularly rich crop. There was the Mad Butcher, a shaven-headed, taciturn fellow of Middle-Eastern origin who always dressed in white and delighted in re-arranging the seating of passengers on buses. There was the Mad Professor, a grizzled chap who wore a greasy overcoat and a headband with feathers in it. He kept all his possessions in a shopping trolley and slept in a bus shelter in front of Sydney University — he was rumoured to have once been a mathematics professor there. He drank at the Marlborough Hotel, and by closing time the floor would be littered with drinks coasters covered in all sorts of strange scribblings and equations. (I have quite a collection of them.) But Newtown's most colourful ornament during these years was undoubtedly Mr Nadar Ponnuswamy, politician/cook and founder of the Uninflated Movement Party.

Mr Ponnuswamy was born in southern India, where he trained as an English and history teacher. He spent some time in Ethiopia, and later Uganda, where he ran a farm, but left when Idi Amin came to power and expelled all the Indians from the country. He arrived in Sydney in 1973. In the first of many tussles with the intractable forces of bureaucracy, the Department of Education would only allow him to work as a casual teacher. To supplement his income he opened Swamy's Uninflated Indian Restaurant at 10 King Street, Newtown, which doubled as his political headquarters. If you ventured into it, you would immediately be presented with a copy of his newspaper, *Popular Sovereignty* — the official "slashing organ" of his movement.

Mr Ponnuswamy could often be seen delivering political diatribes from his slogan-covered car, the Ponnuswamymobile. He ran in several elections, beginning with the Marrickville by-election in 1983. The following year, he received 252 votes in the

Richmond by-election, and told the *Sydney Morning Herald* he was not sorry about the result. "The electors had great respect for me. I knocked on many doors and nobody told me to go away."

I went to Mr Ponnuswamy's restaurant to have a chat to him in 1990. It was dark in there, and the words "Service to mankind is the crown of human blessedness" were painted on the wall. We chatted over cups of tea made by his wife, and he explained to me why he must one day become prime minister. Here are some excerpts from our conversation.

BIZARRISM: Did you intend to become a politician when you came to Australia?

PONNUSWAMY: *The first thing I asked the person who signed the migrant visa on my passport was, "What is the difference between you and me?" There is no difference. The second question I asked him, whether I would be allowed to conduct elections. He could not give the right answer but he looked at my face and he asked me why I am asking that question. I said I am a student of the Australian Constitution. I like Australia, I must see how*

that Federal Constitution is weak and State Constitution is strong. Australia is the weakest confederation in the world, so I wanted to know how this happened. Australia is a continent for a nation and a nation for a continent. I came to the conclusion that the Federal Government is surrendering to the State Governments. Practically it has lost its sovereignty when [Prime Minister Gough] Whitlam was dismissed. From this my political career started.

BIZARRISM: What will you do if you become prime minister?

PONNUSWAMY: *Definitely I'll be the prime minister! Pinpoint a single Liberal Party fellow, a single Labor Party fellow, a single National Party man, a single Democrat to occupy the prime ministership. You pinpoint a single fellow. They're all after money. So I came to the forefront about the salaries, the superannuation, election fund to make a holy war. The prime minister should be a person who should act like a high court judge. If I am elected as prime minister I shall forget about all my party affiliations. I will be the one who will set a new example to the world politicians that Australians are one and indivisible. The moment I am elected all corrupt governments*

N. **Ponnuswamy** Stands for
• The Green Revolution
• Mitigation of Inequality
• Solving the Problems of the Underprivileged
• Elimination of the Unemployment Problem

VOTE
1 N. **Ponnuswamy**
In Every Election

is the only candidate who
RENOUNCED his
Parliamentary salary —

elimination of unemployment, inflation and injustice. Several days and nights I cried before I opened the restaurant, so I am a victim of unemployment. Those people who are intelligent and unemployed, I will make them self-employed.

BIZARRISM: Are there any Australian politicians that you admire?

PONNUSWAMY: *I don't admire these fellows. That is why I am starting from the grassroots. I am getting the mandatory power from the people. If the people say yes I will go ahead. If they say we don't want you I will turn around and ask you to pinpoint why. That they have to answer. If four plus four do not make eight you should explain to me. If you say seven you have to prove it. The burden of proof lies on the shoulders of the people who defeated me at Marrickville, at the North Coast, at Elizabeth, at Vaucluse, at Rockdale.*

BIZARRISM: Were you very disappointed to be defeated?

PONNUSWAMY: *Never! How? There is a famous saying in India — even if the elephant dies the owner gets 100 sovereign pounds. He will sell the bones and the tusks. Even if I am defeated I am still prime minister. Because I am always telling you that I don't want your salary, I don't want your superannuation fund. How will they defeat me? That I want to know. On what grounds? If they defeat me I'll turn around and say we don't want this South African electoral system.*

will fall. The pen is mightier than the sword. I will prove to the whole world. I am not even recruiting anybody here for me. So many people are asking me, I said we don't want martyrs. Just like the Ghandi government, a new approach. People should not organise a terrorist movement or some other movement. Mine is a purely non-terrorist organisation.

BIZARRISM: Can you tell me what 'uninflated' means?

PONNUSWAMY: *Uninflated means*

BIZARRISM: I hear you want to train young people as cooks.

PONNUSWAMY: *Definitely. All, all. I talk to them, I know their parents, their home situations. Their parents, half parents, one half left the family without looking after the children. Moreover, I know poverty. So I can render my total service to mankind — without taking salary. We are not taking the money to the graveyard. What is the use of this money? Work should come from within.*

BIZARRISM: How did you become a cook?

PONNUSWAMY: *When I was a small boy I ate sweet-smelling curries from my mother. Then we became poor afterwards. So many reasons the family became poor. So we could not eat those curry meals. But I have never forgotten the taste which I enjoyed. When I became a school teacher I went to big hotels and ate the same curry. It was very nice. I had a little sister at home and she was waiting for her marriage. In India we have dowry system and we have to give money at the time*

of marriage to the sister. I realised my great responsibility. I told the other young teachers I am not going with you to the hotel restaurant because I am an economist. I have abandoned my tasty curry meals from the restaurant. I started learning cooking every morning and evening. There were old ladies, I watched them in the classroom. I used to ask what you should do. They used to tell me you try these things, then you put the chicken or vegetables in and you use this curry powder, that curry powder. I experimented and I became a top-notch cook. Today I am selling the best curry meals at the cheapest rates. Since 1984 I have made a promise I will not increase the price. I curtailed inflation in my place, I solved my unemployment and I will abolish the injustice of the Labor government.

Alas, Mr Ponnswamy never made it to Parliament. A year or so after our chat, he abandoned his political ambitions, closed his uninflated restaurant and returned to India, where I was told he intended to run a hotel.

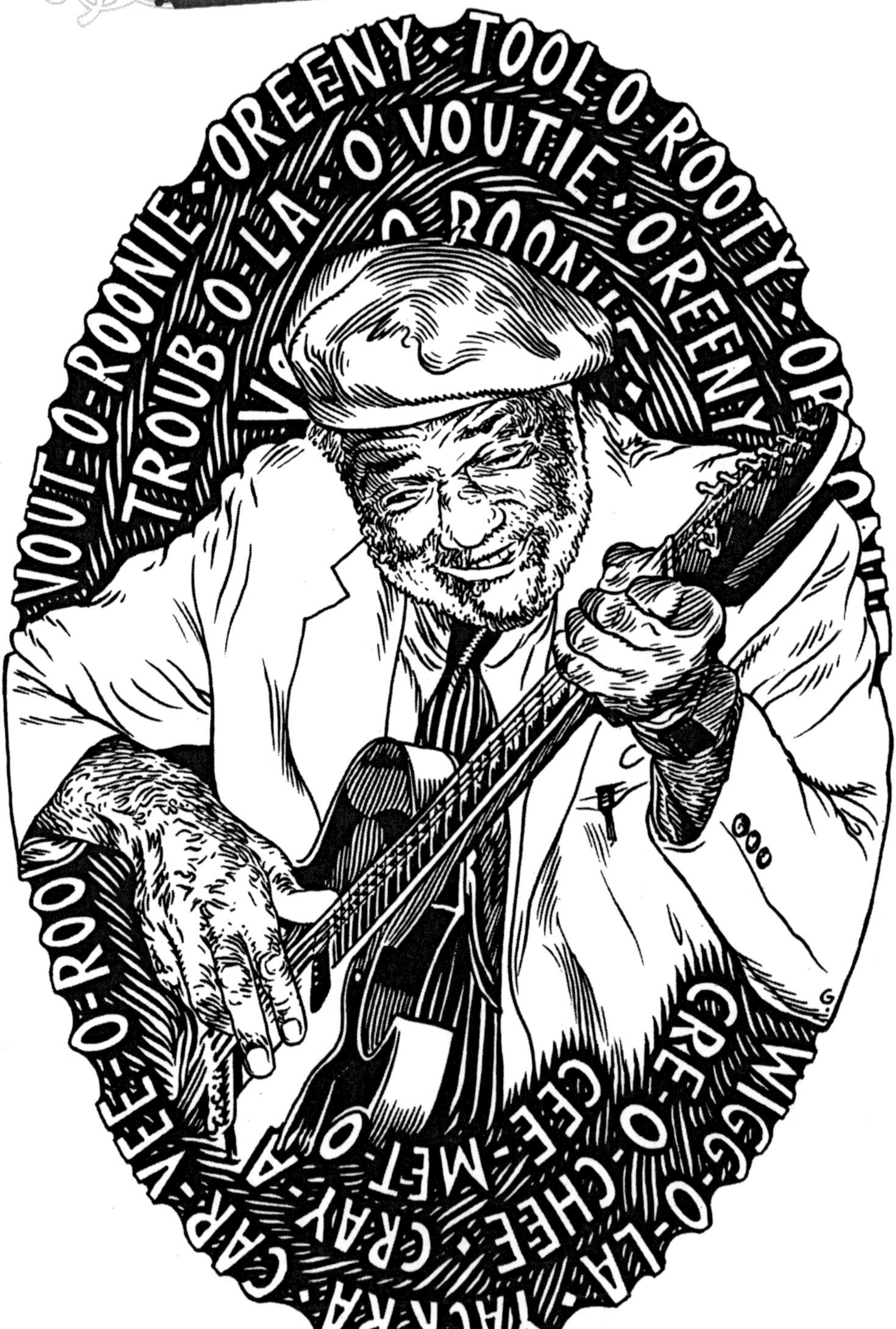
VOUT-O-ROONIE · OREENY · TOOL-O-ROOTY
TROUB-O-LA · O VOUTIE · OREENY

VOUTOROONIE!
THE SLIM GAILLARD STORY

*We're going to cook up a fine dish, real groovy.
Wrap up some fine grape leaves and chip up
a little lamboroonie. Sprinkle on a little fine
riceorootie and a little pepporoonie, a little
peppovoutie. And sprinkle on a little saltoroonie
to put the seasoning in there, that makes it really
mellow. Then you take and you nail an avocado
seed up in the ceiling and let it vout for a while…*

From the intro to 'Gaillard Special' (1946)

azz is so goddamned serious,
tasteful and self-reverential these
days, it's easy to forget a time when
it was dangerous, morally suspect
and, at times, just plain mad. Jazz
history teems with all sorts of eccentric, larger
than life characters, from the shadowy figure
of Buddy Bolden, reputed inventor of jazz,
who is said to have lost his mind while playing
in a parade, to Sun Ra, who claimed to hail
from Saturn. But the most surreal imagination
ever to spread itself over a syncopated rhythm
undoubtedly belonged to a singer, dancer, multi-
instrumentalist, fast food gourmand and god to
the beatniks by the name of Slim Gaillard.

Bulee 'Slim' Gaillard was born on 4 January
1916 in Detroit, Michigan, or maybe Florida,
or perhaps Cuba, where he is said to have
spent much of his childhood (his mother was
Afro-Cuban, according to some sources). His
father, a steward on an ocean liner, used to

take Slim with him during the school holidays
and, when Slim was 12-years-old, accidentally
left him behind on the island of Crete. Slim
was there six months before becoming a
merchant seaman (and sometime ship's cook)
and working his way — slowly — back home,
picking up along the way at least some of
seven languages including Spanish, Greek and
Arabic. To these he would soon add one of his
own devising — Vout.

Back in Detroit, Slim was a boxer and
entertainer (one early specialty was playing
guitar and tapdancing simultaneously). He sang
in speakeasies and drove an illegal booze wagon
for the notorious Purple Gang. In 1937, he went
to New York where he teamed up with bass
player Slam Stewart. As Slim and Slam they
made regular radio appearances, broadcasting
live breakfast shows from the Criterion Hotel.
Decca gave them a recording contract and
their first release, 'Flat Foot Floogie (With a
Floy Floy)' became a number one hit. It was
considered redolent enough of its times to be
placed in a time capsule at the 1939 World's
Fair, along with Gershwin's 'Rhapsody in Blue'.
Slim and Slam followed it up with another
hit, 'Tutti Frutti', and appeared in several films,
notably the incredible, anarchic Oleson and
Johnson comedy *Hellzapoppin'* (1941).

Jazz singers had been scatting and making up
nonsense words before this — Cab Calloway
immediately springs to mind — but Slim

Slim and Bam

Gaillard took the artform to new heights. "I'm going to schooloreenie to study chemistereenie and voutie," he sings on 'School Kids Hop', demonstrating two of the main principles of Vout, namely (a) add 'oroonie' or 'oreenie' (or something like it) onto the end of every other word, or every word if you wish, and (b) say 'vout' or one of its variations whenever possible, assigning to it any meaning you want. MacVoutie? Solid! Listening to a Slim Gaillard recording is like eavesdropping on a convention of Tourette's Syndrome sufferers where the coffee has been laced with acid. Songs are regularly interrupted by other songs, snatches of nursery rhyme, parodies of Spanish radio broadcasts or outbreaks of wild Cuban rhythms. It's a style which in some ways foreshadows the sampling found in rap records today

For Slim, song ideas could come from anywhere. One night he began to sing the menu in an Arabian (or perhaps it was Armenian) restaurant and the result entered his repertoire as 'Yep Roc Heresy'. A record company having commissioned him to record four songs, he

turned up at the studio with only three, then heard a cement mixer out in the street. 'Cement Mixer Putti Putti' became his third big hit. And if there was nothing else to inspire him, there was always food. Countless Gaillard songs extol the joys of eating — 'Fried Chicken O Rootie', 'Matzoh Balls', 'Dunkin' Bagels', 'Avocado Seed Soup Symphony', and 'Potato Chips' ("Crunch crunch, I don't want no lunch / All I want is potato chips!") to name but a few. Slim's amazing verbal inventiveness sometimes obscured the fact that he was no slouch as a musician either, although of a suitably eccentric bent. Recalls jazz historian Arnold Shaw, "He could play the piano with the backs of his hands, palms up; the vibraphone with swizzle sticks… He could play 'Jingle Bells' on a snare drum, producing the pitch by sliding the fingers of one hand along the drum head as he beat out the rhythm with the other hand."

Slim and Slam broke up when Slim was drafted in 1943. He served in the air force as a radio operator and mechanic. Invalided out after a year, he went to California, where he found another bass player in the rotund form of Bam Brown and a drummer, Leo Watson, who was a pretty good scat singer in his own right. They got a residency at Billy Berg's nightclub. Stars like Clark Gable, Marlene Dietrich and Gregory Peck would come in to see the "skyscraping, zootie Negro guitarist" (as *Time* magazine called him) who sang about cement mixers and avocado seeds. Slim would spot them in the audience and do little musical parodies of whatever happened to be their current film. Stories about him abounded, such as the time, turning up a whole week late for a nightclub engagement, he attempted to pacify the irate

owner with a genuine doctor's certificate stating, 'In my opinion this man is perfectly sane.'

Slim and Bam had another hit with the sing-song 'Down By the Station' (which has since become a children's standard) and followed it up with 'Opera in Vout', an insane masterpiece spread over four 78 rpm sides, in 1947. They broke up when Bam, sadly, went insane for real (running on stage one night, high on something and waving a knife around, he was carted off to a mental institution where he died eight years later). Fortunately, one of their live performances was preserved in the 1948 short *O'Voutie O'Roonie*.

Jazz was changing. The bebop revolution had begun — young musicians playing a harder, faster more complex sound which most of the older musicians hated. Slim became identified with the movement, more for his quintessential hipster attitude than his musical style (although he did record with bebop greats like Charlie Parker and Dizzy Gillespie). He was a natural role model for the Beats. Jack Kerouac and Neal Cassidy used to go and see him in a San Francisco nightclub called the Safewind, and Kerouac immortalised a Gaillard show in *On the Road*.

But one night we suddenly went mad together again; we went to see Slim Gaillard in a little Frisco nightclub. Slim Gaillard is a tall, thin Negro with big sad eyes who's always saying, 'Right-orooni' and 'How 'bout a little bourbon-orooni'. In Frisco great eager crowds of young semi-intellectuals sat at his feet and listened to him on the piano, guitar and bongo drums. When he gets warmed up he takes off his shirt and undershirt and really goes. He does and says anything that comes into his head. He'll sing 'Cement Mixer, Put-ti Put-ti' and suddenly slow down the beat and brood over his bongos with fingertips barely tapping the skin as everybody leans forward breathlessly to hear; you think he'll do this for a minute or so, but he goes right on for as long as an hour...

Slim sits down at the piano and hits two notes, two Cs, then two more, then one, then two, and suddenly the big burly bass-player wakes up from a revery and realizes Slim is playing 'C-Jam Blues' and he slugs in his big forefinger in the string and the big booming beat begins and everybody starts rocking... Finally the set is over; each set lasts two hours. Slim Gaillard goes and stands against a post, looking sadly over everybody's head as people come to talk to him. A bourbon is slipped into his hand. 'Bourbon-orooni — thank-you-ovauti...' Nobody knows where Slim Gaillard is... Now Dean approached him, he approached his God; he thought Slim was God; he shuffled and bowed in front of him and asked him to join us. 'Right-orooni,' says Slim; he'll join anybody but he won't guarantee to be there with you in spirit. Dean got a table, bought drinks, and sat stiffly in front of Slim. Slim dreamed over his head. Every time Slim said, 'Orooni,' Dean said, 'Yes!' I sat there with these two madmen. Nothing happened. To Slim Gaillard the whole world was just one big orooni.

Slim continued to make appearances as a singer, comedian and MC, but his musical career began to wind down during the '60s. He did a stint as a hotel manager in San

Diego, grew apples on a farm in Washington State and made occasional appearances as an actor on TV, popping up in *Roots, The Next Generation*, for example, but by the early '80s he had pretty well dropped out of sight.

Cut to London, 1984. I was visiting there for the first time and, never having seen any Slim Gaillard records in Australia, was extremely pleased to find three of his albums in Ray's Jazz Shop in Shaftesbury Avenue, a few minutes' walk from Trafalgar Square. When I went to pay for them the guy behind the counter said, 'Do you want these signed?'

"What do you mean?" I asked.

"He's downstairs."

"Huh?"

"Yeah, I'll go get him."

Mightily impressed by the service you got in Ray's Jazz Shop, I stood and watched as an immensely tall, slightly stooped figure with a grizzled Santa Claus beard slowly ascended the stairs. Grinning broadly he extended a huge hand like a cured ham which I shook. At this point, I'm afraid, I dissolved into your typical fan, mumbling inanities as Slim signed my records.

I raced back to the Chelsea flat where my girlfriend Louise and I were staying. "I met Slim Gaillard! I met Slim Gaillard!" I said, bursting through the door.

"Who's Slim Gaillard?" she said.

Oh well.

Slim, it transpired, had been in London since the previous year, after Dizzy Gillespie had suggested he play some of the European jazz festivals. He'd gone to Paris, then London, and liked the welcome he got so much he decided to stay. London rejuvenated Slim's musical career. He played all the jazz clubs, recorded for the first time in 25 years, wrote advertising jingles for TV and encountered punk rock. "Sometimes I go on a Tuesday when they have the punk bands," he told the *NME* in 1985. "I like what they do, it's far out in a way… They lie down on the floor and jump on each other… It's something to see." In 1989 the *Arena* TV programme set out to make an hour-long documentary on Slim, but found his life so fascinating that *Slim Gaillard's Civilisation*, as it was eventually called, clocked in at four hours.

Slim Gaillard continued to tour Europe and the U.S., dispensing voutie to all and sundry, until his untimely death from cancer on 26 February 1991.

Well done-oroonie!

OF DEROS AND TEROS

BEHIND THE SHAVER MYSTERY

andomness has never been a popular concept. People don't care for the idea that things just happen, and the more unfortunate and tragic an event, the greater the need to find a reason for it. In the past, a whole host of invisible agents — gods, demons, spirits, vampires — were thought to be working assiduously behind the scenes, and whenever something rotten happened to you, from your cow dying to your village being struck by the plague, you could always find someone to blame. With the rise of rationalism and the modernisation of Christian beliefs, these unseen stagehands have for the most part disappeared, but the void they have left is an unsettling one. This is the reason why existentialism has never achieved the popularity of, say, badminton.

On the night of 10 August 1960, the Great Northern Empire Builder ploughed into another train in Michigan, North Dakota, killing 17 and injuring a hundred. A man named Richard Shaver heard the news on the radio at his farm in Wisconsin and smiled to himself. While others might ascribe the accident to fate, chance or the imponderable will of God, he knew better. He knew that beneath that part of North Dakota lay a huge cavern, part of an underground highway that stretched from Pennsylvania to New York. In

Richard Shaver

this cavern there was a gigantic and ancient machine in the shape of a six-armed human figure, and at its controls sat a deformed, stunted, malevolent little fellow named Max. Max's particular pleasure was to wreck the trains that roared above him on the surface of the earth. By manipulating the controls of the machine he had sent out rays which confused the railway signals, changing a red light to an all clear, and causing the Great Northern Empire Builder to crash. He, Shaver, knew all this because, well, he just knew it and, dammit, he was going to reveal the truth to others. So he sat down at his typewriter to hammer out another instalment in what had become known as the 'Shaver Mystery'.

It had all begun one day in 1943, when Howard Browne, a managing editor of the science fiction pulp *Amazing Stories*, opened a letter in the magazine's offices. It contained an alphabetical code which purported to be both the original language of Atlantis and a simple key to finding "the exact meaning of any word". Browne, who wrote hardboiled detective stories under the name John Evans, muttered something about crackpots and tossed the letter into the bin. In the next room, the magazine's editor, Ray Palmer, overheard the remark (this is how he told the story anyway), rushed in and retrieved the letter. He *loved* crackpots.

Born in Milwaukee in 1910, at the age of seven Palmer was involved in an accident which left him a hunchback. He spent years of his childhood strapped face down in a device to prevent further injury to his spine, reading non-stop — up to 15 books a day. At 16 he chanced upon the first issue of the first science fiction pulp magazine, Hugo Gernsback's *Amazing Stories*, and was smitten. He became active in the embryonic field of science fiction fandom, and in 1930, with Walter Dennis (reputed to have been the inspiration for Clark Kent, no less) he published the world's first fanzine, *The Comet*. After producing further amateur publications, and writing stories for the pulps in his spare time, he obtained his dream job in 1937 — editing *Amazing Stories*.

As its editor, Palmer favoured 'space operas' — action-filled adventures featuring spaceships, ray guns, square-jawed heroes, evil aliens and a dash of sex. More cerebral readers turned their noses up at such fare, but Palmer didn't worry as long as *Amazing's* circulation continued to rise. He also liked to mess with his readers' minds —

stories he had written would be published under pseudonyms, with fake photos and biographies of their supposed authors. But it wasn't until he found Richard Shaver that he *really* started to mess with their minds.

He published Shaver's letter in the next issue and was surprised at the response. Hundreds of people wrote in to say that they had applied the code and it had worked. Intrigued, Palmer wrote to the letter's author, Richard S. Shaver, and received in return a 10,000-word article entitled 'A Warning to Future Man'. Rewritten and considerably expanded by Palmer, it was published under the snappier title 'I Remember Lemuria', and the public got its first taste of the Shaver Mystery.

Shaver was one of those people, like H.P. Lovecraft or L. Ron Hubbard, who have taken it upon themselves to create a mythology. His went something like this. Thousands of years ago, the earth was inhabited by a race of giant superbeings from outer space called variously Titans, Atlans or the Elder Gods. They had found the secret of prolonging life indefinitely and they possessed technologies vastly superior to our own. Using genetic engineering they had created various races to be their slaves or 'robots', and controlled them telepathically using a device called a 'telepathic augmenter' or 'telaug' (Shaver shared with L. Ron Hubbard the habit of familiarising outlandish concepts by slapping technical-sounding abbreviations on them). At some point, for some reason, the sun began to emit 'detrimental radiation', and the Elder Gods found the surface of the earth was no longer habitable. At first they moved underground, excavating huge caverns to live in, but when this solution proved inadequate they boarded their

They caused wars, assassinations and industrial accidents. They kidnapped women, dragged them down to their underground lairs and sexually tortured them. In fact, just about everything bad that happened to anyone could be blamed on the nefarious deros. They also had machines to inflame the sex drive — 'stim rays' — which they would point at hapless men, while others turned the rays on themselves and lived their lives in a crazed debauch which could physically deform them. ("…for words will not tell of the pleasures of stim-death, of the pleasures of sadism made infinitely more so by the augmentation of all the body's and mind's impulses.") While most of the underground dwellers were deros, there were a small number of beings who survived the radiation intact. These were the 'teros' ('integrated robots') who tried to help mankind and waged a constant guerilla war with the deros.

space ships, which could travel at the speed of light, and moved to another solar system. They left behind their underground cities full of amazing mechanical devices ('mech') as well as many of the 'robots'. Some of these returned to the surface and became our ancestors. Most stayed underground where they degenerated under the influence of the 'detrimental radiation' into ugly, malformed creatures called 'deros' (short for 'detrimental robots').

The deros, making use of the Elder Gods' abandoned 'mech', liked nothing better than to wreak havoc in the lives of the surface dwellers. They had televisual devices with which they could observe every inch of the earth, and a battery of weapons at their disposal including rays which could kill, hypnotise and sabotage, and 'mental machines' which could create compulsions and delusions.

So how did Shaver know all this? He was born in Pennsylvania in 1907, one of five children of Ziba and Grace Shaver. Ziba worked for a car company, and later owned a restaurant, while Grace was a schoolteacher who also wrote for popular magazines. In his early years, Shaver had a variety of jobs, including meat cutter and landscape gardener, then studied at an art school in Detroit. He fell in love with a Russian immigrant, Sophie Gurvitz, and under her influence joined the Communist Party. Against the wishes of both their families, they married.

The art school closed during the Depression

and Shaver was forced to take a job as a welder in a hellish-sounding car factory. The death of his adored older brother Taylor in 1934 unbalanced Shaver. He developed the belief, on no evidence, that Taylor had been murdered, and began to hear voices. He became aware of a 'hidden world' which was somehow controlling this one.

At the factory, he found that one of the welding guns he was using acted as a 'teleradio' which enabled him to hear the thoughts of his fellow workers. He knew "what was in Bill's lunchbox; what girl Bumpy was going to take out that night". More disturbingly, he heard voices that badmouthed him, calling him a communist and a homosexual, and his fellow workers could hear them, too. When he could take it no longer, he fled back to Pennsylvania, leaving behind Sophie, who was pregnant.

Disturbed by accounts of Shaver's behaviour, Sophie's father, Ben Gurvitz, moved to have him committed, and Shaver's parents acquiesced. In August 1934, he was sent to an asylum, Ypsilanti State Hospital in Michigan, where he was subjected to then fashionable treatments for the insane: hydrotherapy (lots of baths, showers and being 'packed' in wet sheets), massages, electric light and radiation therapy. The regime at Ypsilanti was fairly light, though, and he was occasionally allowed out to visit his family. Sophie, who was supporting herself as a commercial artist, gave birth to a girl, Evelyn Ann. In December 1936, when Evelyn Ann was two, Sophie was electrocuted when a heater fell into her bathtub. Ben Gurvitz adopted her daughter, and attempted to cut Shaver out of their lives.

Allowed out of Ypsilanti again, Shaver failed to return. The voices continued to babble in his head, and behind them he could hear something else — the screams of women in agony.

I could hear a woman cursing and the lash of a whip — and feel a pleasure in the scream of the person getting the lash. It was all so mad, but I kept hearing such things, over and over. It got on my nerves, so I quit. I quit and went on the bum…

He travelled around America and Canada on freight trains, taking odd jobs, surviving on coffee, bacon and eggs. Wherever he went, he was pursued by the rays. His chief tormentor was the dero, Max, but he was also aided by a beautiful, blind tero girl named Nydia. He avoided big cities, where he found that the rays were strongest.

Shaver admitted that he sometimes got into fights, and it may have been one of these that led to his being arrested and sent to Ionia State Hospital for the Criminally Insane. Unlike Ypsilanti, patients at Ionia were never allowed out, and most remained in there till they died. Shaver feared this would be his fate.

During his time at Iona, Shaver learned much about the hidden world, thanks mainly to Nydia, with whom he had had fallen in love. (In a bizarre detail, Shaver described how, while he having what sounds like a wet dream about Nydia, his thrashing about in

One of Shaver's rock paintings

breasts lightly with their spread hands as though to keep the growing buds from blooming suddenly into some wild flowering of culmination — and all their faces were…Nydia.

Nydia told him all about the deros, and even took him through cave entrances to the underground world where he witnessed some of their torture sessions. Here was the reason for the women's screams he had been hearing.

In May 1943, rather amazingly, Shaver was discharged from Iona. He went back to Pennsylvania and the small farm where his parents were living (his father soon died). He got a job as a crane operator, and acquired a wife through a lonely hearts advertisement (the marriage lasting just as long as it took his bride to find out about his spells in asylums). He then met a lively, down-to-earth woman named Dottie, who moved in with him (they would marry in 1945). He was rekindling an old ambition, to be a writer, and began firing off manuscripts to various magazines, including *Amazing Stories*.

bed upset the chamber pot beneath it. He woke up to find that a picture of Nydia had formed in the spilt urine. He showed this to a friend who, while complimenting him on his artistic ability, said, "But isn't it a disgusting medium?") Nydia, to Shaver's delight, returned his love, although this wasn't without its perils. She liked to point stim rays at him, sending him into paroxysms of ecstasy.

The air was heavy with my sensual thinking, or was it the thinking of the whole city? A dark and ancient red being permeated these houses and streets, a hanging odor of coiling, strangling caresses, of strange orgies and strange visions. Every past image of the desired bodies of women, all women I had ever known stretched out their hands to me, and writhed gleaming limbs in a slow dance of longing, holding their red tipped

Ray Palmer followed 'I Remember Lemuria' with further Shaver extravaganzas in *Amazing Stories*, and found that each time he printed one, the circulation of his magazine soared. He realised he had struck a deep chord with his readers, many of whom wrote in to say they had long suspected the sorts of things Shaver was writing about. For Palmer, the whole thing was very much a dry run for the UFO hysteria

which he would soon help to create.

Shaver was thrilled to have found someone who finally took his discoveries seriously, and he and Palmer became friends. In March 1945, Palmer visited Shaver and Dottie at the farm in Pennsylvania. As he lay in bed that night, he heard Shaver in the next room, apparently in a trance, speaking in other voices.

The 'Shaver Mystery' series culminated with the June 1947 issue of *Amazing Stories*, which was entirely made up of Shaver stories. But the magazine's publisher, Ziff Davis, had been under serious pressure to drop it. Not only was science fiction fandom in an uproar about 'Shaverism', but FBI agents had been visiting the publisher's offices, asking questions. Palmer was told that he could continue publishing Shaver stories, as long as they were printed as fiction. By then, Palmer didn't much care. He had been secretly planning a new magazine called *Fate*, in which he would publish what he wanted. Its first issue in 1947 featured an article by Kenneth Arnold — again heavily rewritten by Palmer — on his sighting of 'flying saucers', the incident which kicked off the whole shebang.

It's not hard to see why the Shaver stories proved so popular. They tap into all sorts of beliefs about nasty creatures — dwarfs, goblins, trolls and the like — who live beneath the earth, as well as embodying atomic age technofear. They were obviously tailor-made for paranoids everywhere. And, as can be seen from the above passage about Nydia, they were sexy. Palmer, who cheerfully admitted he expanded many of Shaver's writings, noted that he often had to cut things out when it came to the sexy stuff.

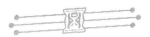

We remember one love scene, some 85 pages long, which we dropped in toto, and which our secretary, a young lady just about to be married, picked up off our desk during her lunch hour and innocently read enough of to throw her into the most amazingly disturbed condition we have ever seen. She tossed the manuscript onto our desk with flaming cheeks and said: "Don't ever let me get hold of anything like that again — I just can't take it." We have always wondered if there was any connection with this and her subsequent moving up of her marriage date by three months.

Palmer continued to publish stories by Shaver in various magazines he edited, and they remained friends. In 1949, Palmer and his family left Chicago and moved to a property in Wisconsin which adjoined the farm where Shaver and Dottie were living. The craze for Shaver had long since passed, but to keep the story alive in the early '60s Palmer published 16 book-length issues of a magazine called *The Hidden World* devoted to Shaver.

For all the outlandishness of his beliefs, Shaver was basically a materialist who was always looking for proof that his inner world existed. Then he realised that all the proof he needed was literally lying at his feet.

One day I noticed a boulder I had sat on a dozen times in my pasture was in fact a gigantic weathered eagle's head. Then I found carved

stones; due to my wife's preoccupation with the 'pretty, strange pebbles' I finally found what I needed. The pebbles are engraved, are artworks in themselves! Tiny, the Elder World's version of modern microfilm, the very pebbles under my feet were screaming at me.

Shaver was a little disconcerted when he found that others could not see these pictures. But, being an enterprising fellow, he developed a technique of slicing rocks into very thin layers, transferring their patterns onto cardboard or plywood and painting over them, bringing out the details which seemed perfectly obvious to him. He called the paintings produced in this way — remarkable, crowded scenes of gods and monsters — Pre-Deluge Rock Art, and sold them by mail order until his death from lung cancer in 1975. (Largely ignored in Shaver's lifetime, his rock paintings have recently been hailed as significant works of outsider art.)

While most writers agree that Shaver genuinely believed in his deros as real flesh and blood creatures manning real machines, Palmer's role in the affair is usually described as that of a hoaxer (which is how he has gone down in science fiction circles). Palmer certainly spent a lot of his time promoting ideas he must have known could not be true — he was, for example, big on the idea that UFOs came from the interior of a hollow earth, which they left through holes in the Poles — but his involvement with Shaver seems to go deeper than this. His late compendiums of Shaveriana, The

Unseen World series, were lavish publications which can't have made any money, and the tone Palmer adopts towards Shaver in them is reverential. He'd spent years promoting Shaver's much-ridiculed beliefs, and it's hard to believe he didn't think Shaver was onto something. And yet, just about everyone who ever met Palmer came away puzzled by what the man actually believed.

The most intriguing aspect of the Shaver Mystery lies not in Shaver's extraordinary and occasionally hilarious descriptions of the dero and tero, but in the personality of Shaver himself. Reading his stories, you would think their author was either a certified paranoid schizophrenic or an out-and-out charlatan. But in person, he presented as neither. He is described by those who knew him as charming and intelligent, and while his early years were restless he lived contentedly with his third wife Dottie, a Christian who did not take his ideas at all seriously, until his death. In some ways he was as down-to-earth as you'd expect an ex-welder to be. (When asked by someone about the possibility of life after death, he dismissed the question by saying, "A dead man is dead, a live man is alive. How can two opposites be the same?") Yet here was a man who could barely have a headache without thinking that a dero headache ray was to blame. Faced with someone like Shaver, a psychoanalyst would no doubt prescribe years of analysis to get to the bottom of the man's delusions and rid him of them. Shaver was in no need of such treatment. He was clearly a man plagued by more than the usual number of doubts and fears, but having articulated them, and in the process created a weird and wonderful mythology, he lived happily ever after.

The sick world of SIGMUND FREUD

n Alfred Hitchcock's 1941 psychological thriller *Spellbound*, Gregory Peck is J.B., a man suffering from amnesia who is tormented by a sense of guilt and the possibility that he has killed a man, while Ingrid Bergman is wonderfully miscast as a psychoanalyst bravely trying to unlock his past. By analysing one of his dreams (a sequence famously art-directed by Salvador Dalì) she ascertains that he has witnessed a murder while skiing. They go to the valley where this took place and J.B. remembers the source of his guilt — as a child he had accidentally killed his brother, and this has led him to assume the guilt for the murder in the snowfields. Once the memory of killing his brother has surfaced, all his other memories come flooding back. He is cured.

Spellbound neatly encapsulates all that is compelling and attractive about the methods of Freudian analysis. I remember being enormously impressed by it as a kid. A psychoanalyst was like a detective, searching for clues and solving the deepest mysteries of all — the ones inside our own minds. It was very cool stuff.

To his supporters, Freud is a great scientific pioneer along the lines of a Newton or Darwin, a fearless investigator who has opened up whole vistas of knowledge. If it's the unconscious mind you want to understand, Freud's your man, and terms such the 'Oedipus complex', 'anal personality' and the ubiquitous 'Freudian slip' are common currency. The theory of the mind first expounded by Freud in the 1890s was undeniably one of the great pillars of 20th century thought. Unfortunately for the 20th century, it's all bollocks.

INTO THE WORLD A FREUD IS BORN

"At the time of my birth," writes Freud in *The Interpretation of Dreams*, "an old peasant woman had prophesied to my proud mother that her first-born child would be a great man." He was born in 1856 in Freiberg, then part of the Austro-Hungarian Empire, and that he would indeed be a great man was something which his parents would never let him doubt. He studied medicine in Vienna, graduating in 1881, and while he would have preferred a career in research, financial pressures (he had just become engaged) forced him to take up a position us a doctor at Vienna General Hospital.

Freud spent some time working in wards filled with the victims of cholera, typhus and other awful, now eradicated diseases, but he soon gravitated towards psychiatry. He worked under Professor Thomas Meynert, who was doing pioneering work dissecting the

bodies of deceased mental patients, noting the abnormalities in their brains and matching them with the symptoms they had suffered in life.

All this time Freud was searching for a subject which would make him famous. In 1884, he read an article on a little known drug, cocaine, and thought he had found it.

Freud purchased a quantity of cocaine, took some of it, and was amazed by its invigorating effects. He began to press it on his friends, colleagues, even his fiancée. He also gave it to a doctor friend named Fleischl-Marxow, in the belief that it would cure him of the morphine addiction he had acquired after his hand had become badly affected during an autopsy. He immediately became a huge coke addict. Fleischl-Marxow would die six years later, still hopelessly addicted to cocaine and morphine. Despite this disastrous result, Freud published a paper in which he claimed to have cured a morphine addict, who can only have been Fleischl-Marxow, in 20 days with the use of cocaine. This was the first of many instances of Freud claiming to have cured someone when no cure had in fact taken place.

Freud grew so euphoric about the promise of cocaine he started to claim it could cure just about every human illness (a state of mind, it has been suggested, possibly caused by his own use of the drug). His euphoria was short-lived however, as word of cocaine's addictive qualities quickly spread. He was forced to backpeddle furiously, while Freudian scholars have glossed over the whole affair as an unfortunate case of youthful enthusiasm.

In 1885, Freud won a grant which enabled him to travel to Paris to observe the work of the famous neurologist Jean-Martin Charcot.

CHARCOT'S CIRCUS

Charcot was famous for the work he had done among the patients of Paris's Salpêtrière hospital for women. Like Freud's previous mentor, Meynert, he had done important work in tracing nervous conditions to physical diseases or damage in the brain, but by the late 1870s had had begun to make a colossal mistake. Believing, erroneously, that he had identified all the organic causes of such illnesses, he was left with a group of women whose fits, seizures, paralysis and other conditions had no apparent cause. He came to the conclusion that these 'hysterical' patients, as they were called, were suffering from a mental, not physical, illness. In some unknown way, their minds were making them sick.

The concept of hysteria, a condition almost entirely associated with women, has been around since the Ancient Greeks. It had been noted that an hysterical fit often started with a sensation in the area of the womb, which gradually rose up through the body, ending with the feeling of a ball rising through the throat and choking the victim. From this it was surmised that hysteria was caused by women's wombs actually breaking free and roaming around their bodies. This belief was held by doctors well into the 18th century.

While studying his 'hysterical' female patients, Charcot became interested in hypnotism. He found that it was easy to hypnotise his patients and induce in them what were considered the typical symptoms of hysteria — convulsions, paralysis, abnormal rigidity in the limbs. Thus began 'Charcot's Circus', the name given to the regular

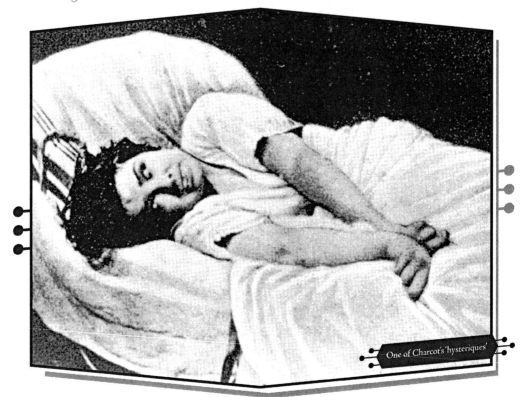

One of Charcot's 'hysteriques'

demonstrations Charcot gave during which his 'hysteriques' would be, as it were, put through their paces. Not only doctors but politicians, writers, actors and anyone else who could get in gathered to watch Charcot play his patients like musical instruments. They watched fascinated as they rolled their eyes, foamed at the mouth and threw themselves into incredible postures, such as the show-stopping 'arc-de-cercle' in which the patient's head and heels remained on the ground while her body arched violently into the air. Some of the younger and prettier 'hysteriques' even became minor celebrities in their own right.

What was really going on here? Because such spectacular displays of hysteria have rarely been seen since, some of Charcot's critics have suspected fraud. Yet, while it is possible that some of his patients were playing to the crowd, the whole phenomenon seems to have been largely a product of misdiagnosis. The tools which Charcot and his contemporaries had to examine brains were primitive by today's standards, and much of the neurological damage which can lead to nervous symptoms simply couldn't be seen. Many of the women were probably suffering from temporal lobe epilepsy, a form of the disease which induces fits beginning with the sensation of a rising womb, which was not properly understood until the introduction of the electroencephalogram in the 1940s.

Others may have had multiple sclerosis, syphilis or a host of other diseases which were either not yet discovered or not yet fully understood. As knowledge of these diseases has grown, the diagnosis of hysteria has virtually disappeared from medical textbooks.

Building on his initial error, Charcot observed physical symptoms such as ulcers or bleeding in his patients and concluded that these too were the products of hysteria. He also began to examine male victims of industrial accidents, in particular railway accidents, who seemed to have suffered no lasting physical damage, yet showed symptoms reminiscent of epilepsy. He decided that the men were suffering from 'hysterical trauma'. (What most of them were actually suffering from, it's now clear, was what is today called 'closed head injury', which occurs when the brain is banged against the inside of the skull.) By the time Freud came to visit him, Charcot was firmly of the belief that the mind could induce in the body just about any symptom.

Freud was greatly impressed by Charcot's demonstrations, but he was even more impressed with the idea that the mind could create physical illness. He left Salpêtrière after six months with the second big idea which could make him famous. He just had to work out the mechanism behind the process.

BREUER AND THE TALKING CURE

Freud returned to Vienna, married his fiancée, and set up a practice treating nervous patients, but grew frustrated with his lack of success. Finding he had no knack for hypnosis,

he decided to try a technique first used by a friend of his, a Viennese doctor named Joseph Breuer. In 1881, Breuer had treated a 21-year-old girl he called 'Anna O.', who had fallen ill while nursing a father dying from tuberculosis. Anna O.'s illness had begun with a simple cough, but developed into a bewildering parade of symptoms including (to name but a few) paralysis of parts of the body, a squint and double vision, an inability to recognise faces, deafness, regular lapses into a trancelike state during which she hallucinated, and an inability to speak her first language, German, so that she had to communicate in English.

Breuer decided early on that most if not all of her symptoms were hysterical. He found that she seemed to benefit from talking during the evening of the hallucinations she had experienced earlier in the day, and it was Anna O. herself who coined the term 'talking cure'. The apparent breakthrough came when she developed an intense aversion to drinking water. During one of their sessions, she recalled her disgust at seeing a friend's dog drinking from its mistress's glass. As soon as she remembered this, according to Breuer, she was able to drink again.

Here is the psychoanalytical method in a nutshell, the moment dramatised in *Spellbound* where a memory resurfaces and a symptom is swept away. The moment which was later dubbed 'abreaction'.

These days it seems perfectly natural to compare the brain to a computer (a comparison which may seem laughably simplistic in the future). Freud and Breuer, influenced by the technology they knew, drew their analogies from hydraulics and electricity. They suggested that a strong emotion which had, for whatever reason, been suppressed caused a build-up of energy in the brain. This excess energy was then somehow channelled through the nervous system, and resulted in a physical symptom. As long as the memory remained unconscious, the symptom would continue. As to how this process actually worked, Freud and Breuer were vague. But it's clear they were harking back to an old model of the nervous system as a network of hollow tubes through which flows a 'life force' or 'spirit', giving life and movement to the body (ideas which were still very much alive at the time).

As each of Anna's symptoms was traced back to a primal memory, they ceased, and at the end of the treatment Breuer declared her cured of her hysteria. The case became enshrined in Freudian mythology as the first triumph of psychoanalysis. The only problem here is that Anna O. had not really been cured.

Anna O.'s real name was Bertha Pappenheim, and in later life she became a famous social reformer. When her medical records were finally tracked down by a researcher in the early 1970s, they showed that, after her treatment by Breuer ended, she was sent to a sanatorium, still suffering from hallucinations and convulsions, and continued to be seriously ill for years afterwards. What she was actually suffering from it is now impossible to say, but meningitis, multiple sclerosis and temporal lobe epilepsy have all been suggested.

Reading through Breuer's case history of Anna O., it's clear what was really happening. Most diseases go through periods of spontaneous remission when symptoms decrease or disappear. When the disappearance of one of Anna's symptoms coincided with her recovery of a particular memory, that memory was deemed to be the cause of it. This was a mistake which was destined to be repeated endlessly in psychoanalysis.

Despite the fact that Breuer had completely failed to cure Anna O., he allowed his account of his supposedly successful treatment to be published in *Studies on Hysteria* (1895), alongside Freud's own first attempts at the new 'cathartic' method. Among these were the case of 'Fraulein Elizabeth von R.', who came to Freud suffering from pains in her legs which made it difficult for her to walk. She presented a typically melancholy 19th century life history. Like Anna O., she had nursed her father through a long illness until he died, then looked after her mother after an eye operation, then watched her sister die. Freud, who was convinced her symptoms were hysterical, decided that they stemmed from her giving up a potential relationship with a young man to nurse her father. He also deduced that she had an unrequited love for her brother-in-law (the husband of the sister who had died). He decided that the pains in different parts of her body could be traced back to different traumatic memories. The cause of the pain in her right thigh was easy to trace — that was where her father had rested his swollen leg when she changed his dressings — but he was initially stumped by her other pains. Then he realised that, as Fraulein Elizabeth was undergoing her various traumatic experiences, she was generally walking, standing or lying, which are, he notes reasonably enough, functions of "parts

of the body which in her case comprised the painful zones, namely her legs". Having made this connection, Freud found it relatively easy to trace the events which caused her other pains, culminating in the moment when she was standing — standing, mind you — by her sister's death bed, and realised that her brother-in-law was now free to marry her. "So for a long time you had been in love with your brother-in-law," Freud put to her, with the air of a policeman nailing a suspect. Fraulein Elizabeth denied this vehemently, but he eventually convinced her it was true. He pronounced her cured.

Unfortunately, as Freud admits, the pains in her legs continued.

Reading this case history today, it's hard to say which is more ridiculous — Freud's absurd diagnosis of a patient who was quite possibly suffering from rheumatism, or the fact that someone with sore legs was seeing a psychotherapist at all. What it clearly shows — and this is something that has generally been forgotten about Freud — is that he began his career as a medical doctor treating physical illnesses.

Soon after the publication of *Studies on Hysteria*, Freud broke with Breuer over the subject of sexuality. Freud had up to this point shown no particular interest in sex, but in a paper published in 1896, 'The Aetiology of Hysteria', he claimed that, of the 18 patients he was treating at the time, all of their symptoms could be traced to some aspect of their sexual life. Never one for intellectual half-measures, Freud now took it as given that repressed sexual ideas were responsible for all neuroses. The reason for Freud's sudden

change of tack has been much debated, but Richard Webster, in his monumental (and succinctly titled) *Why Freud was Wrong* (1995) suggests it might be quite simple.

In order to develop their own notion of cathartic therapy…Breuer and Freud found it necessary to delve into their patients' past experiences in order to identify the particular factors which had supposedly given rise to hysteria… Since they deliberately set out to find aspects of their patients' lives which were hidden, these premises led almost inevitably, in view of the degree of fear and reticence which surrounds sexuality in almost all human society, to the conclusion that sexual factors were among the prime causes of hysteria.

Another important factor in Freud's sudden interest in sexuality was the intellectual partnership he had begun with a charismatic doctor and pseudoscientist of the highest order named Wilhelm Fliess.

THE STRANGE SAGA OF FREUD AND FLIESS

Fliess was a nose and throat specialist two years younger than Freud, and the proud discoverer of the 'nasal reflex neurosis'. Having noticed that many of his patients seemed to exhibit a swelling of the mucous membranes in the nose, he had associated this with a wide variety of symptoms including headaches,

Freud and Fliess in the 1890s, "an inordinate interest in the state of each other's nose."

stomach pains and menstrual irregularities. The nose, he suggested, was connected in some unknown way with other parts of the body, particularly the genitals, and noted that if the mucous membranes were anaesthetised with cocaine, the symptoms associated with the 'nasal reflex neurosis' would subside. (Ironically Freud, in his earlier enthusiasm for cocaine, had missed the only medical use that the drug actually had — as a local anaesthetic.) If the cocaine did not effect a cure, he advocated an operation to remove the tiny, scroll-shaped turbinate bone from inside the nose. From his studies of menstruation, Fliess had also developed a complicated numerological theory which explained the life

cycles of all living things, and indeed all events in the universe, in terms of the numbers 23 and 28.

Freud and Fliess conducted a correspondence which can only be described as passionate. Freud considered Fliess his intellectual equal and subscribed to all his theories (he even used the numerological theory to predict — wrongly — that he would die aged 51). Suffering from migraines and a variety of other ailments at the time, Freud himself was diagnosed as suffering from the nasal reflex neurosis, and Fliess may even have operated on his nose. Both men firmly believed they were on the verge of making discoveries which would change the world.

Freudian scholars are understandably embarrassed by Freud's relationship with Fliess, although even Ernest Jones, Freud's worshipping official biographer, permits himself a chuckle at how "an inordinate interest was taken on both sides in the state of each other's nose". It took one of Freud's more ingenious critics, E.M. Thornton, the author of *Freud and Cocaine*, to grasp what was really going on here. For Fliess, in devising his cocaine treatment for the nasal reflex neurosis, had not realised that cocaine applied to the mucous membranes of the nose enters the bloodstream almost immediately (which is why, of course, people snort the stuff). This is why the application of cocaine alleviated the symptoms Fliess identified with his neurosis. It also means that during these years, Fliess (who also believed he suffered from it) and Freud spent much of their time coked off their brains. It's little wonder the ideas they came up with were increasingly grandiose.

THE SEDUCTION THEORY

We now come to one of the most interesting and misunderstood stages in the development of psychoanalysis. The view of this put forward in Freudian mythology is neatly summarised by a feminist supporter of Freud, Juliet Mitchell, in *Psychoanalysis and Feminism*.

Studying hysteria in the late 1880s and '90s, Freud was stunned to hear women patients over and over again recount how, in their childhood, their fathers had seduced them. At first he gave

an explanation in which the repressed memory of actual childhood incest was reawakened at puberty to produce the neurosis. He realised then that the whole thing was a phantasy… Freud found that the incest and seduction never in fact took place.

Freud's adoption and subsequent rejection of the so-called 'seduction theory' became a full-blown intellectual scandal with the publication of Jeffrey Moussaieff Masson's *The Assault on Truth* in 1982. Masson was a young Canadian trainee analyst who had charmed his way into the upper echelons of the psychoanalytical establishment. He had been appointed Projects Officer of the Sigmund Freud Archives, and here had gained access to Freud's letters to Fliess. These had survived, despite Freud's strenuous attempts to suppress them (he had eventually fallen out with Fliess), and a selection of them had been published in 1950. Masson was interested in the letters which Freud's heirs, in particular his daughter Anna, had deemed unsuitable for publication. Many of these dealt with his discovery, announced in his 1896 paper, that the neuroses of his female patients were caused by sexual abuse as children, most commonly by their fathers. By the following year, Freud decided he had made a huge mistake, and the stories were fantasy.

Masson's interpretation of this about-face was that advocating the seduction theory meant Freud was branding the fathers of his generally wealthy patients with child abuse,

that this would have put him on a collision course with the Viennese establishment and jeopardised his career, and, realising this, he had abandoned it. Freud, in an act of moral cowardice, had turned his back on the real sufferings of his women patients. The whole edifice of psychoanalysis was therefore built on a lie, and Masson was more than happy to bring it all down.

Masson's thesis looks persuasive at first glance. Its flaw is that, paradoxically, it gives Freud too much credit for psychological insight. For the female patients whom Freud was treating were not coming to him with stories of being abused as children. If they had, these memories could not, according to Freud's theory, be the cause of their illnesses — only *repressed* memories could do that.

What was really happening was that Freud, having decided that the seduction theory was true, then found evidence for it by reconstructing his patients' memories in his usual manner, analysing dreams and slips of the tongue and making fantastical word associations. When he finally presented his reconstructed scenes of seduction to his patients as real events, they inevitably rejected them. Freud makes this quite clear in 'The Aetiology of Hysteria'.

Before they come for analysis the patients know nothing of these scenes. They are indignant as a rule if we warn them that such scenes are going to emerge. Only the strongest compulsion of the treatment can induce them to embark on a reproduction of them.

It is of course possible that some of the 18 patients Freud mentions were abused as children (despite the fact that they had no recollection of it). It is highly unlikely that they all were. The crucial point is that Freud, in his usual all-or-nothing way, went from believing that *all* his patients had been abused, to the certainty that *none* of them had. From this point on, psychoanalysts were conditioned to treat memories of physical abuse as fantasies. It's a development which can only have increased the misery of those victims of childhood abuse unlucky enough to find themselves reclining on a psychoanalyst's couch.

FREUD SEES HIS MOTHER NAKED ON A TRAIN

Abandoning the seduction theory left a big hole in Freud's system. How was he to account for all this fantasising about seduction? It was at this point that he began to develop the theory of infantile sexuality which became the cornerstone of psychoanalysis. In doing so, he built on some ideas put forward by Fliess, who was in turn influenced by the 'biogenetic law' formulated by a Darwinian scientist named Ernst Haeckel. And here is one of the most embarrassing skeletons in the Freudian closet.

Haeckel's law started from the observation that a human foetus, as it develops in the womb, appears to replay the evolution of the species. It starts out as a few cells and passes through stages where it looks like a fish then various other mammals before becoming recognisably human. During this time, he believed that the 'soul' (by which he meant what we would call the mind) was dormant. But once a child is born it replays the *sexual* evolution of the species. In the theory of infantile sexuality eventually developed by Freud, a child goes through 'oral', 'anal' and finally 'genital' stages which allegedly mimic, respectively, the reproduction via the mouth practised by some primitive organisms, the anal or cloacal intercourse practised by birds and reptiles, and finally the genital sex of mammals. If a child develops normally, it passes through the oral and anal stages to reach the genital stage and achieve 'normal' sexuality. But if, for some reason, it becomes stalled at the oral or anal stages, it may become a fetishist or pervert or, if these impulses are repressed, a neurotic.

What all of this boils down to, to simplify (but only a little), is that today a person who keeps their house obsessively neat is labelled an 'anal personality' because birds have sex by rubbing their bums together.

The arrival at the genital stage is said to coincide with the onset of the Oedipus complex, probably Freud's best-known bit of business. He discovered it not through any study of real children, but during the lengthy self-analysis he embarked on in 1867. This is portrayed in psychoanalytical literature as an epochal event, the first time in history that the secrets of the unconscious were exposed to the light of day. Freud, whether it was due to cocaine addiction or not, was undoubtedly a sick man at this point, suffering from headaches, chest pains and periods of deep depression. By analysing his dreams and childhood memories, he attempted to discover why. The breakthrough came when he recalled a long train trip undertaken when

Freud with his mother (clothed)

he was very young, during which he and his mother, as he wrote to Fliess, "must have spent the night together and there must have been an opportunity of seeing her 'nudam'". (This incident is usually reduced in Freudian literature to the statement that "Freud saw his mother naked on a train", but it's clear that what he did here was reconstruct a repressed memory of his own, of an incident which may never have happened.)

The Oedipus complex is basically the idea that between the ages of three and five a boy develops a sexual attraction to his mother, becomes jealous of his father and, having noted that girls lack penises, fears his father will castrate him. In it, Freud found the reason for his own intense feelings towards his mother. Having discovered it in himself Freud, being Freud, immediately assumed

Freud with his couch

psychoanalysts accept it in the form put forward by Freud. But Freud considered it the breakthrough he had been looking for throughout his career and he was undoubtedly right. By 1905, when he first elaborated the theory in *Three Essays on Sexuality*, he had already gathered a group of Viennese medical men who met regularly to discuss his ideas, and who became the basis for the first Psychoanalytic Society in 1908. Freud was on his way to fame and respectability.

Why was the theory of infantile sexuality so successful? For a start, unlike the seduction theory, which applied only to individuals who had suffered sexual abuse, it was a universal theory which could be applied to everyone. It is, at first glance, a radical theory, but Richard Webster notes the similarities between Freud's concept of the unconscious mind, seething with repressed guilt from the Oedipus complex or perverse thoughts about oral and anal sexuality, and the Christian concept of children being born in a state of original sin. Freud is often portrayed as a great liberator of sexuality, and it is true that some of his comments on, say, homosexuality were liberal by the standards of his day. But it must be remembered that Freud's concept of normal sexuality was an extremely narrow one. Any practice or desire which veered from your basic missionary position sex was a throwback to animal sexuality which it was the job of psychoanalysts to cure.

It's often been noted that the psychoanalytic movement which Freud founded quickly took on the form of a church, with Freud at its head, issuing papal statements on doctrine,

that everyone suffers from it, and made it the centrepiece of the theory of infantile sexuality.

Despite Freud's airy assertions that the effects of the Oedipus complex may be clearly observed in children, it seems safe to say that, in the many empirical studies of children's behaviour undertaken over the years, little if any evidence has come to light that young children want to have sex with anyone, their parents included. A human being's sexual development is governed by hormones (which Freud knew nothing about). A sudden increase in the production of these hormones is what triggers puberty, but they are produced in such low levels in young children it is difficult to see how they could be 'sexual' in any real sense.

There is so little evidence for the theory of infantile sexuality that these days few

and a priesthood of psychoanalysts who were ordained by being analysed by Freud himself or someone who had been analysed by him. Whenever anyone strayed from the rigorous laws laid down by Freud — usually by questioning the all-important theory of infantile sexuality — they were branded as heretics and expelled from the movement (as Jung was in 1925).

If taking up Freud's ideas was like embracing a new religion, there was another, simpler reason for their success. Freud developed a system of thought virtually unique in the way that it turns any attacks on it back on the attacker. From the beginning, Freud characterised critics of his theories as themselves repressed individuals, unable to face the awful truths about the unconscious. A classic example of Freud's imperviousness to criticism can be found in *The Interpretation of Dreams* (1900), one of his most influential books. Freud begins his study with the analysis of a long, convoluted dream of his own which he decides is, despite first appearances, an example of wish fulfilment. He immediately decides this is what all dreams represent. It's a view which, he notes, his own patients find difficult to believe. They recount to him dreams which seem to be the very opposite of wish fulfilment, but he is always able to analyse them in such a way as to make them conform to his theory. Finally a female patient recalls a dream in which she has to spend the summer with her mother-in-law, whom she despises. How can this represent wish fulfilment? Freud is initially stumped, but then he realises that his patient wishes to prove him wrong about

the nature of dreams, and in having this dream, she is getting what she wanted. So the dream was wish fulfilment after all.

It is, of course, impossible to argue with logic like this.

While Freud had moved from the treatment of physical illnesses to what we think of as 'mental' illnesses, depression, phobias, obsessions and the like, one thing remained constant — the complete inability of therapies based on his theories to cure anyone. It's worth looking at one more case history to see the mature Freud in action — the story of the evocatively named 'Wolf Man'.

OF WOLVES AND WHITE UNDERWEAR

The case of the Wolf Man is called in the introduction to the Penguin edition "the most elaborate and no doubt the most important of all Freud's case histories". Not, unfortunately, a case of lycanthropy, the Wolf Man was a Russian aristocrat named Sergei Pankieff, and he was undoubtedly the most interesting person Freud ever analysed.

He was born in 1887 into a family of wealthy landowners with a history of depression and suicide. Sergei seemed to be a healthy enough young man, but when he was 18, a bout of gonorrhoea, followed by the suicide of his sister, plunged him into a deep depression. In 1908, while being treated in a sanatorium in Munich, he met and fell in love with a nurse named Therese who was some years older than him, divorced and had a daughter. They embarked on a passionate, on again, off again affair, with marriage

Sergei Pankieff, the Wolf Man

between them opposed by Sergei's family, friends and doctors.

At the suggestion of his doctor, Sergei travelled to Vienna in 1910 to meet Freud. His major symptoms at the time were a feeling that he was separated from the world by a 'veil', and a really terrible case of constipation which could only be relieved by enemas. For the next four years, Sergei lay on Freud's couch for an hour every day except Sundays.

Freud found the key to Sergei's problems in a dream he remembered having around the age of four. Awakening suddenly in the middle of the night, he saw his bedroom window open. On the branches of the tree outside sat six or seven white wolves which stared at him silently. Terrified of being attacked by them, he screamed and woke up.

Freud read into this dream the disguised memory of Sergei seeing, at the age of one-and-a-half, his parents having sex — the whiteness of the wolves represented the white underwear his parents were wearing. In the elaborate 'primal scene' he reconstructed, Sergei was sleeping in a cot in his parents' bedroom when he woke to see his father take his mother from behind, three times, with his father upright and his mother bent over. The scene ended when the little boy "passed a stool as a sign of his sexual excitement". According to Freud's extraordinarily convoluted analysis of the effects of this event, Sergei at the time craved sexual satisfaction from his father and therefore identified with his mother in the primal scene. His defecating Freud interprets as producing a gift for his father, noting "I believe there can be no difficulty in substantiating the statement that infants only soil with their excrement people whom they know and love; they do not consider strangers worthy of distinction". (!) Later, in repressing these homosexual urges, Sergei developed a childhood phobia about wolves with whom, via fairy tales, he had come to identify with his father. It was this repression which, years later, caused the problems with his bowels. Meanwhile, the fact that he had seen his mother bent over led to a sexual attraction to servant girls whom he would often see in this posture, scrubbing floors and so on, and this accounted for his falling in love with the nurse Theresa.

Freud conceded that the primal scene may never have happened, but went on to suggest that such a scene exists in everyone's mind as a sort of Jungian archetype which we're

born with. But if the primal scene with its particular details — such as the mother being bent over — never took place, Freud's analysis falls apart.

The Wolf Man's first period of analysis ended days before the outbreak of World War I. After the war, he underwent a further six months of treatment to clear up some 'nonanalysed residues', after which Freud discharged him, declaring him to be cured.

In 1973, an Austrian journalist named Karin Obholzer tracked down the Wolf Man, who was then living in obscurity in Vienna. In a fascinating book, *The Wolf-Man, 60 Years Later*, she records their conversations. The Wolf Man's life had indeed been a tragic one. He had lost his fortune after the Russian Revolution and, although he had eventually married Theresa, she had committed suicide in 1938. Far from being cured, his mental state had continued to be much the same after Freud had discharged him. He had been dependent on analysts all his life, and, at 86, was still in analysis. Looking back on his time with Freud, he didn't think much of the latter's analysis, noting that, when a child, his cot had been in his nanny's room, not his parents', so the primal scene could not have happened as Freud described it.

In my story, what was explained by dreams? Nothing, as far as I can see. Freud traces everything back to the primal scene which he derives from the dream. But that scene does not occur in the dream. When he interprets the white wolves as nightshirts or something like that, for example, linen sheets or clothes, that's somehow farfetched, I think. That scene in the dream where the windows open and so on and the wolves are sitting there, and his interpretation, I don't know, those things are miles apart.

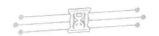

WHY PICK ON FREUD?

Freud's stocks have certainly fallen over the last few decades, with his more vehement critics dismissing psychoanalysis as a pseudoscience. Analysts of the classic school are a dying breed (outside France, at least), and these days Americans are more likely to pop a Prozac than head for a shrink, but the legacy of Freud lives on. The sloppiness of his thought and his cavalier interpretations of symbolism have pervaded every branch of the humanities from anthropology to art criticism. By focusing on early childhood, and arguing that we can be traumatised and damaged by events we don't even remember, he has created a whole industry catering to victims (all the hysteria about 'recovered memories' during the 1980s and '90s can be directly traced to his methods). The ultimate irony is that Freud, who set out to cure sickness, ended up creating brand new categories of it.

FOMENKO!

 e goes by many names: the Wild Man of Wujal-Wujal, the King of the Coral Sea, the Last of the Wild White Men. He's Michael Fomenko, the Russian aristocrat who's held down the job of being Australia's very own Tarzan for over half a century.

He was born in Soviet Georgia in 1930, the son of a former athlete turned academic, Daniel Fomenko, and Princess Elizabeth Machabelli, a member of the pre-Revolution aristocracy. Fleeing the country in the late '30s, his family travelled to China, then Japan where Fomenko led a gang of refugee boys who fought it out with the local toughs. They eventually settled in Sydney where his father became a teacher at the exclusive Shore school and a wartime radio commentator. Fomenko became a student at Shore, but being a foreigner — the only one in the school — with an imperfect grasp of English, he naturally felt alienated. The only other boy he made a connection with was Tim Bristow, who would later become an infamous enforcer, private detective and pants man. In a 2003 biography, *Bristow: Last of the Hard Men*, ex-journalist Kevin Perkins described a fight between the two of them which is still legendary among old boys from the '40s.

Bristow recalled that Michael Fomenko started it and they went into the dressing sheds after school to have it out. It lasted two or three hours. Fomenko would not stay down and wanted to continue on, even when obviously beaten. His blood would leave stains on the floor and wall seats. He stopped only when physically exhausted. Tim felt sorry for him because the fellow would not admit defeat. It was a fair fight, no kicking or gouging, only punches as sportsmanship required then.

Tim was amazed when Michael came to school next morning looking like a mummy, his face swathed in bandages, wanting to continue with the support of his father, who was a teacher at the posh school and also a coach in sport there. "We are Cossacks, we never give up," said his father. Here was a scholarly master wanting to referee a fight between his son and another student. Tim had nothing to prove, he'd won, and to avoid more bloodshed he said, "I'd rather shake hands." After some hesitation Fomenko shook hands with him and they became friends.

Fomenko was no scholar, but like his father he was a star athlete, and there was even talk of his competing in the decathlon at the 1956 Melbourne Olympics. His most marked characteristic, however, was a violent aversion to the 20th century. In 1955, his head full of Odysseus, he left the family home. He

Fomenko in his dugout canoe

Cooktown to Thursday Island. For the next leg of his epic journey — the closest thing Australia had to the Kon-Tiki expedition — he planned to paddle to New Guinea, then on to the Solomon Islands. Strong currents took him off course, though, and for months nothing was heard from him. He finally washed up in Merauke in Dutch New Guinea in December 1959, suffering from dysentery and malnutrition. His father, who had mounted a search for him, arranged for him to be brought back to Sydney, where he recuperated in Royal North Shore Hospital. Fomenko's voyage garnered wide press coverage, with one newspaper hailing him as "a symbol of non-profit seeking rugged individualism in an age of comfort".

With the legend of 'Tarzan' (a name first bestowed on him by Torres Strait Islander kids) firmly established, Fomenko returned to his jungle haunts. The stories about him continued to multiply over the years — how he fought off sharks with his bare hands, killed crocodiles with a bowie knife, covered himself with ash at night to ward off mosquitoes...

Tim Bristow, admittedly not the world's most reliable source, claimed that at one point Fomenko's father engaged him to track him down and bring him back from the wild. He managed to do this, but Fomenko was promptly thrown into a mental hospital. Bristow obtained permission for him to be released at weekends and took him to parties, where he encouraged him to paw the female guests and generally wreak havoc. Afterwards, Bristow would put him up in his house where, as might be expected, he was no ordinary

wore a flannelette shirt, jeans and sandals, and had a haversack on his back containing a New Testament, a book on marine life and a tomahawk. He was headed for the jungle — to the rainforest between Wujal-Wujal and Cooktown in northern Queensland, to be precise. Initially he made return visits to Sydney (he still had a girlfriend there, and would summon her by standing outside her house and blowing on a conch shell). But eventually the visits home ceased.

He lived on his wits, catching fish and mudcrabs, taking down wild boar with a machete, toasting coconut on the fire for a treat, and gained the respect of the local Aborigines, whom he referred to as 'my people'. He first made headlines in 1958 when he carved a canoe out of a sandalwood log and paddled 640 km (almost 400 miles) from guest. As Bristow's biographer tells it, "Michael wanted to sleep roughly, not in a bed, so Tim put him under the house with his dog. There was a terrific commotion and yelping when the dog tried to steal Michael's tucker."

In April 1964, police began to receive reports of a 'wild white man' wearing a lap-lap and armed with knives who was terrorising women in homesteads in Cape York Peninsula, begging or stealing food. Tracked down by an outback policeman, Fomenko — who was suffering from septic wounds, the legacy of a wild boar attack — was declared insane by a Townsville doctor and banished to an asylum in Ipswich where he was subjected to electroshock therapy. Michael's father, who had generally supported his son's lifestyle choices, was now dead, and unfortunately his mother agreed with the doctor's diagnosis. After two years, though, Fomenko was released with a certificate stating he had never been insane, and not surprisingly high-tailed it back to the jungle.

Interviewed by the *Sunday Telegraph* in 1985, a grizzled Fomenko, wearing his favourite leopard-skin underpants and plastic sandals, was quoted as asking, "Just what is this nuclear war?" His life was pretty good, he said. He survived by hunting and fishing (although he obtained some food from the local store as well), liked a beer and had a lot of lady friends. "Let's just say I'm up to scratch in every possible way," he joked.

It was around this time that his sister, Nina Oom, managed to find him. Encountering him on a beach, she flung her arms around him but he didn't recognise her. Shouting "I have to do my exercises!" he ran away. She left a sign on

Fomenko with Aboriginal friends after his aborted voyage to New Guinea

the beach asking him to contact her, which he did, and they spent a couple of days together. He returned to Sydney for the last time in 1988 to attend his mother's funeral. According to Nina Ooom, shortly before her death she said she regretted having her son committed.

It is interesting to see the different ways that Fomenko has been portrayed over the years. In the '50s the former private schoolboy gone bush was a heroic figure, in the '60s a potentially dangerous one. By the time he made an appearance in a 1996 TV programme called *Alternatives*, he had emerged as an exponent of alternative lifestyles, rubbing shoulders with tantric therapists, holistic counsellors and witches. The programme's producer, Patrick Lindsay, having tracked Fomenko down, persuaded him to agree to an interview in a darkened

Fomenko in 1985

a doctor. He also said that he'd like to get married if he found a girl who is good enough. ("But I'm only young and I haven't worried about this until now, see.")

Journalists continued to seek him out, and sometimes they found him. Jason Gregory of the *Courier Mail* came upon him jogging along the Bruce Highway in 2003. Some of the locals who took an interest in Fomenko's welfare had told Gregory they feared for his health — they had recently seen him catching buses and taxis. As Gregory jogged along beside him, Fomenko dismissed their fears. "I am still young. They are concerned about nothing and you should not worry about that talk."

Now in his 80s, Fomenko continues to live near Cairns. His principle residence is within the roots of a giant strangler tree, but he moves around a lot and can sleep anywhere. He makes forays into town every few weeks to pick up supplies, a hessian sugar bag over his shoulder, the jog now more of a shuffle. After cashing his pension cheque he'll have a meal of fish and chips and, especially if it's the wet season, may even check into a hotel for the night. He continues to make dugout canoes and dreams of embarking on one last great voyage, and as he's still a young man he may well do it.

hotel room, shot with a handicam. In the interview, which was screened with subtitles, a fit-looking but rather hard to understand Fomenko, who had only four teeth left (one of his few concessions to the 20th century being a fondness for Coca-Cola) spoke of the dangers he faces each day — lightning, sharks, falling off things; the food he ate — mainly seafood; and raised the possibility that, should he ever leave the jungle, he may become

"DON'T BUY THIS MAGAZINE!"

THE OFFICIAL UFO STORY

FO enthusiasts refer to periods when flying saucer sightings dramatically increase as 'flaps'. One of the biggest flaps, during the 1970s, was fuelled by the massive success of Erich von Däniken's *Chariots of the Gods*, tales of the Bermuda Triangle et al, and eventually big-budget films like *Close Encounters*. Newsagents were flooded with UFO magazines, some serious, most thrown together to cash in on the craze. Of these magazines one, *Official UFO*, is in a class of its own.

I have 10 copies of *Official UFO* and its sister publication, *Ancient Astronauts*, dating from September 1977 to December 1978. The earlier issues are the usual stuff — fuzzy photographs of supposed flying saucers, pseudoscientific articles on the Nazca lines, rehashes of the classic UFO cases. Then things begin to go haywire. The stories become more absurd, moving into territory that readers of the late, lamented *Weekly World News* would have been familiar with. 'Saucers Loot and Burn Chester, Illinois.' 'Mayor Koch Reveals Alien Nest Under Empire State Building.' 'Nudism — An Open Door For Alien Attacks.' 'Are Your Neighbours Insane?' Etc.

So far, so good. What makes this mag unique however is the penchant the editorial staff had for concocting stories about themselves. No one is safe from the 'space aliens', least of all the intrepid *Official UFO*

team. The January 1978 issue, for example, records the story of their offices being ransacked by the infamous men in black. The trouble started, it seems, when the art department hired a paste-up artist named Ron. This Ron acted strangely, knew things he shouldn't have and, worst of all, when he ate "he used his knife and fork clumsily, as if *he was using them for the first time*". After Ron mysteriously disappears, staff photographer David Blakely is lucky enough to witness three space aliens materialising in a field, and snaps a whole roll of film. The photos, which feature

Take this simple test to determine whether or not space aliens have turned your neighbors insane. Check YES or NO in the appropriate boxes.
DOES YOUR NEIGHBOR DO THE FOLLOWING:

SIT ON FRONT PORCH DRINKING BEER	YES ☐ NO ☐
HONK HORN LATE AT NIGHT	YES ☐ NO ☐
INDULGE IN TOO MANY LOUD ARGUMENTS	YES ☐ NO ☐
TRADE IN CARS WITH GREAT FREQUENCY	YES ☐ NO ☐
EAT TOO MANY BETWEEN-MEAL SNACKS	YES ☐ NO ☐
OWN TOO MANY PETS	YES ☐ NO ☐
WATCH TOO MUCH T.V.	YES ☐ NO ☐
ALWAYS SPY ON YOU THROUGH WINDOW	YES ☐ NO ☐
ATTEND TOO MANY PTA MEETINGS	YES ☐ NO ☐
ALWAYS BORROW THINGS FROM YOUR HOME	YES ☐ NO ☐
PLAY THE RADIO TOO LOUD	YES ☐ NO ☐
HOLD CONSTANT PARTIES WITHOUT INVITING YOU	YES ☐ NO ☐
KEEP ODD HOURS	YES ☐ NO ☐
HAVE MANY STRANGE VISITORS	YES ☐ NO ☐
LIVE BETTER THAN YOU DO ON SAME INCOME	YES ☐ NO ☐
HAVE HOBBIES THAT SEEM WEIRD TO YOU	YES ☐ NO ☐
IS OVERLY FRIENDLY WHEN GREETING YOU	YES ☐ NO ☐
IS A REAL KNOW-IT-ALL	YES ☐ NO ☐
HAVE CHILDREN THAT WALK ON YOUR PROPERTY	YES ☐ NO ☐
WEAR BUSINESS SUITS EVEN ON WEEKENDS	YES ☐ NO ☐
SPEND TOO MUCH TIME IN SWIMMING POOL	YES ☐ NO ☐
LOOK IN MIRRORS TOO OFTEN	YES ☐ NO ☐
CARRY AROUND BIG RADIO OR TAPE RECORDER	YES ☐ NO ☐
CARRY LIQUOR IN PAPER BAG AND DRINK IT IN STREET	YES ☐ NO ☐

SCORING: less than 5 YES answers—**PROBABLY NOT INSANE**
    between 5 and 10 YES answers—**ON THE BRINK OF INSANITY.**
over 10 YES answers—**NO DOUBT ABOUT IT, CONSIDER MOVING!**
    But remember, even a single **YES** answer could spell trouble — **BE ON YOUR GUARD AT ALL TIMES!**

close-ups of the beings from another world, are hidden away in the magazine's top priority file. The very next day three men wearing dark suits and sunglasses burst in. While two of them begin pulling out desk drawers the third confronts editor Jeffrey Goodman.

"You have one minute to decide whether or not you want to continue living. One minute. And every second brings you one second closer to your own death."

Luckily, just as Goodman's fate seems sealed, the men find the folder of photos and depart. But worse was to come for the hapless editor. The December 1978 issue finds him in a coma after having caught sight of a flying saucer one morning, occasionally regaining consciousness enough to rant and rave about the incredible visions he is having. Most of the story consists of a transcript of these visions, accompanied by numerous photos of Jeffrey lying on the floor, lying on a bed, lying in a hallway, and pacing around the room with a 'strange device' over his mouth "wanting to know if Einstein had left a message for him".

Editor Jeffrey Goodman again popped out of his coma. This time, however, he began to drink and smoke heavily. He then started speaking in Irish, recalling his merry days on the Blarney Stone. Soon thereafter these bizarre side effects wore off, and when the beleaguered editor was quizzed on what happened, he exclaimed, 'Why I've never been to that green land of Irish Spring' and fell back into unconsciousness, once more a victim of the fiendish coma.

DON'T BUY THIS MAGAZINE! screams publisher Myron Fass in an October 1978 article entitled "Ancient Astronauts on the Brink of Financial Ruin".

"That's right. You heard it. Don't buy Ancient Astronauts or Official UFO, *because we actually lose money when we sell copies. The printing bills, editorial costs; who needs it? We can't afford it.* WE ARE SEEKING THE TRUTH!"

On the subject of their financial status, the magazine's writers become what can only be described as schizophrenic. On the one hand they work out of "a large, bunker-like building disguised as a factory to avoid discovery" which contains "the most sophisticated equipment in the world to investigate UFOs and aliens from other planets". (We're shown photos which look remarkably like nuclear reactors and power plants.) Yet in the very same article we are told that the editorial staff must sit on cardboard boxes because they can't afford desks, wait patiently in line for the one electric typewriter they own, and put out the garbage themselves because they had to lay off the janitor. All this is accompanied by photos showing the staff performing such menial tasks, occasionally stopping to wipe "gobs of sweat" from their brows. The most poignant is the one of editor Jeffrey Goodman (in his pre-coma days) begging for supplies from neighbouring offices. ("He became lucky that day when the company down the hall from us were kind enough to give him four pencils.")

Broke or not, *Official UFO* certainly came up with some impressive scoops. The most impressive of all, and undoubtedly the magazine's finest hour, was the saga of Elvis's clone which dominates the May 1978 issue, and which Albert Goldman mentions in his indispensable biography of the cheeseburger king. It predates the 'Elvis is alive' hysteria by almost a decade.

Elvis's clone is at large and potentially dangerous. In his crazed condition there is no telling what he is capable of doing. He's a public menace and we're responsible for whatever happens.

BEFORE

AFTER

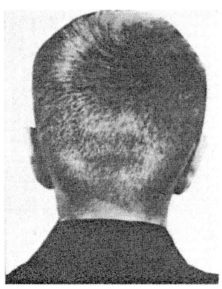 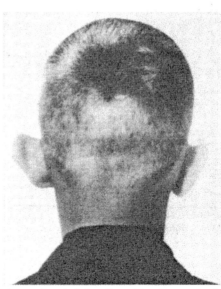

This is one of the unfortunate victims whose body was invaded by alien spirits. As a result of practicing karate wearing loose-fitting clothes, he left himself wide open for alien invasion. The most pronounced results of his attack are a gradual thinning of the hair, and enlarging of his earlobes.

This is 'Dr D.' speaking. He describes how Elvis, knowing that he would soon die, came to him with a request that a clone be made of himself which could take over his career "without anyone but his closest friends knowing the real singer had passed away". Dr D. is sceptical, but with Elvis offering unlimited funds he agrees to give it a try.

I will not lie to you and say that the first experiment was a success. In fact, we had to go through a cloning process at least seven times before we had a perfect Elvis. The first few times were dismal failures, with our creations looking quite monstrous… Finally, attempt number seven got us what we wanted — a 100 percent perfect Elvis.

Alas, while the clone looks just like Elvis, he soon begins to exhibit hostile behaviour. He leers into open space, curses the doctors, and asks for "vanilla ice-cream cake". As usual with *Official UFO* there's plenty of photographic evidence to back all this up, with pictures of the clone which indeed look remarkably like the real Elvis (like the real Elvis in some of his movies, in fact). Finally, shortly after Elvis's death, the clone goes completely berserk and escapes. The thought of a crazed, tremendously strong ("he can easily fend off three or four burley men") clone of Elvis Presley roaming the country is no laughing matter, and *Official UFO* offers a $100,000 reward to anyone who can bring the clone in (he may, it's suggested, be posing as one of the Elvis impersonators currently working the nightclubs). There's also a questionnaire to fill in for those who think they might have

spotted the clone, with questions like "Did he look like he was on drugs?" and "If female, did you have any sexual relations with the clone? Yes___ No___ If yes, please describe."

There are lots of other great *Official UFO* stories I could quote from, but I'll leave you with the disturbing facts about vending machines. The space aliens, according to Dr Joseph Cavor, are attempting to drive us mad by installing vending machines "which are NOT OF THIS EARTH." Dr Cavor has many incidents on file.

In one section of Chicago… vending machines loaded with small balls of bubble gum produced some astounding effects on the people who ingested the gum. Their tongues were turned weird colours, which is not an unusual side-effect of such candies. However, their entire faces soon followed suit, as did their entire bodies. There are reports of children running home hysterically panicked because they were totally green, blue, red and other colors. One poor little girl was transformed into a completely chartreuse child. Since she happened to be wearing a chartreuse dress, the effect was most pronounced… She passed out on a large lawn and, because she blended so well into her surroundings, she was undiscovered for several hours.

After a spate of attacks by vending machines, which are trapping people with mysterious magnetic forces and cutting off their fingers when they try to insert coins, the authorities decide to raid a vending machine warehouse. The story builds to a conclusion worthy of H.G. Wells.

ANCIENT ASTRONAUTS EDITOR IN CHIEF IN COMA !!

Secrets Of The Universe Revealed

"Aliens are responsible for the Great Depression; I know, I can prove it. FDR told me so." And so the ranting and raving continues. Is there any hope for Editor Goodman?

We like to think of the *ANCIENT ASTRONAUTS* staff as more than just a mere group of people working together. It is a real family in every sense of the word. We're a closely knit team which was thrown together by one of those strange quirks of fate which eventually touches us all, and, ultimately, changes the course of human events. In this case, our "family" has been chosen to lead the great fight against those that would oppress our freedom to print the truth about "the great UFO mystery." So, you can all well imagine the sorrow we felt when our Editor-in-Chief Jeffrey Goodman caught sight of a flying saucer one morning, and suddenly lapsed into a coma. He was immediately rushed to one of the finest hospitals in our city, where thousands of well wishers have been flooding his room with cards and telegrams praying for his speedy recovery, and wishing his grief stricken staff to have courage in this darkest hour. At times, Jeffrey comes out of his coma and rambles on somewhat incoherently about coming in contact with Albert Einstein and other great figures from history. Is this merely a symptomatic dream induced from his comatose state, or a great vision of things to come? Is Jeffrey a goner, or has he, in fact, met his date with destiny? We present it to you in these pages, as transcribed by staffer Kevin Goodman.

The raiding personnel entered the building, where they were confronted with a puzzling sight. Row upon row of vending machines were within the building. These were unlike any other type of vending machine people had seen before. They were on long stilt-like legs, and they had projections on their sides. As the terrified members of the raiding party watched, the lights within the machines came on... Simultaneously, the machines began to emit strange noises. Then they began to melt; transforming themselves into a liquid substance so sticky that it coated the warehouse floor like glue. The men could not lift their feet... Scientists dispatched to the scene could not disengage the trapped men, or do anything to dissolve the glue. As the glue began

to lose its stickiness, it also began to dissolve into vapor. By the time the men were freed, there was no trace left of the vending machines.

As Criswell says in *Plan 9 From Outer Space*, "Can you PROVE it didn't happen?"

POSTSCRIPT – THE EDITOR EMERGES!

Shortly after this article appeared in the first edition of the *Bizarrism* book in 1999, I was contacted by none other than *Official*

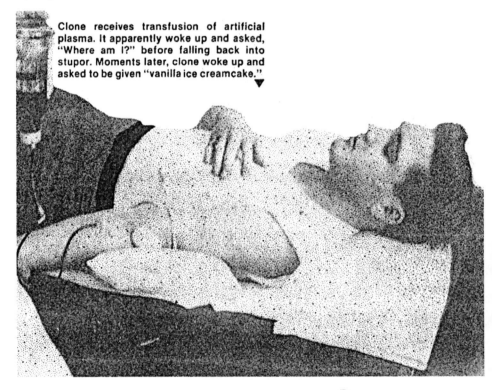

Clone receives transfusion of artificial plasma. It apparently woke up and asked, "Where am I?" before falling back into stupor. Moments later, clone woke up and asked to be given "vanilla ice creamcake." ▼

UFO's editor, Jeffrey Goodman, who had gotten wind of it. I'd been worrying about the poor man's fate at the hands of the space aliens for years, so this was an immense relief. And of course I was interested to learn more about his illustrious publication. What follows is an edited version of several of Jeff's emails.

Glad I found the right guy! I have been trapped in the underground bunker hidden beneath the Empire State Building since 1978 and have been recently revived and again confined in Bellevue Hospital by the men in black. I did manage to read part of your excellent chapter on us courtesy of someone with a fax machine…

I'm making a good living now in mail fraud and from having invented 900 dial a porn. The tinfoil man [Jeff had sent me a mysterious photo of a man sitting at a desk with his head wrapped in tinfoil] was David Fass, Myron's acid-taking, Grateful Dead worshipping, brain damaged son. Myron at last report was running a gun shop. You never heard the story where he shot at his publishing partner, Stanley Harris, through a wall with a "review pistol". Did you know Myron was a fairly well known horror cartoonist before embarking on a publishing career?

One of our greatest amusements was not only writing the articles, but fielding incoming phone calls. We had a routine where some deranged reader would call with a "UFO sighting". I remember one Haitian or Jamaican sounding guy called to say there was a "fish man" in his back yard, from outer space.

We had a well-rehearsed spiel where the callers would think they called a vast organization rather than our garbage-strewn cubicles on Park Ave South.

Buddy Weiss would answer the phone, take the "report", then transfer the call to Hannah Spitzer, our "operations secretary". She would transfer him to me, I would be "investigations division", and I would take the report, seriously ask questions such as "Was the fish man naked? Tried to have sex with you? Wearing nylon?", and so forth. After being bounced to many people (we published about 60 magazines from porn to dogs) they were convinced they had reached an immense global operation.

The caller would be put on hold many times and work himself into a state of apoplexy, thinking he has discovered the greatest thing since sliced bread.

We would then tell him his $10,000 sighting reward might be on its way if everything "checked out".

By the way, the Weekly World News copied our story ideas only days after ours would come out. I knew one day our genius would be appreciated…build it and they will come…ha ha.

– Jeff

KELVER HARTLEY

THE STORY OF A RECLUSE

It's a scenario which crops up in the media every year or so. A house is entered and the body of its former inhabitant found, he or she having died days, weeks, sometimes years previously. It's usually an elderly person, a recluse with little or no contact with others, no family to notice their disappearance from the world. Certain motifs recur in these stories. Sometimes a diary is found, its final entry pointing to the time of death. Sometimes the deceased is discovered sitting in front of a TV which is still, eerily, on. (This was how the comedian Benny Hill — increasingly reclusive and depressed after political correctness forced his programmes off British TV — was found some years ago).

In the media's reporting of these stories, two subtexts are usually present. Firstly, the assumption that the behaviour of recluses is baffling, incomprehensible. How can any rational person choose to cut themselves off from society like this? Secondly, the fact that some considerable time may have elapsed before a body is discovered is taken as a sad reflection on the uncaring nature of modern society. Thus, the discovery of the two-year-old corpse of retired seaman Clement Williams in Sydney in 1995 (with the radio still on) led to calls from the NSW Premier for a register of elderly people who lived alone so that their well-being might be periodically checked, while

a policeman was quoted as saying "I think it's a pretty sad indictment of our community that he hasn't got any relative or somebody to identify him, or report him missing."

I find both these notions curious. Since when are human beings so wholly admirable that someone's decision to be done with the whole lot of them can only be explained as crazy? And as for the length of time that may pass before a recluse's body is found, well, frankly I can't think of a more fitting way for a recluse to go.

Speculating about the psychology of recluses is always a risky business for the simple reason that once they have turned their backs on society, they rarely return. If we are to make anything at all of their motivations, we must usually rely on the things they have left behind.

On the afternoon of 29 February 1988, the landlord of a cheap boarding house in the Sydney suburb of Glebe broke into one of his rooms and found the body of its occupant, Kelver Hartley, who had obviously died some days previously. There had been little contact between Hartley and his fellow boarders, although it was rumoured that in a former life he had been a professor. Among the meagre possessions found in his room were numerous unpublished manuscripts and a will. This showed that Hartley exemplified a particular, and particularly intriguing, species of recluse

— the individual who lives in extreme poverty, yet has a fortune salted away. In Hartley's case this came to almost a million dollars in stocks and shares.

Kelver Hartley was born in Adelaide on 3 January 1909. He studied French at Sydney University, taught briefly in schools, and in 1933 was awarded a two-year scholarship at the Sorbonne. While in Paris, he wrote a thesis on Oscar Wilde and met Wilde's lover, Lord Alfred Douglas. He also dabbled in right-wing politics, and later claimed to have fought with the fascist group Action Française in street riots. (Hartley's often-voiced right-wing sympathies would later get him into trouble when, back in Australia, he briefly came under police surveillance during World War II.)

It must have been quite an anticlimax for Hartley, doctorate in hand, to return to Australia and go back to teaching in high schools. He had postings in Newcastle and various other places before becoming, in 1955, Senior Lecturer in French at Newcastle University College, which later became the University of Newcastle.

Hartley had by now acquired a reputation as a somewhat eccentric teacher. While the emphasis he placed on rote learning and the translation of great slabs of French made his lectures often less than exciting, they would occasionally be enlivened by reminiscences of his Paris days, impromptu demonstrations of fencing, or hints of his familiarity with the occult. Outside the classroom he was crippled by shyness and did everything he could to avoid contact with other people, especially women. If a woman happened to pass him in a corridor he would flatten himself against the wall in an apparent attempt to dissolve into it. Yet, despite the forbidding exterior which he attempted to construct, he inspired in many of his colleagues and students great affection, as the essays in a memorial volume published after his death make clear. His private life, however, remained a complete mystery and rumours about him abounded. Some said that he earned money on the side writing sexy thrillers, others that he was acquainted with every prostitute in Kings Cross.

Hartley's particular corner of scholarship was comparatism, the painstaking tracing of sources and influences in literature. He had a fair few papers published in academic journals, but it's clear he never scaled the intellectual heights he had expected to. In 1968 he announced his retirement, making the odd request that his superannuation — some $30,000 — be paid in cash. Taking his money he walked out of the university and, with the exception of one former student whom he would meet twice yearly for a literary chat, he never saw any of his colleagues or students again. He had two goals in mind. The first was to become, of all things, a science fiction writer. The second was to invest his money and turn it into a fortune.

He didn't have much luck with his first goal, for it seems only one of the many science fiction stories he wrote was ever accepted for publication ('The Mallinson Case', which appeared in *Worlds of Tomorrow* no 24 in 1970). In his second goal he had far more success. Hartley lived frugally, ate little more than oranges, dressed in clothes bought from K-Mart and walked everywhere rather than spend money on public transport. Every available cent was poured into investments. His dream was to make a million dollars, to be donated to Newcastle University and spent on sending promising students to study in France, as he had in his youth. By 1987 he had achieved his goal, with the value of his share portfolio exceeding a million. Then came the October 1987 share crash, which wiped tens of thousands of dollars from the value of his shares. This last apparent failure was, it seems, too much for Hartley to bear. He swallowed a large quantity of barbiturates, washed them down with alcohol and died. Ironically, movements in the share market soon took the value of his investments over the million mark again. By 1994, when the Hartley Bequest programme went into operation, they were worth two million.

Among the manuscripts found in Hartley's sparsely furnished room were two books. The first was a long philosophical tract called *Optimism*, which denounces the idea that all men are equal and advocates a society run by intellectuals. He was so convinced of the importance of this work that dates in it are expressed in terms of the half-life of radium so that future civilisations will be able to make sense of it, but Professor Kenneth Dutton, Hartley's successor at Newcastle University, has called it "almost unreadable". The second was a novel called *Remus Leaping*. This was published (as *The Haunting of Dr McCuaig*) by the Hartley Bequest Program, and it's a fascinating book. It tells the story of a university professor in his late 30s named Ian McCuaig who becomes involved with a group of spiritualists, and falls in love with one of their number, a 19-year-old waif named Elinor. She dies suddenly when, while acting as the medium in a séance, she is grabbed by one of the sitters. McCuaig then begins to hear voices in his head which threaten to drive him mad, until a nostalgic trip back to the country town where he grew up helps him regain his senses. McCuaig is obviously closely based on Hartley himself (although you have to laugh at his easy way with women — the book contains more than a few erotic passages — compared to Hartley's own abject terror of them). It's a densely written novel, bristling with obscure words ('incolumity', 'catercorner' and 'ugolinish' come at you in the course of two pages) and with some quite brilliant descriptive passages. At times it reads like a Victorian novel of ideas, so that the occasional reference reminding you that it's set in the 1970s — when it was apparently written — can come as a surprise. It doesn't all quite hang together as a novel, and its arcane subject matter means it would probably never have been published under normal circumstances, but that makes it all the more interesting to read now. Hartley demonstrates an intimate knowledge of the world of spiritualists in his novel, and one can only wonder what the experiences were that inspired him to write it.

The Hartley Bequest Program has published further volumes of 'Kelveriana', including a collection of short stories entitled *Eerie Tales*, while the first Hartley scholar left for Paris in 1997, to be followed by many more. Clearly Kelver Hartley, who by the end of his life had no regard for people in person, has in his own strange way done rather a lot for them.

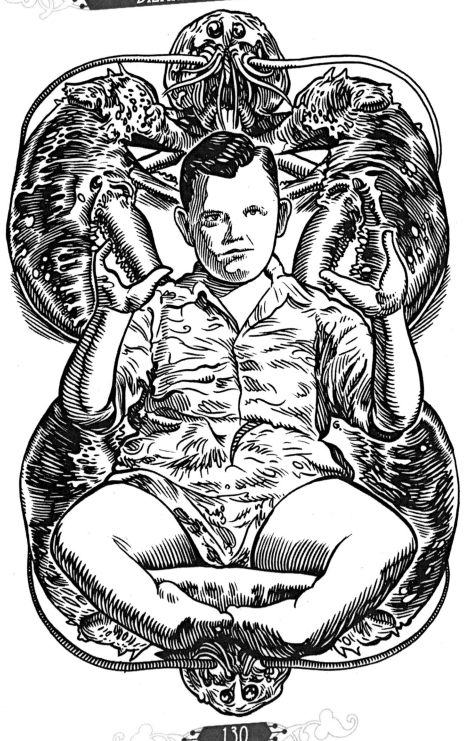

The life & death of
A LOBSTER BOY

The freakshow as an institution has all but disappeared. The carnivals that carried them have been in steady decline since the advent of television, while disabilities activists, crying 'exploitation', have made gawking at gross physical deformities socially unacceptable (no matter what the freaks themselves think about the matter). While it's true that a few hardy individuals may still be found exhibiting themselves in America's more out of the way places, and acts like the Jim Rose Circus Sideshow do an excellent job of conveying old-time carny thrills to new generations, the freakshow is largely a thing of the past.

Yet, if the freakshow as an institution is no more, as an idea it is still very much alive. The last few decades have seen an explosion of interest in freaks. Numerous books have appeared, from scholarly tomes to potboilers which display their galleries of freak photos like a tattooed lady showing off her skin illustrations. Freaks have become a pop culture staple, their images on record covers and posters, in comic books and films.

"A good freak would top every outfit on the midway," writes the great Daniel P. Mannix in *Freaks: We Who Are Not As Others*, "even the nude posing girls, and it's mighty hard to beat sex as an attraction." What accounts for this fascination? Firstly, of course, there is the I-could-have-been-born-like-that genetic shudder that goes through you when viewing one of 'nature's mistakes'. Also important, I think, is the glimpse that freakshows provide into a closed world, a fraternity you can never be part of because you have to be, quite literally, born into it. Everyone is interested in secret societies with their own rules, traditions and language (and there are few languages as colourful as carny slang). Freaks, as we have learned from the books about them, stick together through thick and thin. They tend to marry each other, leading to quite a few 'world's strangest couples' over the years. They are resilient and good humoured, looking upon their lot with equanimity. They are not the monsters portrayed in the final scenes of Tod Browning's landmark 1932 film *Freaks*, but, as the title of a '70s bestseller put it, 'very special people'.

This, however, is the story of a freak who was a real sonofabitch.

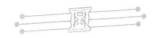

Grady Stiles, Jr. was born on 17 July 1937, a victim of ectrodactyly or 'lobster claw syndrome', a condition which had run in the Stiles family for generations. Grady's hands were pincer-like claws while his legs ended below the knees in flippers. Grady, Sr. had the condition too and made a living

LOBSTER BOY

Born in Pittsburgh, Pennsylvania
4th Generation
Condition has run for 5 Generations
Condition in the feet every other Generation

Grady Stiles

spectacular, graceful movement. His claws were strong too, and hard. When he was drinking, which he did from an early age, he got mean. He'd hit out at people who annoyed him with his claws, and he was good at headbutting too. Grady's claws came in handy for other things as well as fighting. A lot of women were attracted to him, he once boasted, and what they all wanted to do was have sex with his claws.

Grady married at the age of 17 but the marriage didn't last. Then he met a girl called Teresa who worked in the carnival as, among other things, a Blade Box Girl (whose job was to stand inside a box as a magician stuck swords through it) and an Electrified Girl. Teresa moved in with him and they married a few years later.

They had two children who died young, followed by two daughters, Donna, who was born normal, and Cathy, who had lobster syndrome (ectrodactylics have a 50 per cent chance of passing it on to their children). Grady was by now spending most of his waking hours guzzling whisky and regularly using his family for punching bags. Teresa, by all accounts an incredibly passive woman, never retaliated, but one day she snapped and walked out with Donna and Cathy. Grady immediately filed for divorce and won custody of his children — to their dismay. He took them to live in Pittsburgh with his new wife, a skinny piece of white trash named Barbara, with whom he had a son, Grady Stiles III or 'Little Grady' (who was not lacking in the

exhibiting himself as the Lobster Man, so it was inevitable that his son should soon join him on the platform as the Lobster Boy. In the winter months, when the carnivals shut down, the Stiles family, like many carnies, retired to the tiny Florida town of Gibsontown. Here their neighbours included Jeanie Tomaini the Living Half Girl, Dolly Scott the Ossified Woman and Percilla the Monkey Girl.

Grady's deformities may have been severe but they were not incapacitating. He got around on his arms, which became immensely strong, or in a wheelchair. He could swing himself off the floor onto a chair in one

lobster department). Teresa had meanwhile taken up with a carnival midget and friend of Grady's, Glenn Newman, aka Midget Man, and had a son with him named Glenn Newman, Jr.

Teresa missed her daughters but Grady wouldn't let her see them. One day in 1976, she and Glenn went to see Grady to try and persuade him to allow the girls to visit at Christmas. Grady pulled a revolver on them and whistled for his henchman, a 600-pound Fat Man named Paul Fishbaugh, who walked in carrying a shotgun. As Fat Man covered Midget Man, Grady went to work on his ex-wife with his claws.

In 1978, Grady's daughter Donna, aged 15, ran off with an 18-year-old boy named Jack Layne, Jr. Grady was furious, but none of his threats persuaded her to return home and the private detectives he hired couldn't find her. Finally, after Donna had lied to him that she was pregnant, he relented and agreed to sign a paper which would allow them to marry. On 27 September, the day before the wedding, Donna, her stepmother Barbara and brother and sister were busy making preparations for the reception, while Grady was in the local bar, getting drunk. Donna and the others returned after putting some money down on a wedding dress, to find that Grady's wheelchair had apparently been stolen from the front of the house. He sent them to look for it, but as they were leaving called Jack back inside. A few minutes later Grady pulled a .32 revolver from beneath the cushion he was sitting on

Grady with Cathy and Grady III

and shot Jack in the chest, then in the back as he tried to get out the door. Donna heard the shots and ran back to see Jack stagger out and collapse in front of her. He died on the way to hospital. As Grady was being taken away by police he said to Cathy, "Yeah I did it, and I'm glad I did it. I'd do it again."

Grady hired an expert defence attorney and shamelessly went for the jurors' sympathy, playing up his disabilities for all they were worth. He testified that, before the shooting, Jack had mocked him, then lunged at him threateningly, and he had shot him in self-defence. The jury found him guilty of manslaughter, but at the sentencing the judge said that Grady's condition made it impractical for him to be imprisoned, and he was released.

So little of Grady Stiles's life makes sense, it's hardly surprising that, a few years after the shooting and having divorced Glenn the Midget Man, Teresa decided to go back to Grady. He was now running his own 'Ten-in-One' show (10 acts under the one roof) with Grady its star attraction, and making good money — up to $80,000 a season. He was again based in Gibsontown and off the booze, and claimed to be a changed man. He even persuaded Donna to forgive him for shooting her fiancé. But the new Grady didn't last long. Soon after Teresa remarried him he was drinking again and getting as violent as ever. During one memorable bender he beat up Cathy, who was pregnant, so badly she was rushed to hospital where she gave birth to a premature lobster baby named Misty.

Teresa started to talk about having Grady killed.

Glenn, Jr. had a 17-year-old friend named Chris Wyant, a delinquent who claimed to have killed people. Glenn approached him and agreed to pay him $15,000, which Teresa had saved up, for the hit. Chris went out and bought a gun, but didn't do anything for several weeks. Glenn grew impatient and confronted Chris on the evening of 29 September 1992, demanding the money back. Chris said that he had already spent it and, showing Glenn the gun, told him he would fulfil his part of the bargain that night. At 11 pm he entered the Stiles' trailer home by the back door and found Grady in his accustomed place in the living room, in front of the TV with the day's supply of whisky under his belt. Grady, who knew Chris, yelled at him to get out of the house and turned back to the TV (he'd been watching *Ruby*, the movie about Lee Harvey Oswald's killer). Chris shot him three times in the back of the head.

As nothing was stolen, this obviously wasn't a robbery gone wrong, and the lack of grief among the family members quickly made them suspects in the eyes of the police. Glenn failed a lie detector test and broke down under questioning. Chris Wyant was tried and convicted of second degree murder and sentenced to 17 years. Teresa's lawyers used 'battered wife syndrome' as her defence, but she was found guilty of first degree murder and sentenced to 12 years, while Glenn was convicted on the same charge and got life.

As with any even mildly interesting murder case in America these days, a quickie paperback soon appeared — in this case *Lobster Boy* by Fred Rosen, a journalist who covered the trial. Leafing through its "16 pages of shocking photos", as the cover puts it, produces conflicting emotions. It's not often that the gaudy worlds of freakshow and murder collide, as they do in the story of Grady Stiles, Jr. Looking at the photos of his misshapen body lying in the morgue, and the three bullet holes neatly drilled into his bald head, you think, nobody who was born like that should have to die like that. But then you think, well, maybe in Grady's case you could make an exception.

BOVVER!

his is not a pretty story. It has violence, extreme right-wing politics, Japanese robots and a death no one should have to suffer. But it was Bovver's story, and he was stuck with it.

I first became aware of Wayne 'Bovver' Smith in the mid-1980s as a somewhat menacing presence in the Mod scene. Mod was one of the most visible youth subcultures in Sydney at the time, having taken off in the wake of a similar movement in Britain, itself a reaction against the scruffiness of punk. The Mods had revived and codified all the most stylish bits of the original Mod movement of the '60s. The boys dressed in impeccable suits, the details of which were minutely defined down to the number of buttons and the length of the vents, the girls wore mini-skirts and ski-pants and plastered their eyes with gooey black mascara. At night, having popped a few amphetamines, they rode on scooters to Mod gigs where the bands played a mixture of soul, ska and Who-style power pop. On the weekends they went on scooter runs to Brighton-le-Sands, the closest thing Sydney had to Brighton.

Bovver edited a fanzine called *Big Brother*, one of several which chronicled the Mod lifestyle. He hardly looked like your typical fresh-faced Mod however. A hulking, lugubrious figure, instead of a tight suit he

wore an army greatcoat, in the pocket of which nestled a spanner in case of trouble. My friends and I were somewhat surprised when a girlfriend of ours accepted a ride home from the Trade Union Club with him on his scooter one night. We were even more surprised when she started going out with him. After that we saw a lot more of Bovver.

I suppose because he was going out with a friend of ours, Bovver was always on his best behaviour in front of us. While you could never entirely ignore a certain underlying wildness in him (his fondness for speaking

Bovver the party animal

in *Clockwork Orange* slang was a bit of a giveaway), he came across more like a little kid than anything else. The first time he visited my house, he was so fascinated by my collection of Japanese robots — the sort that transform themselves into other things like cars and planes — that he spent hours rolling around on the floor playing with them, gleefully shooting little plastic missiles at me. On another afternoon we watched a video of the movie *Street Trash*, which Bovver liked so much he rewound it as soon as it had finished and watched it again, then continued to watch it for the rest of the day. Some people believed Bovver had suffered some brain damage, the result of a car accident in his youth. This had been followed by several scooter prangs and, later on in the '80s, a further car accident which left him with a crippled leg. After that

he walked with a cane, which came in handy for other things as well. One day, passing an acquaintance on the street, he swung the cane on a whim, smashing the other's wristwatch. This was Bovver's idea of humour.

Bovver was such an over-the-top individual in every way we tended to think of him more as a sort of cartoon character than a human being. Stories and rumours about him abounded. He had grown up in the Western suburbs, where his father had been a motor mechanic, and we imagined him as a toddler with the wrecks of cars for toys. We could hardly believe it when he got a job, through a government employment scheme, as a gravedigger, relishing the image of him tramping over graves in his Doc Martens. While doing this job, it was said that he had been struck by lightning, without ill effect.

Ah, we said, as with Frankenstein's monster, this would only have made him stronger. We were entertained by the tantrums he sometimes threw. One afternoon we were busy filming a Super-8 splatter film and had persuaded his girlfriend to appear naked in a fridge (it's a long story). This made Bovver very cranky indeed. He stomped all over the house, played a record of *TV's Greatest Hits* at full volume (with the result that the theme from *F-Troop* figured prominently in the finished film) and finally kicked a large fibreglass brain down the stairs (as you do).

Leaving an inner-city party one night, my girlfriend and I grew rather apprehensive at the sight of three skinheads approaching us down a dark street, only to hear a cheery hello from the biggest of them. At a certain point the Mod subculture blended into the more openly violent Skinhead one, and this was the direction in which Bovver had naturally drifted. Then, in 1988, he joined the right-wing extremist group National Action, led by Jim Saleam. Bovver had always been fascinated by militaria and Germany, so this political incarnation didn't come as too

much of a surprise. National Action's campaign consisted of plastering bus shelters and lamp posts with blue and white stickers bearing the Eureka flag and slogans like "Asians Out", throwing bricks through windows, and making the odd death threat. Bovver was rumoured to have taken part in one of their more notorious acts — the firebombing of a car owned by Bronwyn Ridgway of the NSW Nurses Federation. But it seems that Bovver was too fierce even for National Action. The other members were scared of him, and eventually voted to expel him. They were too frightened to tell him though. By this time Bovver had grown disillusioned with the group, and was passing information to the police about its future activities. This was his downfall.

If Bovver's life was surrounded by rumours, there is no dispute about the facts of his death. For it was all tape recorded.

On the afternoon of Saturday, 20 April 1991, Bovver was at National Action's headquarters in Tempe with another member, Perry Whitehouse, with whom he had been arguing. Bovver, who was wearing a singlet bearing the slogan "No to the new gun control

laws", was trying to make a phone call when Whitehouse came in from another room with a .22 rifle. The phone, which ASIO (the Australian Security Intelligence Organisation) had bugged months before, was left off the hook. The transcription of what was recorded, later read out in court, speaks for itself.

WHITEHOUSE: *I'll show you what I got to say.*
SMITH: *All right.*
A pause is followed by six gunshots, then crashing noises.
WHITEHOUSE: *That's what I got to fuckin' say… I just killed the prick.*
Sounds of laboured breathing. Footsteps.
WHITEHOUSE: *Do you think I'm fuckin' scared of going to jail?… I'm not scared.*
Traffic noises heard, then a gasp.
WHITEHOUSE: *Shut up…*
Smith hiccups. His breath can be heard.
WHITEHOUSE: *Is that you, prick? Looks as though your brains are coming out. Isn't that bad luck? You police informer…Bit o' bad luck, mate. Eh? The old brain come out the back.*
Groans and breathing throughout.
WHITEHOUSE: *Hope ya die, you dog bastard. That's right…*
Breathing becomes weaker.
WHITEHOUSE: *(Sings) "When I was 16… just a young boy going round and round in circles."*

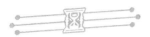

In October 1992, Perry Whitehouse was sentenced to a minimum of 13 years jail for Bovver's murder. Jim Saleam had already been sentenced to three-and-a-half years for another crime. National Action slowly faded away, to be replaced by other right-wing extremist groups.

There are others better equipped to tell Bovver's story, but I fear they'll never get around to it, so this is my version, make of it what you will. Bovver was 25 when he died, uneducated, easily led and aggressive. He was, when you get down to it, as Peter Cook would say, a cunt. But he would go out of his way to help people, he made you laugh, and he was always good to his mum.

The intergalactic
ADVENTURES OF KIRK ALLEN

 ne day in the late 1940s, a pleasant looking, blond-haired man walked into the office of psychoanalyst Robert Lindner. This man, whom Lindner called 'Kirk Allen' when writing about the case, was in his 30s, and was employed as a research scientist in a secret government facility. His superiors there, noticing that he seemed to be preoccupied with something that was affecting his work, questioned him about this and, receiving the assurance that he would "try to spend more time on this planet", were worried enough to have him flown to Baltimore where Lindner could treat him.

Kirk Allen, who seemed to Lindner on first impression perfectly sane, had grown up on a small Polynesian island where his father, a stern and uncommunicative naval officer, had been commissioner. He had an isolated and mostly loveless childhood. Ignored by his mother he was raised by a succession of Polynesian nurses and imported white nannies (one of whom had sex with him when he was 11, apparently causing in him an intense aversion to sex). From an early age he had escaped into fantasy. A voracious reader, his imaginative life received a tremendous boost when he discovered a long series of science fiction romances whose protagonist shared his name. He found that he could actually remember the incidents in these books, and came to believe that they were his own story, even though this other 'Kirk Allen', the ruler of a

distant planet, a legendary warrior and lover of beautiful princesses, lived sometime in the future.

Kirk Allen became obsessed with this alternative biography. Where there were gaps in the narrative between books he filled in the details himself, and when this was done he picked up the story where the books left off, being careful to distinguish between what he really remembered of his future life and what he had merely imagined. Then one night, as he wracked his brain for a particular memory, he found he could will his way into the mind of the other Kirk Allen and experience his adventures as reality. Astonishingly, he was able to keep all this up through his university studies and scientist work. To ensure that he had the details of this other world straight, he meticulously recorded everything he recalled, and these records he turned over to Lindner. They included a 12,000-page 'biography' of Kirk Allen, divided into 200 chapters, with a further 2,000 pages of explanatory notes attached; a glossary of names and terms running to 100 pages; 82 maps of planets, countries and cities; tables of dates and names of battles and other historical events; astronomical charts; 44 folders containing information on various aspects of the planetary system, with titles like 'The Fauna of Srom Olma 1', 'The Transportation System of Seraneb', 'Parapsychology of Srom Borbra X' and 'The Sex Habits and Practices of the Chrystopods'; hundreds of sketches and paintings and

innumerable scraps of paper covered with jottings and mathematical equations.

Lindner, being the good psychoanalyst that he was, didn't take long to identify the roots of his patient's obsession in childhood traumas, but now he had a problem. Kirk Allen was convinced that his intergalactic adventures were real, that he was a sane man with an extraordinary gift. Given that these experiences were infinitely more exciting than anything his real life had to offer, how could Lindner possibly persuade him to give them up? Lindner decided that the only course of action he could take would be to go along with his patient's fantasies for a while, to enter into them to a certain extent, and, when inconsistencies cropped up, use them to create doubts in his patient's mind. So Lindner immersed himself in the records. Whenever he came upon an apparent error or mistake in a calculation, he pointed it out and demanded Kirk Allen fix it, which usually involved him making a trip to his home planet to consult the records there. As Lindner (who had once witnessed a meeting between two women, both of whom believed themselves to be the Virgin Mary) explained, there's usually only room for one person in a fantasy like this.

Lindner was a former prison psychologist used to dealing with violent criminals and juvenile delinquents (his 1944 study *Rebel Without a Cause* gave the James Dean film its title) but he didn't realise the dark waters he was entering here. He wasn't up against flick-knives now, he was fighting fantasy, and it wasn't long before he too was caught in its web. As he continued to search through the records for inconsistencies, he began to feel increasingly anxious that these be cleared up. When, as occasionally happened, Kirk Allen was unable to resolve a discrepancy, Lindner devoted his own spare time to doing it. Phrases from the 'Olmayan' language that Kirk Allen had created began to pop unexpectedly into his head. The worlds of Seraneb and Srom Olma 1 were increasingly in his thoughts, and his own work began to suffer. Events came to a head during a session one day, when Lindner noticed that his patient was not showing his usual interest in their work. Kirk Allen suddenly admitted that he had given up "that foolishness" weeks ago, that he had realised that none of it was real, and had been feigning interest in it solely for Lindner's benefit. It was the patient's turn to cure the psychoanalyst.

Lindner described the case in a book, *The Fifty-Minute Hour*, published in 1955. He died the following year and the identity of Kirk Allen has never been revealed. He obviously had all the prerequisites for a career in science fiction, and it has long been rumoured in science fiction circles that he was Paul Linebarger, a political scientist who wrote a book on brainwashing techniques called *Psychological Warfare*, as well as producing a series of science fiction stories under the name Cordwainer Smith. Sinologist and science fiction scholar, Leon Stover, claimed that Lindner told him Linebarger was Kirk Allen in the early '50s, while Robert C. Elms has found many parallels between the families and careers of the two men (making allowances for the fact that Lindner, for reasons of patient confidentiality, had to disguise the details of Kirk Allen's background in his book). However, no conclusive proof that the two men were one and the same has yet emerged.

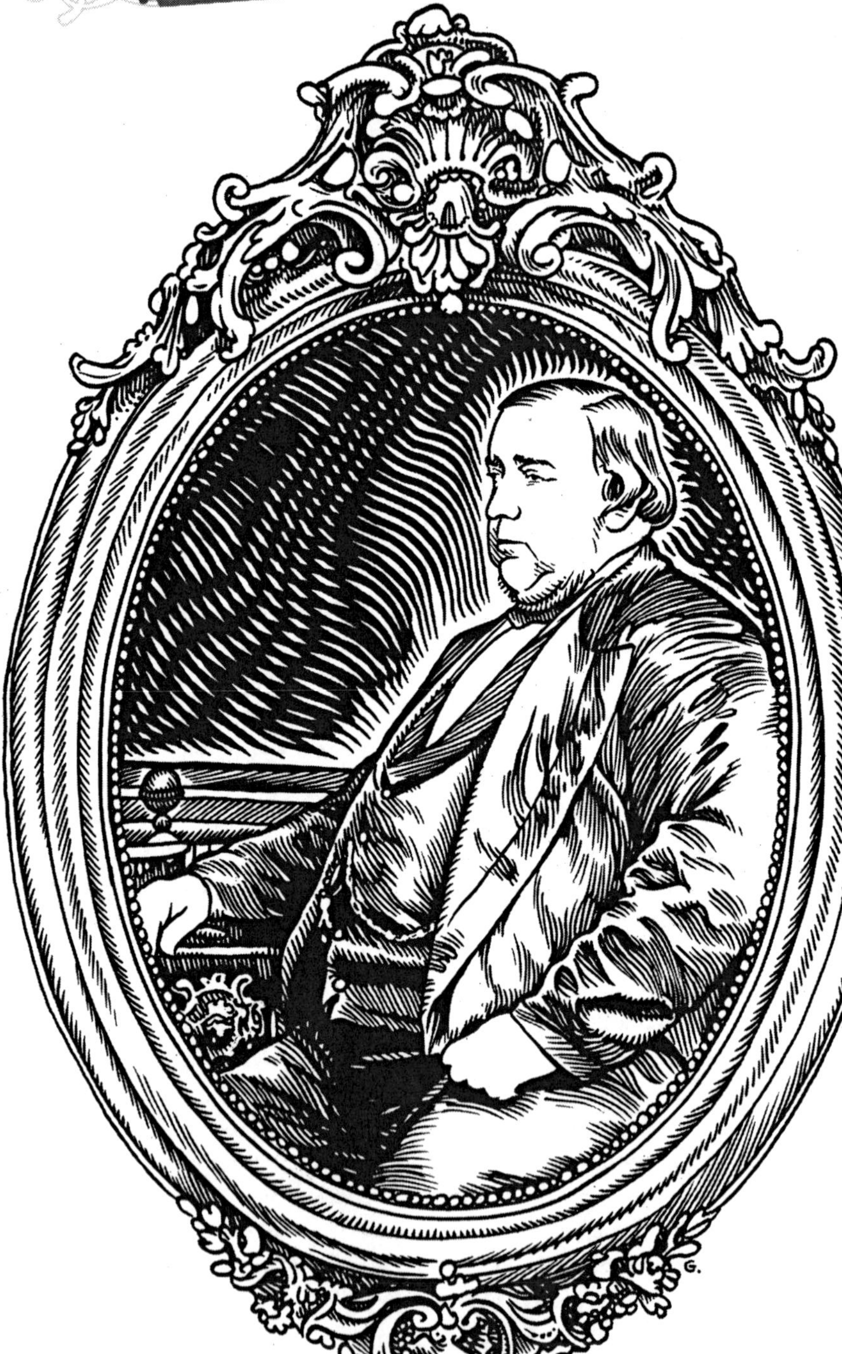

TICHBORNE-MANIA!

n 1866, an overweight and amiable butcher from a country town in Australia arrived in England to press the claim that he was Sir Roger Charles Doughty Tichborne, heir to a fortune and long believed lost at sea. It was the beginning of a decades-long farce which would divide the country, lead to two extraordinary trials, and culminate in a radical political movement which threatened to overthrow the British government. Along the way, the Tichborne Claimant, as he was known, became famous around the world, his appearances in public guaranteed to draw crowds, the mere mention of his name a cause for spirited argument among strangers.

But let us begin this tangled tale with the brief but eventful life of Roger Tichborne — the real one, that is. He was born in Paris in 1829, and was the son of James Tichborne, baronet and member of an old Catholic family, and Henriette, his French-born wife. Henriette hated England and the English with a passion, and kept Roger in Paris until he was 16, when his father managed to spirit him away to England. He was educated at Stonyhurst, then joined a dragoon regiment, the Carabineers. He also fell in love with his young cousin, Katherine Doughty. Her parents initially objected to a marriage, for Roger, despite his prospects, was a moody, twitching, thin-chested, sallow-faced young

man with a taste for hard liquor and spicy French novels. Katherine's father eventually agreed to the match, but only on the condition that the couple wait for three years. Roger announced that he was off to South America. Before leaving, he gave his best friend, Vincent Gosford, a sealed packet for safekeeping.

Roger spent 10 months in South America, shooting exotic birds and sending their skins back to England to be stuffed. He also posed for two daguerreotypes which he sent to his family, and which would eventually assume great importance. Arriving in Rio de Janeiro, having drunk away most of his funds, he booked passage to Kingston on a ship named the *Bella*. She set sail on 20 April 1854, and was never seen again.

Roger's father accepted that his son was probably dead. His mother did not. When James died in 1862, Lady Tichborne placed advertisements in newspapers around the world seeking information about Roger. One of her ads was seen by the wife of Walter Gibbes, an attorney who lived in Wagga Wagga, a country town in New South Wales. Gibbes was, at the time, handling the bankruptcy of a local butcher, Thomas Castro, who was newly married with two children to support. He suspected that Castro was not the man's real name, and had also been intrigued by the butcher's carelessly dropped hints that he had once been shipwrecked, and owned property in England.

Gibbes mentioned these hints to his wife, and it was she who suggested that he might be the missing heir. When he put the suggestion to Castro, the butcher looked apprehensive, saying, "I do not want my family to know." Yet he made no attempt to hide that fact that the pipe he was smoking was engraved with the initials 'RCT'.

Despite the apparent reluctance of Castro (who will, in time-honoured fashion, be henceforth referred to as 'the Claimant'), Gibbes persuaded him to write to Lady Tichborne. His letter, poorly written and full of spelling mistakes, was duly sent in June 1866. It contained a request for £200 for his passage to England.

Two months later, the Claimant's third child was born. Gibbes was supporting him financially by now, thus becoming the first in what would be a long, long line. In return, he persuaded the Claimant to draw up a will naming him as a beneficiary. The resulting document, in which the Claimant managed to get his mother's first two names wrong, also listed several nonexistent properties. Having received his letter, Lady Tichborne was initially sceptical, but she did send £40 which got the Claimant and his family to Sydney. Here, in a moment of overexcitement, he bought a hotel for £10,000 with funds from an imaginary bank account. He also passed his first real test, for living in Sydney at the time was an elderly negro, Andrew Bogle, who had been a servant of the Tichborne family and knew young Roger well. Bogle met the Claimant and recognised him immediately (after all, he reasoned, the Claimant had recognised *him*). When the Claimant had raised enough money to take himself, his wife

and month-old child to England, he took Bogle along, too.

They arrived in London on Christmas Day, 1866. That night, the Claimant slipped away from the hotel where they were staying and paid a visit to the dockside suburb of Wapping. Here, he made inquiries about a local butcher named George Orton. He learned that George and his wife were dead, as were four of their sons, but there were still two daughters living in the East End. The Claimant was eager to have their addresses.

A few days later, the Claimant set off for Paris and the long-awaited meeting with Lady Tichborne. The affair had received wide coverage in the newspapers and a crowd gathered at London Bridge to see him off — a taste of things to come. Upon his arrival, Lady Tichborne summoned him, but the Claimant said he was feeling too ill to go to her (as well he might have been). Instead, she went to his hotel. She found him lying fully clothed on his bed, a handkerchief over his head, and recognised him immediately. Her servant, who was present, later testified that her exact words were, 'He looks like his father, and his ears look like his uncle's.'

Back in England, the Claimant visited the Tichborne estate in Hampshire, where he was generally well received by the locals and recognised by the family's solicitor and doctor. A few members of Roger's former regiment also came to the party, as did his cousin, Anthony Biddulph, who became one of the Claimant's staunchest supporters. The

rest of the family proved harder to persuade. Roger's uncle, Henry Seymour, questioned the Claimant in French and found that he had forgotten it (despite the fact that it had been Roger's first language); showed him a sample of Roger's father's handwriting which he failed to recognise; and asked him about a mutual friend whom he could not recall. This was enough for Seymour who declared, "I cannot recognise you in any way."

The Claimant explained his memory lapses as a result of the hardships endured during his missing years. According to his story, after the *Bella* was wrecked, he survived in a lifeboat until he was picked up, delirious, by a ship bound for Australia. Arriving in Melbourne in July 1854, he adopted the name of Thomas Castro and went to work as a stockman on a cattle station in Gippsland. Over the next few years he was a horse breaker, mail rider and gold prospector, before moving to Wagga Wagga and taking up the butcher's trade.

The Tichborne family dispatched a solicitor named Mackenzie to Australia to check this story. Producing photos of the Claimant, he soon found people who recognised him, but they identified him as Arthur Orton, a butcher from Wapping. Mackenzie reported back to England, and the family sent a detective to Wapping who uncovered the story of the Claimant's visit there and inquiries about the Ortons. When confronted with this, the Claimant said that Arthur Orton had been a friend of his in Australia, and had asked him to look up his family while in England.

Lady Tichborne died in March 1868, a disaster for the Claimant. Not only was she his chief supporter, but her weekly cheques for £20 had been his only regular source of income (and as usual he was heavily in debt). Salvation came in the form of the good gentry of Hampshire. They had been mightily impressed by the Claimant's prowess in shooting, fishing and other country pursuits, and reasoned that he *must* have been born one of them. After Lady Tichborne's funeral, they got together and voted him a yearly income.

Meanwhile, preparations for a trial by jury to settle the matter were under way. Two commissions composed of lawyers for the family and the Claimant travelled to South America and Australia to interview witnesses. The Claimant was supposed to go too, and actually made it to South America but, complaining of ill health, he returned almost immediately. This didn't go down well with his supporters, most of whom quit. Faced with the loss of income, the Claimant's solicitor had the brilliant idea of issuing 'Tichborne Bonds' which had a face value of £100 (the amount to be paid to the bearer when the Claimant came into his inheritance) but which were sold for much less. They were a great success, raising some £40,000 for the cause.

If the Claimant had forgotten much of his past, he had clear memories of his time in South America, and in particular his stay in the small Chilean town of Mellipilla with the family of one Tomas Castro (whose name he had adopted in Melbourne). Interviewed by the South American commission, people in Mellipilla did remember the visit of an English boy. Alas for the Claimant, they had

Roger Tichborne (left) and the first photo of the Claimant sent to Lady Tichborne.

believed him to be poor, knew him as Arturo, and had never heard the name Tichborne. The commission sent to Australia had more mixed findings. The family's lawyers found plenty of people who recognised the Claimant as Orton, with some of them suggesting he had changed his name to cover up some past crime such as sheep stealing. But the Claimant's lawyers found witnesses who swore that Orton and Castro were two different men. What was abundantly clear was that identity was a fluid concept in Australia at this time. People often changed their names, rarely gave surnames, and it was not done to question someone too closely about their past.

The trial finally began in May 1871, with

the solicitor-general, Sir John Coleridge, acting as chief counsel for the family. Coleridge's main goal was to demonstrate the Claimant's ignorance of Roger Tichborne's early years, and in this he was successful beyond his dreams. The Claimant was totally, spectacularly, blissfully ignorant of vast areas of Roger's life.

COLERIDGE: *Have you studied Greek?*
CLAIMANT: *Yes.*
COLERIDGE: *Did your studies in Greek go as far as the alphabet?*
CLAIMANT: *I don't know.*
COLERIDGE: *You surely remember that?*
CLAIMANT: *I went there unprepared.*

COLERIDGE: *Could you make out Greek at that time?*

CLAIMANT: *Perhaps a sentence.*

COLERIDGE: *Could you read the first chapter of St John?*

CLAIMANT: *No.*

COLERIDGE: *Does any of this linger in your mind now?*

CLAIMANT: *Not a bit of it.*

COLERIDGE: *Could you give us the Greek for 'and'?*

CLAIMANT: *No, I am not going to do anything of that kind.*

COLERIDGE: *Did you get on better with Latin?*

CLAIMANT: *I believe I got further with Latin.*

COLERIDGE: *Did you learn the Latin alphabet?*

CLAIMANT: *Of course I did.*

COLERIDGE: *Could you read a line of Latin now?*

CLAIMANT: *I'm certain I could not.*

The most notable aspect of the Claimant's testimony was not his inability to recall minor incidents, which might be expected, but his ignorance of facts on the public record like the details of Roger's school and regiment. It had now been four years since he embarked on his claim — surely in that time he would have taken the trouble to check such things. So profound was his lack of knowledge, though, that some people began to feel he might be genuine. The Claimant himself remained completely unfazed by Coleridge's onslaught, and it seemed that no demonstration of his failings of memory could upset him in the slightest. Coleridge

had expected an easy opponent, but was soon confiding in his diary, "He will kill me before I do him. I am seriously wearing out and getting ill."

The Tichborne trial was the biggest news story in Britain. Each day's proceedings were eagerly discussed, and everyone had an opinion. The trial was celebrated in pantomimes and burlesques, satirical songs and illustrated booklets. Quotations from it, such as Coleridge's favourite opening gambit when questioning the Claimant, "Would it surprise you…?", became catchphrases, while the despairing cry of "No Tich!" meant that the speaker couldn't bear to hear another word about it. People queued to see a waxwork of the Claimant at Madame Tussaud's, clad in a set of clothes he had donated himself, and you could buy plaster figurines of him and other notable participants in the trial. Contributing greatly to the sense of fun was the Claimant's physical appearance. A heavily built man on his return to England, his weight had now ballooned to a massive 26 stone (165 kg), making him an instantly recognisable subject for caricature. The contrast between the thin, sallow-faced and missing Roger, and the fat, cheery and ever-present Claimant, was

irresistible. He was like a sort of one man Laurel and Hardy.

The Claimant now made a grave tactical error. This involved the sealed packet which Roger had given to his friend Gosford before leaving for South America. The Claimant had previously made a statement to his solicitor, and after sustained questioning by Coleridge he repeated this in court. What he said amounted to this: that prior to his departure, he had seduced his cousin, Katherine Doughty, and she had told him she was carrying his child, but he had not believed her. As Gosford, who had rejected the Claimant soon after meeting him, had already stated that he had destroyed the packet long ago, the Claimant had nothing to gain by saying this. But his real blunder was to thus blacken the name of Katherine Doughty, who was now the respectably married Lady Radclyffe (and present in the courtroom). These charges were shocking stuff in those days, and even many of the Claimant's supporters could not forgive him for making them.

The Claimant's lawyers began their case by calling over a hundred witnesses to back up his claim. Coleridge, in his opening address

for the family, which lasted a month, said he would call 250 to deny it. The trial had been going for seven months now, and judge and jury were growing weary.

Coleridge's first witness, Lord Bellew, introduced a new and startling development. He testified that Roger had tattoos of a cross, heart and anchor on one arm, and that he himself had added the letters 'RCT' to these when they were at school together. Other witnesses corroborated this (although their recollections of the tattoos differed somewhat). The Claimant, needless to say, bore no such marks. This was enough for the jury, and they let it be known that they had heard enough to declare him an impostor. The judge, Bovill, agreed with them, and ordered that the Claimant be arrested for perjury.

That the jury had clearly decided the case on the tattoo evidence troubled many. If Roger really had been tattooed in this way, then no further proof was needed that he and the Claimant were different men. Why then had the family or anyone else not spoken up about the tattoos earlier, saving everyone an awful lot of time and money? Could it be true, as the

Claimant's supporters maintained, that there was a conspiracy against him?

Released on bail, the Claimant made a barnstorming tour of the country, speaking to thousands and soliciting money for his defence fund. It was from this point that the Tichborne cause became a great popular movement. From the beginning, opinions about the case had been polarised along class lines. While the upper classes, with a few exceptions, looked on the Claimant with undisguised contempt, the masses took an instant liking to 'Good Old Sir Roger', with his love of sport and ability to get on with anybody. The newspapers, which for the most part toed the establishment line, looked on aghast as support for the Claimant soared. How could people be so stupid?

The first point that needs to be made about all this is an obvious one — if the claimant really was a missing baronet, returned to have his inheritance, he makes no sense at all as a working class hero. But this is to misunderstand what was going on. The Tichborne case was not about identity, but transformation. The Claimant, in the eyes of his supporters, started life as an aristocrat, turned his back on his heritage to rough it in wild and woolly Australia, then returned to regain his birthright. He was the man who had transcended class barriers.

And then, too, there was probably a more mundane reason behind popular support for the Claimant. When the establishment attacked him for his ignorance, his boorishness,

Edward Kenealy

his illiteracy and lack of manners, they could easily recognise a slap to their own faces.

The Claimant's supporters had trouble finding a barrister to represent him in the coming criminal trial, and it was only a few weeks before it began, in April 1873, that Edward Kenealy stepped forward. Now this Kenealy was almost as interesting a character as the Claimant. He was an Irishman, a fiery orator and dabbler in radical politics, and was already identified with lost causes, having taken part in the defence of the notoriously brazen poisoner William Palmer. He was also, in his spare time, a mystic who turned out enormously long religious books, including *The Book of God*, a commentary on the Apocalypse. Kenealy wrote that a new Messiah arises every 60 years. Adam had been the first, Jesus was

another of course, and the twelfth one was now due. This new Messiah, he strongly suggested, was Kenealy himself.

In the criminal trial, unlike the previous civil trial, the prosecution's object was to prove not only that the Claimant was not Sir Roger Tichborne, but that he also was Arthur Orton. The prosecuting counsel, Hawkins, began by calling numerous witnesses who had known Orton in England, including his former girlfriend.

Kenealy, having come to the case late, never mastered its complexities. He made up for ignorance with bluster, painting the picture of a massive conspiracy against his client involving lawyers, the government, the Tichborne family and the Catholic Church (it had been rumoured that, should the Claimant be recognised, he would halt the family's regular donations to the Church). He accused the prosecution witnesses of being paid to lie. In building his case he received no help whatsoever from the Claimant, who seemed thoroughly bored with the whole business. A peculiarity of the law at the time was that defendants in criminal cases could not testify, so the Claimant sat mute as the lawyers argued, sketching caricatures of the courtroom personalities, waiting for each day's adjournment so he could get out and about and enjoy himself. He laughed uproariously at the jokes Hawkins made at his own expense, and seemed oblivious to his fate should he lose the case. Faced with such a useless client, Kenealy adopted a two-pronged strategy. On the one hand, he painted the young Roger Tichborne as a dissolute wastrel, thus making his transformation into the Claimant more

plausible. On the other, he portrayed the Claimant as an utter fool who lacked the intelligence to come up with such a fiendish imposture. In doing so, he disputed many of the things the Claimant had said in the first trial. As it was perjury that the Claimant was now being charged with, this was an unusual strategy, to say the least. Kenealy also made much of a matter only fleetingly mentioned in the first trial, the fact that the Claimant had what is known as a retractile (or usually hidden) penis. (In fact, he claimed that Lady Tichborne, seeking to assure herself that he was genuine, had once asked him to take his trousers down, then grabbed his crotch.) Kenealy tried to prove that Roger Tichborne also had this malformation, with little success.

In his month-long summing up at the trial's conclusion, Chief Justice James Cockburn made no bones about the flimsiness of the Claimant's case. He concentrated on his ignorance, the dissimilarities between the baronet and Roger, and the matter of the tattoos. He also registered his disgust at Kenealy's behaviour. (Kenealy would be disbarred after the trial.)

Cockburn's summing up was due to end on 28 February 1874, and a verdict was expected almost immediately. Fearing civil unrest, even rebellion, the government dispatched 600 police to Westminster, but the crowd took the guilty plea calmly. Historian Michael Roe suggests that "the Claimaint's supporters wanted his freedom less than they wanted confirmation that he was a victim of conspiracy". The case had lasted 180 days, making it the longest trial in British history, and it would remain so until the so-called McLibel Trial of the 1990s.

Britons all come pay attention
And list awhile to my sad song
And when you've heard some facts I'll mention
You'll say they've proved that right is wrong
That the claimant is the right man
To many people is quite clear
But the jury found him guilty
His sentence is 40 years.

From the ballad
'We'll Not Forget Poor Roger Now'.

The establishment breathed a collective sigh of relief that the case was over, but they had not reckoned on the bloody-mindedness of Kenealy. Riding on the back of the incredible popularity that the trial had given him, he started a newspaper, *The Englishman*, which combined pro-Claimant polemics with other populist causes such as crusades against compulsory vaccination, the Contagious Diseases Act (which gave the police the power to examine alleged prostitutes for venereal diseases) and the lunacy laws (which were said to make it too easy for doctors to commit people). Kenealy's paper was a great success, as was the political movement he founded — the Magna Charter Association — which called for the dismantling of the party political system and the abolition of taxes on the working classes. Some 250 branches sprang up across the country, and 200,000 gathered for a Magna Charter demonstration in Hyde Park in March 1874.

Kenealy's movement was beginning to look like a real threat to the social order. In the following year, he was elected to Parliament where he quickly moved for a Royal Commission into the Tichborne case (it was defeated in a vote of 302 to one). But then the movement began to falter due to a lack of funds, the vast majority of its members being poor. Kenealy achieved nothing further in Parliament, and was defeated in the 1880 election. He died two weeks later, and the Magna Charter Association eventually petered out.

The Claimant was released from prison in 1884. He immediately resumed touring the country and once again thousands turned up to hear him speak. Many of his appearances were now in music halls and circuses, which some of his supporters found demeaning. The Claimant loved music halls, though, and even found a new, young wife in one of them (having become estranged from his first wife while in prison). With Kenealy and other staunch supporters dead, however, the Tichborne movement was in decline. Seeking funds, the Claimant travelled to New York in 1886, was treated with indifference there, and ended up working in a saloon. Back in England, still strapped for cash, he signed a confession for a newspaper in which he admitted to being Arthur Orton. As soon as he had received payment, he retracted it. He was living in as abject a state of poverty as he had ever known when, on April Fool's Day, 1888, he was found dead in his bed. He was buried in a coffin with "Sir Roger Charles Doughty Tichborne" on its lid.

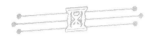

It is now almost universally agreed that the Claimant was Arthur Orton, born in Wapping in 1834, who had travelled to South America like the real Roger Tichborne (only four years earlier). All the evidence suggests that, when he first made his claim from the safe distance of Wagga Wagga, the most he had hoped for was to squeeze a little money out of Lady Tichborne, and he had certainly never expected to actually go to England in the guise of Sir Roger. But then the affair developed its own momentum, spurred on by the greed of others hoping to get a piece of the Tichborne pie. And Orton, a man who seems to have lived only for the moment, went along with it.

Yet other mysteries remain. An enormous amount has been written about the case, and Orton was, for many years, perhaps the most closely observed man in Britain, but he remains an enigma. How did he cope, every day, with the knowledge that a vast machinery of humanity had arisen, all built on the idea that he was someone he was not?

Why did so many people recognise the Claimant as Roger Tichborne, including many who had known Roger well? It's hard to believe there was no physical resemblance between them, yet it's impossible to see any in the photos of them.

And then there is the transformation that took place in the Claimant over the years. He arrived in England inarticulate and barely literate, the very model of a country butcher, yet he became an effective public speaker, and by the end of his time in prison,

his letters were as expressive and elegantly written as anything the real Roger Tichborne had written — perhaps more so. While he remained ignorant of many details of Roger's life, at the same time he was constantly coming up with snippets of information about Roger which convinced people he was the genuine article. To explain this, some have surmised that Orton was an illegitimate son of one of the Tichborne men. Others have suggested that Roger survived the wreck of the *Bella* and made it to Australia, where he met Orton. Douglas Woodruff, author of *The Tichborne Claimant*, is inclined to believe this, and cites persistent rumours that Orton and Tichborne were bushrangers together. Yet there is no real evidence for any of these theories. And as recently as 2000, an Australian author wrote a book in which he argued that the Claimant really was Sir Roger.

In 1989, 25-year-old Darren Tichborne, who said he was the Claimant's great-great grandson, was interviewed in his London squat. Calling for DNA testing on the Claimant's body, he said that when he became Lord Tichborne he would retain his punk hair style and earring. "I will kick out rich yuppies from our villages so ordinary people can live in them again."

He was later revealed to be an impostor.

THE JOE MEEK EXPERIENCE

oe Meek was one cool guy. The first independent record producer in Britain, his life was a heady mix of pop, pills, occultism, gangsters and mounting paranoia, culminating in a grand and violent finale. It's one of the strangest sagas in the history of popular music.

He was born on 5 April 1929 in the small town of Newent, near Gloucester, the son of fish and chip shop owner George Meek and his wife Biddy. By the age of 11 he had developed an interest in music, and asked for his first gramophone for Christmas. He spent his childhood tinkering with bits and pieces of secondhand electronic equipment, constructing radios, amplifiers and the first TV set in his town. After a stint in the RAF and work as a repairman for various electronics shops, he moved to London where he scored a job travelling around the country recording variety shows for Radio Luxembourg.

Working as a sound engineer, Joe began to experiment, playing around with reverberation and echo to create sounds that no one had ever heard before. These were the days before multitrack recording, when making records involved little more than the taping of a single performance. Joe pioneered the technique of recording multiple takes of each instrument then laying down the best ones, one at a time, gradually building up the song. It seems perfectly obvious now but all of this was quite revolutionary at the time, and it horrified Joe's fellow recording engineers. What was undeniable was the sound he was able to get. In 1956 the first disc he produced, a jazz number by Humphrey Lyttelton called 'Bad Penny Blues', made it into the Top Twenty, and this was soon followed by his first Number One with Anne Shelton's 'Lay Down Your Arms'. Using primitive, patched-together equipment, Joe was the only man in Britain able to match the full, lush sound of American recordings.

It was around this time that Joe became interested in spiritualism. He began to hold regular séances with his musician friends, and during one of these received the message that Buddy Holly was to die on the third of February. Joe was a big fan of Holly, and when the singer toured Britain he made a point of going backstage to deliver a friendly warning. Holly thanked him politely, but had no doubt forgotten all about the incident by the time he bundled his entourage onto a plane on the stormy night of 3 February 1959. After that, Joe became obsessed by Holly, and came to believe that the dead rocker's spirit was helping him with his music.

In 1960, Joe set up a recording studio at 304 Holloway Road, Notting Hill — three floors above a leather goods shop — and formed a company called RGM. A recording studio in a busy street, with traffic roaring outside and irate neighbours banging on the walls,

doesn't sound like a brilliant idea, but for Joe it meant being able to live with his recording equipment 24-hours-a-day. The middle room, reached by a narrow staircase, became the studio and control room, but Joe utilised the whole flat when recording, and would often have a string of violinists down the stairs and the singer shut in the bathroom for added echo effect. In this unconventional setting, amid a mass of secondhand machinery and handmade speakers, with electrical wires and unspooled tape trailing all over the floor, Joe set about making hits.

A textbook obsessive, Joe was temperamental and difficult to work with. A little switch in his brain would flick and he'd go from sweet and charming to completely irrational. A tyrant in the studio, any obstacles to getting a sound he wanted sent him into insane rages which echoed those his father — a WWII shellshock victim — had suffered from. Whatever hours of the day he wasn't actually producing records were spent experimenting with sounds (anything from a jar being tapped to a fingernail running along the teeth of a comb might find its way into one of his recordings) or writing songs, tunes running through his head constantly. Being incapable of singing or playing any sort of instrument, he had to communicate these songs to others as best he could, humming in a high-pitched whine and banging out the rhythm with anything that came to hand. Any signs of amusement from the musicians who were supposed to play these compositions would cause Joe to explode. He'd chase them down the stairs, hurling tape recorders and other heavy pieces of equipment after them.

Joe's first big success after establishing his studio came with an actor named John Leyton. He could barely sing, but this was no problem for Joe who, with a bit of knob-twiddling, could make anyone sound good. The first Leyton release, 'Johnny Remember Me', was a song written by Joe's friend and fellow spiritualist Geoff Goddard (who also thought he was getting a posthumous song-writing hand from Buddy Holly). One of the so-called 'death discs' of the 'Tell Laura I Love Her' school which were inexplicably popular at the time, it was a big hit, as was the follow up, 'West Wind', and for a while Leyton was something of a star.

'Son, This Is She', the third Leyton disc and one of Joe's masterpieces, may be taken as representative of the 'Joe Meek Sound'. For a start it's LOUD, so loud that the needle threatens to jump out of the grooves. It's all swirling orchestra, girly backing vocals, stuttering rhythm and messages from beyond the grave, and Leyton's voice sounds magnificent. Hard to believe it was recorded in a lounge room with little more than a four-piece band, four violins, a harp and a French horn.

Then came 'Telstar' and Joe's greatest success. Joe was fascinated by space travel and the possibility of extraterrestrial life (he had previously recorded perhaps the world's first concept album, a suite of electronic songs on the subject of life on the moon entitled *I Hear a New World*, which had unfortunately gone unreleased). 'Telstar' was inspired by the launch of a communications satellite of that name. Joe got a session group he had formed called the Tornadoes to perform it, with the main melody played

Meek with equipment

on an early electronic keyboard instrument called a clavioline. Released in August 1962, 'Telstar' was a huge worldwide hit, and became the first record by a British group to reach Number One in the U.S. Joe's eccentric methods were vindicated — he'd beaten the Americans at their own game.

'Telstar' sounds pretty dinky today, but back then, with its spacey effects and strange organ sound, it was the last word in futurism. In a 1991 *Rolling Stone* interview, Church of Satan founder Anton LaVey cited it as an example of a truly satanic song, as opposed to the supposedly satanic but empty music of certain heavy metal bands. (His other example, incidentally, was 'Yes, We Have No Bananas'!)

There were other hits after 'Telstar' but it was downhill time for Joe now. The beginning of the end came when Joe, who was gay and found most of his partners in the streets around his studio, was arrested in a public toilet. He was charged with "importuning with an immoral purpose" and let off with a fine of £15, but the incident made the papers. Joe became a target for blackmailers and his paranoia, always healthy, grew. He had hidden microphones planted all over the studio and any musicians overheard making jokes about his homosexuality were booted out.

Musical tastes were changing, too. The Beatles had broken through and across the country hundreds of groups had sprung up to play the new Merseybeat sound. Records like 'Telstar', which had sounded so modern a few months before, were suddenly old hat.

Joe's problems were beginning to pile up like the tracks on one of his records. Revved up on amphetamines he continued to churn out

discs by a large number of singers and groups, but the hits were getting harder to find. He was still hooked on the occult, imagining that ghosts were roaming the studio, and grew so paranoid that record companies were trying to steal his secrets that he would sometimes communicate only with notes. He conducted regular searches of the studio for bugging devices (and in one instance found one, showing it wasn't entirely paranoia). He believed he had discovered a way of driving people mad with a high frequency electronic signal, and was convinced his enemies were using the same technique on him. Sometimes, in the middle of a recording session or a conversation, he would drift off into a trance…

By 1967, Joe was almost broke. The lease on his studio was up, and he suspected he was going to be thrown out. There were gangsters threatening him, wanting to take over the Tornadoes. Meanwhile, a teenage boy had been killed (The Suitcase Murder, they called it, because the victim had been cut up and placed into two suitcases) and the police were reported to be interviewing all known homosexuals. Joe had known the boy and feared being dragged into it. He began to burn documents. John Repsch, in *The Legendary Joe Meek* (1989) comes to the conclusion that he was planning suicide.

On the morning of 3 February 1967, Joe's landlady, Mrs Violet Shenton, came to visit him. There was an argument and Joe shot her in the back. She staggered out of the studio, falling down the narrow stairs onto Joe's office assistant, Patrick Pink. Extricating himself from the dead weight of the 54-year-old woman, Pink made his way upstairs in time to see Joe blow the top of his head off, ending the sounds in there forever. It was the anniversary of Buddy Holly's death.

The question remains — why on earth did Joe shoot his landlady, with whom he reportedly had an almost mother-and-son type relationship? Repsch speculates that, in the hope of at least something going right, he had confronted her about the lease, and when she disappointed him, she became the victim of his final insane rage. She was just there at the wrong time.

Joe Meek left behind over 250 records by a wide variety of artists, all of which have his personal stamp on them. Although he was largely forgotten for years, the publication of Repsch's biography revived interest in him. *Telstar*, a play about him, opened in London 2005, and was made into a film in 2008. Most importantly, almost all his recordings have been re-issued (with *I Hear a New World* gaining its first full release in 1991). They still sound like nothing else and are well worth seeking out, the legacy of a very strange, totally obsessed man.

Illustration by Charles Pierce

BELLERIVE THE POET

While the legendary Scotsman William McGonagall is rightly regarded as the world's greatest bad poet, Australia possessed a worthy runner-up in Joseph Tishler. Writing under the name of Bellerive, Tishler toiled in the mills of poetry for almost five decades, producing a body of work which, if it lacks a little in the spelling and scanning departments, more than compensates with sheer exuberance.

Tishler was born in Dunedin, New Zealand, in 1871, and spent most of his life in Melbourne. He worked at various times as a woodchopper, street vendor, auctioneer and factory hand. He played the accordion at larrikin parties and was involved with the theatre as a stagehand and occasional actor (the role of a monkey in *Sinbad the Sailor* being one of his more memorable). The influence of overripe old melodramas can be clearly seen in his poems.

THE STAGE VILLIAN

To and fro he
Did pace the stage
And cursed the hero
In he's rage
'I'll foil the hound,'
He did egaculate.
'By heaven I will
Seal he's fate.

He robbed me of
My sweet Totlinda.
I'll throw him out of
He's top floor window.'

In 1908, Bellerive had the first of many poems published in *The Bulletin*, which would remain virtually his only outlet. So what if his poems only ever appeared in the 'Answers to Correspondents' section, where contributions deemed unfit for publication were held up for ridicule? Bellerive was happy enough to see his work in print.

He soon attracted something of a cult following ("the most popular poet in Australia," *The Bulletin* called him in 1912, tongue firmly in cheek). While he tried his hand at bush ballads and lyrical pieces, it was his bloodthirsty narratives that attracted the most attention.

A WOMAN'S REVENGE

Oh Wilfred why do you shun me
Appealed a woman as her blue eyes met his
Begone Ileen said the artist
My love for thee like a bird has flown
A cry broke from the lips of an unhappy Woman
The false deceiver had ruined her life
As he turned with contempt towards his easel
Into his side she plunged a knife
'Twas a fatal thrust his brow turned livid
As he sank compulsively to the floor

She had fulfilled her deed of revenge and horror
Into a pool oozed the victim's gore.

"Tragedies, Death-bed scenes, Brawls and Haunted houses, etc., are doeful subjects to Dwell on," wrote Bellerive, "and the art of turning ghastly incidents into verse is neither cheerful nor Simpile, but I'm attached to my Art and possess Vivid inspiration, which aids my Task. Wanderings, hardships and bitter trials as blighted my life, but never the less I endeavour to do my best under the circumstances."

Bellerive was a true naïve, with a childlike fascination with the minutae of the world. Anything that happened to him during the day, from a woman accidentally sitting on his hat, to discarding an old pair of trousers, could become the subject of a poem. Over the years he penned tributes to flies, fleas, cockroaches and even the humble denizens of cheese.

CHEESE JUMPERS

They hop o'er your plate
And go as you please
The little white jumpers
That live in old cheese.
Some people loathe 'em,
And others don't care
If they swallow a mouthful.
The truth I declare.
They hop twist and leap,
And go as you please,
The jumpers, white jumpers,
Whom live in old cheese.

A long article about Bellerive appeared in *People* magazine, August 30, 1950. The writer

found a dispirited poet, then aged 80, living with his wife, an amateur painter, in a tiny, unheated cottage near Melbourne's Victoria Markets. He was suffering badly from asthma, the cold, and the accumulated bad reviews of 40 years. He knew some people laughed at his work. "Writing poetry is a hard, cold life and you make more enemies than friends," he said. "I never got any more out of it than a few shillings anyway. And the theayters have killed it. First the theayters, then the films and then radio. People don't want to hear poetry anymore. And now that the Government has talked of banning it I'm pulling out. I'm too old to worry about fame. Fame is for young fellows and I'm going to give it away."

Bellerive wheezed his last in 1957, but received a measure of vindication with the publication in 1961 of a small book of his poems.

BEHIND THE CURTAIN OF MY ART

I dippeth my pen in silence
My verses are no longer seen
Weekly as they were in the answers,
For years in The Bulletin
A victim of fierce speculation
In defence I could only dare,
But never weakened or trembled
In the thralldom of sad despair
A mirthful clown of a circus
Who capers and rolls he's eyes
Wins more friends than a poet,
Be him ever so clever and wise.
I jotteth down verse in silence,
I'm snug in my little den,
Master of my gift from the cradle,
Wizard of ink, paper and pen.

Pushing his pram-wheeled billy-cart along a Melbourne street, Bellerive (Mr. Tishler) cried, "Don't take no pictures of me. I've retired. Fame is not for me. Writing poetry's a hard life."

The wonderful
WORLD OF MORMONS

 love the sight of Mormons in the morning. Haircuts and teeth gleaming in the sun, they stride purposefully forward, confident in their magic underpants, paperback copies of the *Book of Mormon* wedged firmly in the back pockets of their polyester trousers. Unfailingly polite, seemingly mass produced in plastic, they roam the world in pairs, the determinedly nice side to one of the strangest major religions around.

THE TALE OF A MONEY DIGGER

There were so many great new Christian sects springing up in America in the early 19th century, young Joseph Smith (born 1805) couldn't decide which one to join. His family had a reputation for unorthodox religious beliefs and a fondness for magic, and Joseph in particular was known as a 'money digger' who could locate buried treasure with a divining rod. In 1820, according to his later accounts, Smith was visited by God (the Father *and* Son) who told him not to join any of the existing sects — they were 'abominations'. In 1823, an angel named Moroni appeared in Smith's bedroom and told him about an ancient book, written on 'golden plates', which was buried beneath a hill, Cumorah, near Smith's birthplace of Parmyra, New York State. Four years later Smith was allowed to

unearth them. They were inscribed in the hitherto unheard of language of Reformed Egyptian, which Smith was able to translate with a handy gadget which came with the plates, the Urim and Thummim, a sort of cosmic spectacles (although some accounts have Smith with his head buried in a hat containing a 'seer stone'). Strangely, when Smith's earliest followers asked to see the plates, instead of just pulling them out from under the bed — which is where, according to Smith's wife Emma, he kept them — he took the men out into the woods where God provided a vision of them.

Smith spent two years transcribing the *Book of Mormon*, which is essentially a history of ancient migrations from Israel to America. First, in 2250 BC, came the Jaredites who built up an extensive civilisation before wiping themselves out in a series of bloody battles. They were followed by the prophet Lehi and family who settled in South America in 600 BC. Lehi's descendants split into two tribes, the Lammanites who rebelled against God, were cursed with a blackening of the skin, and became the native Americans; and the Nephites who remained faithful, gradually migrated north, and were rewarded in 34 AD with a visit by Jesus Christ.

After a few centuries of peace the two tribes went to war, and in 383 the Lammanites killed all but one of the Nephites in a battle near Cumorah. The sole survivor was Moroni, who gathered the golden plates containing his people's history and buried them.

With the transcription complete, Smith returned the plates to Moroni. A local farmer, Martin Harris, was persuaded to pay the printing costs, and the *Book of Mormon* went on sale in March 1830. The Church of Jesus Christ of Latter Day Saints was incorporated later the same year, with Joseph Smith its leader and prophet.

Mormons who come to your door today wave the thick and impressive looking *Book of Mormon* at you with confidence. Where did it come from? About 10 per cent of it is in fact lifted verbatim from the King James Bible (as this was first published in 1611 it's a little hard to understand how Mormons can seriously argue that the Book of Mormon was completed about 400 AD, but there you go). An early theory was that Smith based it on an unpublished novel by a Presbyterian minister, but this has never been found. Mormons maintain that a man of Smith's age and education could never have written it, but his supporters and critics agree about his prodigious imagination, and as the style matches that of his later writings (especially with regard to grammatical errors — ironed out in later editions) it's now generally accepted that it was mainly Smith's work.

After a year Smith moved 1,000 followers to Kirtland, Ohio, where they built the first Mormon temple. The Mormons were less than popular with the local townspeople — at one point Smith was tarred and feathered — and tensions mounted when Smith founded in 1837 the Kirtland Safety Society Bank (which

became an 'Anti-Banking Society' when the state refused to grant it a charter). To convince investors of its soundness, Smith displayed what appeared to be chests of silver in its vaults (in reality, lead, stones and iron with a thin layer of silver on top). The 'bank' failed after a few months and Smith high-tailed it to Missouri, where many of his followers had already settled, but they proved no more popular here. After the state militia stepped in to stop fighting between the Mormons and locals, they moved again, to a spot on the east bank of the Mississippi where the city of Nauvoo was founded. Its numbers were soon swollen by thousands of converts made in England by one of Smith's more enthusiastic followers, Brigham Young.

Smith organised a 4,000-strong legion of which he was general and, in 1844, declared his candidacy for the U.S. presidency. When some of his critics began to publish a newspaper denouncing the excesses of Church leaders, Smith ordered his men to destroy their printing press. He had gone too far. The owners complained to the state governor and he was again arrested. On 27 June 1844 an angry mob attacked the jail where Smith and his brother Hyrum were being held, dragged them out and shot them. Smith was becoming an embarrassment to the Church he founded. Martyred, he would be much more useful.

A leadership struggle ensued which was won by Brigham Young. Two years later he led the majority of Mormons on their great trek west, while a group loyal to Smith's widow and son, Joseph Smith III, moved to Independence, Missouri, and became the Reorganised Church of Jesus Christ of Latter

Brigham Young

Lee, massacred a wagon train of 140 settlers who were passing through Utah on their way to California. Lee tried to blame it all on the Indians but was eventually executed for the crime. Brigham Young continued to defy the government until his death in 1877, but those who followed him were made of less stern stuff. Congress kept up the pressure, denying voting rights, confiscating Church property and refusing to grant Utah statehood. In 1890 the Mormon leadership caved in and banned polygamy. The way was open for Mormonism to go mainstream.

YOUR OWN PLANET!

Joseph Smith's religious ideas were fairly conventional at the beginning. The *Book of Mormon* contains little in the way of doctrine, and what it does say, about polygamy for example, often contradicts what Smith later taught. (Mormonism is such an inherently inconsistent religion it is little wonder that Mormons place so much importance on their 'testimony' — their personal belief that the tale of the gold plates is true.) As Smith built up his Church, he kept his sometimes unruly followers in line with a stream of revelations from God. When Emma Smith objected to the idea that he take on extra wives, Joseph had a timely revelation in which God not only permitted it, He warned Emma that if she didn't abide by His laws she would be 'destroyed'. Emma abided and Smith had at least 37 wives by the time he died. With each revelation, Smith strayed further from orthodox Christianity. According to his later revelations, the God we know is a flesh

Day Saints, which continues to insist it is the true Mormon Church.

On 4 July 1847 the first Mormon settlers reached the Great Salt Lake in Utah, which Young declared would be the new Jerusalem. A fund was started to finance immigration from Europe and the population of Salt Lake City reached 100,000 over the next three decades. Polygamy had by now become a central tenet of the Mormon faith, and when the gold rush began in 1849, the promise of extra wives was no doubt a strong incentive for the city's men to stay put while the rest of the country was rushing off to California. The usual tensions between Mormons and locals continued, and panic swept the community in 1857 when it was learned that President Buchanan had ordered troops into Utah. Amid fears of a new period of repression, a band of Mormons and local Indians led by Young's deputy, John

and blood being named Elohim who lives on another planet, has (needless to say) numerous wives, and whose spiritual children take up residence in the physical bodies of humans born on earth. What's more, just as Elohim has our planet to rule over, each faithful male Mormon will one day be a God in his own right with his own planet (surely one of the most terrifying ideas to be found in any theology).

To make the grade as a god, Mormons must lead devout lives, abstaining from alcohol, tobacco, tea, coffee and extramarital sex. And don't forget those magic underpants! Otherwise known as 'the garment', this is a one-piece, neck-to-knee number embroidered with symbols derived from Freemasonry (as are many Mormon rituals). The garment is meant to protect its wearer from evil while on the earth, and some devout Mormons are said to never remove one for washing before putting another one on (which must make for an interesting sight on laundry day). According to Mormon folklore, Joseph Smith neglected to put on his garment the day he was killed.

Mormons must marry to gain their piece of cosmic real estate, and these 'celestial marriages' are for all eternity. They also believe, uniquely, that people may be baptised posthumously into their religion, and have gathered in Salt Lake City a vast number of genealogical records from around the world so that the dead may be given their chance to enter the 'celestial kingdom'. This is a task taken very seriously by the Church, so seriously in fact that it's highly likely *you* will one day be baptised a Mormon, whether you like it or not. Mormons are just as interested

in recruiting the living, with young men expected to devote two years of their lives to missionary work.

Its emphasis on making converts had made Mormonism one of the world's fastest growing religions. The practice of tithing, whereby Mormons are supposed to donate 10 per cent of their income to the Church, has also made it fabulously wealthy. Joseph Smith can have had no idea how much money he was going to dig up.

Over the last few decades, Mormon elders have attempted to play down their religion's doctrinal eccentricities and adopt a more moderate image, but they face a few obstacles. Chief among these is a lingering affection for polygamy which, despite the 1890 ban, is still practised openly or secretly by some 20,000 inhabitants of Utah. Its most vocal advocate for years was Alex Joseph, mayor of the small town of Big Water who, amid much publicity, took his tenth wife in 1992.

Men like Alex Joseph (who died in 1998) provide a reminder of just how fundamental a belief polygamy was for Joseph Smith and Brigham Young (who had over 50 wives and said that only men who practised polygamy could become gods), but with the Mormons having sanitised their history so extensively over the years, there are many other things to hide. Which brings us to a dealer in rare documents named Mark Hofmann.

THE MORMON BOMBER

Mark Hofmann was born in 1954 in Salt Lake City. His father was a fundamentalist and polygamist, having secretly taken a second

Mark Hofmann

finds gained him entry into the upper echelons of the Church.

There was less fanfare, however, when Hofmann turned up a letter to Smith which confirmed his long-rumoured involvement in 'money-digging'. Mormon president Gordon Hinckley, who effectively ran the Church, bought this one and quietly deposited it in 'The Vault', the fabled repository for documents which did not tend to 'promote the faith'. Even worse was a second Harris letter Hofmann produced in 1984, containing a description of the golden plates' discovery quite different to Joseph Smith's. Instead of God and the angel Moroni, there was talk of spirits, seer stones and a mysterious white salamander. The 'Salamander Letter', as it became known, was an uncomfortable reminder of Mormonism's early links with the occult. With news stories about its discovery beginning to appear, Hinckley couldn't just buy it and hide it in 'The Vault', so there was relief when it was bought by Steve Christensen, a young Mormon businessman and bishop in the Church. (Although outwardly devout, Christensen was, like Hofmann, secretly ambivalent about his faith and curious about its origins.)

Hofmann made a small fortune selling documents both genuine and faked, but in his endless wheeling and dealing he borrowed a lot of money too. In need of cash he began to talk of having found the 'McLellin Collection' — the long sought after papers of one of Mormonism's earliest and fiercest critics. Here was every fundamentalist Mormon's worst nightmare, and negotiations were soon under way for its purchase. A loan of $180,000 from

wife, an act which his son deplored. Hofmann began to question Mormon beliefs while at school, but still went on his regulation missionary tour, spending two years in England. Upon his return he kept up Mormon appearances, but he had now hit upon a way of getting back at the Church — and making a lot of money in the process. He became a forger of early Mormon documents.

In 1980, Hofmann produced what seemed to be a transcription from the golden plates in Joseph Smith's own hand. This was a sensational discovery, and the Church eagerly accepted it as a 'donation' in return for other documents worth about $20,000. He followed this up with a letter from Smith's early supporter, Martin Harris, in which Harris affirms he saw the golden plates. As well as enhancing Hofmann's reputation as a documents dealer, these highly publicised

a Mormon bank was quickly arranged which paid off some of Hofmann's debts. As the McLellin Collection only existed in his head, however, he now had a big problem.

In October 1985, with his debts exceeding a million dollars and his creditors closing in, Hofmann did the obvious thing and went on a bombing spree. The first of the pipe bombs he constructed blew up Steve Christensen, who had been involved in the McLellin Collection negotiations. To make this bombing appear connected to the troubles of Christensen's former employer, a finance company which had gone spectacularly bankrupt, he planted a second bomb to kill the company's director, Gary Sheets, a man whom Hofmann had never met. It ended up killing Sheets's wife, Kathy. The next day, Hofmann was handling a third bomb in his car when it exploded, severely injuring him.

That Hofmann was the bomber was soon obvious to police. The Mormon elders panicked, with Hinckley denying that he knew Hofmann, whom he had actually met many times. Hinckley knew that the Church's acceptance of the incriminating documents at face value was almost as damaging as if they had been genuine. It seems that certain sections of the legal system were reluctant to mount a prosecution in which the Church was so deeply implicated, and when Hofmann's case finally came to trial in 1987, a plea bargain meant he received a much lighter sentence than might have been expected for two such indiscriminate murders.

THE GOD OF THE WHOLE EARTH

All Mormons are taught to believe that they may receive direct revelations from God, just as Joseph Smith did. It therefore comes as no surprise that Mormonism is a fertile breeding ground for cults, especially when you throw in polygamy for good measure. Typical of recent Mormons who have received a call from God was Jeffrey Lundgren, who was a member of the Reorganised Church of Latter Day Saints (RLDS), the splinter group which had remained loyal to Joseph Smith's wife and son. Lundgren showed little interest in religion as a youth, but began studying the Bible and the *Book of Mormon* soon after joining the navy in 1970, aged 20. He served in Vietnam where his ship came under heavy fire several times without receiving a hit — a fact which led him to suspect that God was protecting him for some special purpose.

Following his discharge from the navy Lundgren worked sporadically and was arrested for passing bad cheques. He kept studying the scriptures and began to gain a reputation among fundamentalists dissatisfied with the liberal direction in which the RLDS was heading — especially its decision to allow women priests. He began to give scripture classes, at first sanctioned by the Church, later in his home. Two of his earliest followers were a docile bank employee, Dennis Avery, and his wife, Cheryl. Lundgren loathed the Averys and made fun of them behind their backs. The Averys considered Lundgren and his wife, Alice, to be their best friends.

Lundgren decided that God wanted him to move to Kirtland, Ohio, where Joseph Smith had built his first temple. In August 1984, he moved there with Alice and their four children, and got a job as an unpaid temple tour guide. He persuaded as many of

Jeffrey Lundgren

in this way until even his most sceptical followers were convinced. Using chiasmus, and with borrowings from the Sean Connery movie *The Highlander*, with which he and Alice had been deeply impressed, Lundgren decided that he was the last of eight prophets created by God. He began to stockpile arms and food for the coming tribulation.

Lundgren found a passage in the scriptures which told him that he had to mount an armed attack on the Kirtland temple and kill everyone living around it. This would trigger an earthquake, Kirtland would be destroyed and Christ would reappear. Studying the temple's decorations told Lundgren the attack should be on 1 May, but not in which year. As May 1988 approached his followers began to grow nervous — especially since he had told them they would not all survive the attack. After he gave strong hints that one of them, Kevin Currie, would be among the casualties, Currie picked up the courage to leave the group and notified the police about the plan. Their inquiries rattled Lundgren, who announced there was too much sin among his followers for the attack to be made that year.

He came up with a new plan. If the group were going to see God, they would have to make a 'blood atonement' sacrifice. Casting about for possible victims, the Avery family were the obvious choice. Lundgren ordered a pit dug in the farm's barn, and on 17 April 1989 the Averys were invited over for a lunch of roast beef. Afterwards Dennis Avery was lured into the barn, knocked down, bound and placed in the pit. As four of the men and Lundgren's eldest son, Damon, stood guard, Lundgren shot Avery in the back. Cheryl

his followers as he could to move to Kirtland, claiming it was Zion, the new Jerusalem to which Christ would return. By the end of 1987, the Lundgren group numbered ten adults and several children, most of them living communally on a farm on the outskirts of the city. On the periphery of the group were the Averys who, Lundgren candidly admitted, had been lured to Kirtland so that he could get their money.

Lundgren went about the business of convincing his followers that he was a prophet with great cunning. His most useful weapon was a method of textual analysis he had stumbled on called 'chiasmus'. By diagramming scriptures and finding repetitions, or what he said were repetitions, Lundgren could find their hidden meanings. Each outlandish claim he made was backed up by scripture after scripture dissected

Avery and her three daughters, aged 15, 13 and six, were led into the barn one by one and given the same treatment. Lundgren had never killed anyone before and did a bit of experimenting with different types of bullets.

The following morning, coincidentally, the FBI and police raided the farm, but didn't know about the killings and didn't find anything. That afternoon, Lundgren and his group of 24 men, women and children packed up and headed for 'the wilderness'. They ended up in a forest in the Appalachian Mountains where they set up tents. After a couple of weeks Lundgren climbed up a mountainside for one of his frequent talks with God and came back pleased. Jesus Christ had appeared, told him he was now immortal, and given him the impressive title 'God of the whole earth'.

Declaring that he had to strip the women in the group of pride, Lundgren ordered them to dance naked before him while he masturbated into their underpants (his ejaculation, he explained, would be the same as Christ shedding his blood). After watching the women dance he announced that one of them, Kathy Johnson, was going to be his second wife and her husband, Keith, had better accept it. Alice had put up with a lot from her mystically inclined husband, but this was too much and she walked out. The group returned to Missouri where it began to break up. Lundgren didn't much care. He was tired of his followers' 'sinfulness' and wanted to start again with another group. He might have done so had not Keith Johnson, desperate to get his wife back, told the authorities about the murders. The bodies were found in the barn and Lundgren and his followers arrested.

Lundgren's trial began in August 1989. Completely unrepentant, he lectured the court on theology for five hours before being sentenced to death. On 24 October 2006, after a last-minute plea that his obesity meant his execution would be 'cruel and unusual punishment' was rejected, he was given a lethal injection.

THE POLYGAMOUS WORLD OF WARREN JEFFS

Of the many groups that broke away from the LDS Church after it renounced polygamy, the largest, and most embarrassing for it, is the Fundamentalist Church of Jesus Christ of Latter Day Saints (FLDS). While it remained little known for most of the 20th century (even among Mormons), the revelations about its activities during the early 2000s, and arrest of its ghastly prophet Warren Jeffs in 2006, made headlines around the world.

The reason that Jeffs and other FLDS leaders got away with what they did for so long can be traced back to the night of 26 July 1953. That's when Arizona governor Howard Pyle sent 200 state troopers into the RLDS community at Short Creek, on the Utah-Arizona border. The community, which began in the 1930s, consisted of 500 mostly dirt-poor farmers, and Pyle was reacting to a public outcry about welfare fraud and child rape within it. He expected to be lauded for the raid, but made the mistake of inviting the press to witness it. The photos that appeared in newspapers showing poor women and children being wrenched from their homes, while their menfolk sang 'God Bless America', resulted in a wave of sympathy for the group. In the aftermath, Pyle was

Warren Jeffs

many men (along with boys as young as 10) were put to work in FLDS businesses for no pay. The result of all this was that the sect's leaders became fabulously wealthy, while the bulk of the community stayed poor. Children were given a rudimentary education, free of science and history (apart from the history of Joseph Smith). Newspapers, television, radio, magazines and non-religious books were banned, so that most within the community knew virtually nothing about the world outside. The FLDS was running what was, to all intents and purposes, its own country. One thing its inhabitants did know, however, was that the world was going to end any minute and they were the only ones who would be saved. When the rest of the world's population cottoned on to that, they would descend on Short Creek and the FLDS would have to kill them — all six billion of them. That would take a while, so in preparation they stockpiled arms and food.

The FLDS teaches that a man needs at least three wives to enter the celestial kingdom and have his own planet (although more are better as that will boost your planet's population). The prophet decided who would marry who, and members in good standing were rewarded with wives as young as 13. The role of women, who wore neck-to-ankle, long-sleeved 'prairie dresses' and were forbidden to cut their hair, was to 'keep sweet' and produce babies. Wives who failed to be almost permanently pregnant were looked down on.

But Rulon and the extraordinarily creepy Warren (increasingly in charge after his father suffered a series of strokes) had a problem — male-female birth rates are stubbornly close to equal. By 2000, they were simply running

thrown out of office and others involved with the raids also lost their jobs. The message to the authorities was clear — interfere with this group at your peril.

Over the next few decades, the Short Creek community grew into the twin towns of Colorado City, Arizona, and Hildale, Utah, with a population of 10,000. When the FLDS's prophet, Leroy Johnson, died in 1988, a lot of Short Creekers were none too pleased when Rulon Jeffs, who had been the sect's chief accountant and was based in Salt Lake City, managed to take over. Johnson had been a fairly easy-going prophet. Rulon, and later his son Warren, were made of sterner stuff.

The FLDS controlled the government, the police, the fire and water departments and public schools in Short Creek, while all property was owned collectively by the sect. Eighty per cent of its members received welfare payments, and

out of women to hand around, and came up with a simple solution — expelling some of the men. On the slightest pretext, parents would be instructed to drive their sons — usually teenagers — out of town, dump them on the side of a highway somewhere, and forget they had ever existed. (One 15-year-old was thrown out in the middle of winter for watching part of an episode of *Charlie's Angels*.) The boys, completely unequipped for life in the real world, sometimes committed suicide or resorted to prostitution to survive. They were known colloquially in Utah and Arizona as 'lost boys', and there were hundreds of them.

When Warren Jeffs took over as prophet after Rulon died in 2002, he wasted no time in snapping up his father's youngest wives, along with many more (some estimate he had as many as 300 by the end). He also dissolved many marriages, assigning wives to new husbands and splitting up their families, and banished hundreds of men he viewed as threats. Other perverse decrees by Warren at this time included the announcement that the colour red belonged exclusively to Jesus, forcing sect members to frantically discard anything they owned that was red, and ordering all dogs in the community to be killed after a young girl was attacked by one.

Jeffs's new world of absolute power began to unravel just months after he became prophet. The trigger came when Ruth Stubbs fled from the community, taking her two children with her. At the age of 16, Rulon and Warren had forced her to become the third wife of a 32-year-old policeman, Rodney Holm. Ruth and her kids had suffered dreadful abuse by Holm's first two wives (one of whom was her sister). With

the help of a lawyer working pro bono, Ruth obtained custody of her children. By then, the case had piqued the interest of Utah Attorney General Mark Shurtleff. He was a Mormon, but he was appalled when he heard that a serving police officer was being accused of bigamy and statutory rape.

Meanwhile a wealthy ex-FLDS member named Dan Fischer decided to bankroll lawsuits against the sect launched by some of the braver lost boys, including one who accused Jeffs of molesting him from the age of five. Jeffs told his followers that their tactic in the face of legal action would be to "Answer them nothing." Court notices, subpoenas and other documents sent to FLDS members were returned with things like "Refused" or "No such address" stamped on them. Of course this wasn't going to make the lawsuits disappear. With $110 million worth of RLDS property in Short Creek under threat of being seized, no one could understand why Jeffs and his men weren't lifting a finger to prevent it.

What they didn't know was that Jeffs had decided to abandon Short Creek — along with many of its inhabitants whom he thought unworthy of salvation. In 2003, the RLDS purchased 1,700 acres near Eldorado, Texas, which was to be its new home. Locals were fed the story that the land would be used for a hunting lodge, then watched as three buildings the size of hotels were frantically erected on it. A journalist soon made the connection with RLDS, and the more Texans heard about the group, the less they liked it. Polygamy and child rape were bad enough, but the idea that most of these people lived on *welfare* was guaranteed to stick in any self-respecting Texan's craw,

In June 2005, Jeffs was indicted for underage sex crimes and went underground. He moved around the country constantly in a variety of vehicles, heading wherever God pointed. He met up with groups of his wives when he could, and conducted hundreds more marriages. The FBI put him on its Most Wanted list and there was a $100,000 bounty on his head, but no one expected he would be caught quickly. Jeffs had unlimited funds at his disposal, and any number of followers who would shelter him. However, on 28 August 2006, a Nevada highway patrolman flagged down a red Cadillac and recognised the skinny fellow inside it as the fugitive prophet. In 2007, after a trial that became a media sensation, Jeffs was convicted of facilitating rape and sentenced to life plus 20 years.

Even with Jeffs behind bars, frenzied building continued at the Texas compound. In April 2008, after police received a phone call from a 16-year-old girl who said she was being held there against her will (later established to be a hoax), around a hundred Texas Rangers and other law enforcement officers raided it and took away hundreds of women and girls. Although court orders meant they were later allowed to return, the raid garnered a mountain of incriminating evidence including marriage records and hundreds of hours of Jeffs's droning tape recordings. The most disturbing discovery came when investigators broke into the compound's gigantic, heavily fortified temple. Next to its altar was a large bed, constructed of hardwood to Jeffs's precise specifications, and surrounded by pads on which spectators could kneel. Also found was a tape recording of Jeffs 'breaking in' a 12-year-old bride on the bed, as up to twenty FLDS men watched.

Warren Jeffs continues to run the RLDS from his prison cell. When he's not busy with that, he spends his time praying, going on frequent hunger strikes and compulsively masturbating.

THE CELESTIAL BALANCE SHEET

The efforts of characters like Warren Jeffs notwithstanding, there is no doubt that the Mormons have largely succeeded in gaining the respectability they have long sought. The critically acclaimed TV series *Big Love* offered a sympathetic portrayal of a polygamous Mormon family, while Mitt Romney's Mormonism barely registered as an issue during his campaign for the presidency in 2012. And in their hit Broadway musical *The Book of Mormon*, *South Park* creators Trey Parker and Matt Stone mix affection with the satire. (Parker and Stone have spoken about how graciously LDS Church leaders greeted the musical, which sends up their most sacred beliefs mercilessly.)

Current membership of the Church is estimated to be around 15 million worldwide, while a 2012 survey confirmed its status as the fastest growing religious group in America. The Church has long had more members outside the U.S. than within it, and has been particularly successful in the Pacific region (in perhaps the most intriguing statistic of all, half the population of Tonga is said to be Mormon). These are the sort of numbers any international corporate enterprise would be crowing about. Sure, you can laugh the next time a couple of Mormons turn up on your doorstep, but how well is your business doing compared to theirs?

A conversation with SIR WAYNE

It's the photos that hit you as you enter Sir Wayne Martin's tiny Darlinghurst flat. There's Wayne whooping it up in nightclubs in the '60s with the likes of Sammy Davis, Jr. and Tom Jones. There's Sinatra with an affectionate arm around Wayne's shoulders. There's Wayne, immaculately suited and sharp as a razor, among strippers, musicians and entertainers of all kinds, or on a boat on Sydney harbour, stark naked, flanked by 20 or more bikini-clad girls, and with the biggest grin on his face you've ever seen in your life.

"Truly," Sir Wayne tells me, "all we used to like in those days was having fun. Having a laugh and a good time." At this point the phone rings. It's a girl who wants to know what he's up to tonight. It's Good Friday, so it's going to be a fairly quiet night, but there should still be some clubs open later on. Why doesn't she come up?

So who is Sir Wayne Martin? Why was he having such a good time back then? And why, aged 67, is he *still* having a good time?

To answer these important questions, we must go back to a time before Sydney's infamous red light district of Kings Cross became the evil-smelling, junkie-infested, vomit-stained, fast food spewing, crime-ridden, characterless shithole it is today. Back to the days when people flocked to 'the Glittering Mile' to soak up its bohemian atmosphere, gawp at its host of colourful

characters, or take in the international acts that played its swanky nightclubs. When drunken young men worried about whether they would be let into a strip club without a tie, and strippers kept their G-strings on. And when the classiest, best-known striptease club in Australia was the Pink Pussycat, ably run by Last Card Louie and Wayne Martin.

Inside the club at night time, the pink plaster discs on the ceiling blink as the spotlight plays on and off the girls doing their strip acts on the catwalk. Music from a record player in a curtained corner of the room blares out and then stops abruptly at appropriate times to give effect to the various performances, while the audiences — usually all male — view with satisfaction, excitement and perhaps other more doubtful emotions the creamy or tanned bodies, the smooth mounds of the breasts and the gleaming bare buttocks of the strippers.

From *The Pink Pussycat* by Lee Meredith (1972)

Wayne Martin was born in New Zealand in 1930, and grew up in an orphanage. At 16 he ran away from it and stowed away on a ship bound for Sydney. Within a week he

had met another young fellow named Louie Benedetto whose mother had a little Italian restaurant in Kings Cross. He washed dishes in the restaurant and worked with Louie at the markets. In the early '50s, Kings Cross kingpin Abe Saffron hired Louie and Wayne to run a coffee lounge in the basement of a hotel he owned at 44 Macleay St. After that, Wayne worked as a chauffeur for promoter Lee Gordon, driving around the visiting stars such as Sinatra, Sammy Davis, Betty Hutton and Bob Hope that Gordon brought out.

On a trip to the States, Wayne saw strippers in action, and came back with a proposition for Abe Saffron.

"'What about strippers?' He says, 'Oh, you can't do that in Sydney.' I said, 'Well, there's no law. I've spoken to a solicitor and there's no law about it. So anyway he says, 'Oh well, we'll give it a try.' And Abe had a coffee lounge type place down in Orwell St. and we opened up a club there called the Staccato, and he put me and Louie in charge of that. That went alright and then… we got this property above the top of William St., above the Hasty Tasty, on the second floor, and decided to turn it into a place that we saw in Los Angeles, the Pink Pussycat."

Painted an eye-catching pink on the outside, the Pussycat was a huge success. In its heyday around eight strippers performed three shows a night, each girl performing for about eight minutes to a selection of records. Among its more celebrated performers were 'Jeddah', an Aboriginal girl who came out with a boomerang and removed her kangaroo-skin outfit to the strains of the then popular novelty hit 'My Boomerang Won't Come Back'; Princess Aloha, who performed to Hawaiian music; and Sandy Nelson, famous for her 40-inch bust, who made headlines in 1964 when she spent a Sunday afternoon strolling around Sydney in a topless dress. "They used to queue up outside to get in," recalls Wayne. "A quid it cost. And then at the end of the show you put on the lights and me and Louie to get rid of the people used to say the next show will be half-an-hour and the place would empty, because we had people waiting to get in. Otherwise they'd just stay there and perv all night."

"To every girl we used to say, what we want you to do is striptease but we want you to reverse the word — tease while you're stripping. You know, just don't go there and get all your gear off. Tease 'em, you know. Pull your stocking half way down and then go to roll it up. Your bra, you know, take it off, no, I'll put it on, no take it off! That was the whole act. You'll find nowadays they come out with nothing on. In our time they used to have a hat on. We'd give them an hour and 20 minute show. So you'd get the girls, they'd take off their hat and then their earring, their glove, then a shoe, and her stockings and then her dress. And then she'd have a slip on, and then she'd have a girdle, a lovely embroidered girdle. She'd take that off and then she'd be down to bra and panties. She'd take her panties off, and then she'd have a G-string, and then she'd take her bra off and she'd have little pasties. And the vice squad used to come in with a policewoman and she used to have a ruler and she used to measure, if the G-string was under an inch give them a warning she'd have them charged with indecent exposure." Wayne's determination to present the Pussycat's customers with a quality show led to the foundation of Australia's first School of Stripping. It was all a bit of a gimmick, he admits today, but it was great for publicity.

'Most women,' said Wayne Martin philosophically, 'just don't know how to undress.'

Being a quiet-living bachelor myself, I wasn't prepared to argue with him. Certainly not on professional grounds, anyway.

For Wayne runs the Staccato School of Stripping in Sydney's Kings Cross.

He is, in fact, one of the few men in Australia outside a doctor's surgery who can tell a girl to take her clothes off without getting a slap in the mouth for his trouble.

His school offers courses in such fascinating subjects as 'Methodology of Teasing and Tantalising'.

'Stripping is a creative form of dancing; it's an art,' said Wayne. 'There's a lot more to it than just throwing clothes everywhere.'

From *Everybody's* magazine, 21 April 1965

Wayne distributes diplomas to graduates of the School for Stripping

"This was a hot club," writes Australian rocker Billy Thorpe, describing his first visit to the Pink Pussycat and meeting Sir Wayne in his rollicking memoir *Sex, Thugs and Rock'n'Roll, A Year in Kings Cross 1963–1964*. "The girls were class, the drinks were thick and the vibe was definitely happening…" The Pussycat's clientele included English lords and visiting cricket teams, servicemen on leave and young country boys on their first trip to the big smoke. "I remember one night a police sergeant come up," says Sir Wayne. "He said, 'G'day, how are you? I got three guys down in the car. Is it alright, they haven't got ties on? We said, 'That's alright, we'll sit 'em over the side there, in the back.' These fellers come up in black suits with no ties on. They were sitting there. We said would they like coffee and a sandwich? 'Just a coffee thanks'. And the sergeant come over, said 'What about that?' I said 'Who are they?' He says, 'They're priests out with the Pope.' They left their collars down in his car. He said, 'Don't say anything.' 'Oh, no, we won't say anything.'"

To find the Pink Pussy Cat you climb up a steep and narrow staircase, It is not the kind of marble and gilt facade traditional in nightclub-land. It

is rather more like visiting someone on the third floor back in a doubtful apartment house. Even in the faint glare of a 60-watt globe, the walls at the side of the steps are frowsy and grease marked. Halfway to the top, on a small landing, there is a knot of unidentified, slick-haired, blue-chinned men gossiping, laughing, smoking, picking their teeth. From one of them (who turns out to be 'Last Card Louis', the manager) you get an admission ticket for 1. You also get a "souvenir card", a pink-printed bit of pasteboard certifying that you have been "duly admitted to the inner sanctum of The Pussy Cat and appointed an honorary Tom Cat of King's Cross". Visitors from the country or more sedate suburbs may treasure it as visible proof of their sophistication.

From *Life at The Cross* by Kenneth Slessor & Robert Walker (1965)

Last Card Louie and Wayne ran a tight ship at the Pussycat. When a drunken buck's party caused havoc early on, Louie decided to ban any groups larger than four, and after that fights were unknown. They developed strategies for dealing with potentially unruly visitors. "We would just have a small guy on the door, because we found out every time we had a big feller two or three guys would come along and say, 'Go on, Billy, you can have him. Call him a cunt, well, fucking biff him.' We always used to have a little guy and just near the door was a button. 'If any guys give you trouble just lean back by the door and press the button a couple of times.' That would go off upstairs. We would just go, 'Helmut, your

wife's on the phone! Quick, hurry up!' 'Oh, excuse me.' So now there's no one to abuse."

"Whenever people used to scream out we'd send the waitress down and then if the waitress couldn't quieten them down we'd go down and we'd get a couple of friends we knew in the audience and they in their suits would stand up at the back with their arms crossed and we'd go, 'Listen the vice squad are up the back. They'll pinch ya for indecent language.' 'Where?' 'There. We'll come and tell you when they're gone.' 'Oh, sorry, mate. Hey, Billy, the coppers are here. Don't yell out!'"

Speaking of his old mate and partner Louie, Wayne says "Not a soul could say anything against him. I remember before each night we'd get to the club at seven o'clock and open it up. And the doorman and the two guys who worked for us would see that the restaurant was set up and the waitress would arrive and then Louie and I would go for a walk through the Cross. And I remember Louis, every night he'd say, 'Just a minute' and he used to get about 10 pound notes and roll 'em up into little balls and put them in his pocket. And the guys would come up, 'Hello, Louie, how are you?' And shake their hand. 'Oh, thanks, mate.' Louie would say, 'There's another, I'll just shake his hand.' In those days we used to walk past every shop. 'Hello, Louie. Hello, Wayne.' 'How are you Pedro?' 'Come and try the salami.' 'Try this piece of cheese.' 'Here's a piece of fruit.' 'I've got some people coming up from Wagga, never seen a strip show.' Louie would get out his thing and write 'Guests of Last Card and Wayne's.' In those days the Cross was so beautiful and nice and lovely." Crime was so rare he recalls he could park his Austin car outside the Pussycat at the beginning of an evening's shift, leave his jacket in the back seat with the window down, and still find it there in the morning.

It seems that everyone had a nickname back then. "There was a guy called the Judge because everywhere he went he was always sitting on a box or a case. Then there was a guy called the Prince, beautiful, debonair looking guy, he had a restaurant. And then there was Two Storey Ted, 'cause he was a cat burglar, he used to go up two storeys when the people were in bed to rob. George the Fibber because, 'Are you fibbing again?' 'No, it's the truth.' Trick Tom because he had a hairpiece, they'd say 'That's a tricky piece.'" Last Card Louie was christened by the radio star Jack Davey, after he won the pot in a card game at the turn of the last card. And Wayne was known as Morals Martin, the legacy of a little incident involving three millionaires, two girls, an apartment in Palm Beach and some police outside with a ladder. The newspaper headline read 'Four Men on Morals Charges' and Morals Martin it was.

In 1972, the Pink Pussycat was gutted by fire — not an insurance job, just an unfortunate consequence of having 1,000-watt spotlights. Wayne and Louie rebuilt the club, but shortly afterwards the block it was in was bought up by Hong Kong businessmen. Louie went off to manage a clothing factory, got married and settled down, while Wayne toured the world's nightclubs as a representative for Bally poker machines.

And it was at this point that Wayne's life takes a weird and wonderful turn. He'd been known as 'Sir Wayne' since the '60s, a reference to the cheeky way he addressed police as 'Sir', so it was really only fitting that he was made a knight for real, and a papal knight no less.

It happened like this. Wayne was in London when he ran into Sir Edward Vellis, the London head of the Order of St John of Jerusalem.

"And he says to me, 'Listen, we're trying to raise money for Biafra in Africa and all that.' I says, 'Aw, yeah, I've got no money.' 'But you know Sinatra, Sammy Davis, blah blah blah.' I said, 'Aw, yeah, I'm going over the States.'

"Sinatra and Sammy were doing a show in England and they did an extra one and the money from that they donated x amount of it to the Knights of Malta. And then Ernest Borgnine from America he donated, they all went in together. Ted Vellis rang me and said, 'Listen, in Rome they are very happy. Would you like to become an honorary member?' I said, 'What's it gonna cost me?' He said, 'No, no, no, because of what you've done they could put you in as a Knight Grand Commander. Not high ranking within the order but you do more good work for us, you'll get promoted, you'll get higher and higher till you become like him, Duke So and So.' I said 'What does it entail?' He said, 'Oh, you get the robes and the badges and the ring and the medals and the sashes and your passport and you get a lovely diploma which you can hang on your wall.' I thought, oh well, it's the odds to nothing. I said 'Thanks very much.'"

Wayne shows me his medal and passport, and a scrapbook full of photos of his investiture in Rome, with him resplendent in a red robe, and a certificate signed by, of all people, Shirley Temple Black. Has the

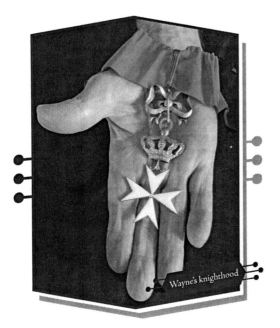

Wayne's knighthood

knighthood opened any doors, I ask. "Lots of people in Sydney call me Sir Wayne, but I don't harp on it."

These days Sir Wayne's life seems to have hardly slowed down at all. He still socialises at night, when he believes people are at their best, and has no shortage of girlfriends. "I'm 67 and I carry on like I'm 37 as far as I'm concerned. The point is I couldn't get aroused by a 55- or 60-year-old woman, but the youngies, 25 on, they come up and they say, 'Shit, look at this'. All the girls." He waves at all the photos. "I say, 'What, you want me to put all boys up there?' Guys today say, 'Wayne, you go out and sheilas flock around you'. Do you know why? Doing the right thing. I've never hit a girl in my life, never abused a girl in my life. Whenever a girl and I don't get on I say, 'Scuse me, I won't be a minute. I left

something in the car. I'll be right back.' I just get out and disappear. 'You left me stranded in that place!' 'Yeah, but I had to move me car and…' The point is I always left 'em sweet."

A couple of U.S. warships happen to be docked in Sydney that weekend, and the Cross is once again swarming with white uniforms. Wayne is telling a story about being invited to have dinner on the USS *Enterprise* by its captain, whom he met as a lieutenant at the Pussycat years before, when he's interrupted by the arrival of Vanessa, a blonde in her 20s. She sits on Wayne's couch as he continues his story. The captain tells him there's an admiral flying in in two days. "And he says can you get some girls for some of the officers? I said, 'Oh, it'll be a little bit hard, but I'll try my best.'"

"Oh, man," says Vanessa, "I had sex with an officer the other day."

"Shut up, Vanessa, we're recording," says Sir Wayne. "He's a reporter. About the old days in the Pussycat. So then they were at the Chevron, these two and five other officers. And I said, 'I couldn't get any girls.' 'Oh, you let us down.' And the girls were out there. They knocked. One, two, three, four, five, six, seven, eight, nine of them come in. He says, 'I told you about this guy. He knows more girls in this town than anyone!'"

Later I ask Vanessa what she thinks of Sir Wayne. "I tell you one thing about Wayne Martin is he will listen to you… He makes you feel comfortable and you can crash on his couch and shit like that. He won't sort of drag you into bed and say 'You can't stay here unless you have sex with me.' He's been very good to me throughout the years."

MARY'S VOICEBOX

he Virgin Mary is, according to Catholic doctrine, the 'Mediatrix of all Graces', the intermediary between God and human beings. It's only fitting, then, that she pop down to visit us occasionally, and she has not left Australia off her touring schedule. In 1994, her image appeared in a piece of rough plaster on the wall above the altar of Christ Church in the tiny South Australian town of Yankalilla, and pilgrims have been going to see it ever since. The following year, a former housewife and primary school teacher, Debra Geileskey, founded what became a thriving religious community in Helidon, outside Townsville, Queensland, built around her regular conversations with Mary and Jesus. But there is no doubt that Australia's best-known and most ambitious Marian intermediary is a short, tubby, bespectacled ex-bank clerk who has been acting as Mary's 'voicebox' since the 1980s, and who goes by the unlikely moniker of the 'Little Pebble'.

William Kamm was born in Cologne, Germany, in 1950. His mother was 17-year-old Gertude Simons, who had fallen pregnant after a brief liaison with an Italian soldier named John. Kamm was born almost two months prematurely, weighing less than a kilogramme, and little he would remain. He later told his followers that he had arrived in this world at three minutes past midnight, the moment when Judas had betrayed Jesus. "It is for this reason that I, too, have been and am still betrayed by so many people, so often."

Gertrude married Hans Scheuttler, and they had a daughter, Karen. When Kamm was four, they immigrated to Australia, and like many Germans settled first in South Australia. In 1963, Gertrude divorced Hans and took her children to Victoria, where she married Hans Kamm.

The young Willie Kamm, according to his own account, was a pious boy frustrated by his parents' lack of interest in religion. While attending a mass in Wollongong on the NSW south coast, where his family moved when he was 15, he received a message from God who said, "You will suffer much and become a great saint." He made inquiries about joining the priesthood, but these came to nothing. Instead, he began forming prayer groups with a focus on devotion to the Virgin Mary. Kamm claims to have had his first message from Mary in 1968, while he was washing dishes.

Kamm moved to Sydney when he was 22 and worked in a factory. He later held a series of jobs in banks and financial institutions, but none lasted very long. In 1979 and 1981, he paid visits to Bayside, New York, known as the 'Lourdes of America', where a woman named Veronica Leuken had been receiving messages from the Virgin since 1970. During his second visit, many of Leuken's female

followers complained that Kamm had been making unwanted sexual advances to them. He had, for example, been wandering among the women who were stuffing envelopes for a mail-out, kissing their ears and breathing on the backs of their necks. Leuken told one of her lieutenants to order him out. Also present when Kamm was confronted with the allegations was a Canadian journalist, Anne Cillis, who was briefly involved with the sect and later wrote a book exposing it. She described what happened to the *Sydney Morning Herald* in 1993.

"He was arrogant and scornful and so cynical in his response. We eventually said: 'Either you leave now or we'll get you thrown out in the morning.'

"He then walked over to the door and put his hand on his hip in this sexy pose and said: 'Well, I guess it's time that Australia got its own seer.'"

Kamm's financial situation at this point was precarious. He had borrowed a large sum of money from a friend some years earlier, and still owed her over $10,000. In 1982, unemployed and with debts of almost $20,000, he declared bankruptcy. But his religious movement was growing quickly. By 1983, he had 14 prayer groups in Sydney, Wollongong, Canberra and Perth. Kamm presented himself as an orthodox Catholic, albeit one with a direct line to Mary (followers were able to give questions to him, and he would hand-write Mary's answers to them).

His was a traditional sort of Catholicism, and many of his followers were conservative Catholics upset by the reforms of Vatican II.

His group, based on property owned by two of his most dedicated followers in Cambewarra near Nowra in NSW, was originally called the Marian Work of Atonement, later the Order of St Charbel. As for the name the 'Little Pebble', Kamm claims it was bestowed on him by Mary herself. It's usually taken to be a play on St Peter's nickname, 'the Rock' (Kamm says that one day he will be the last pope, Pope Peter II). The Pebble and his right hand man and head of security, Jim Duffy, had houses in the Cambewarra compound, while its other residents, eventually numbering 200, lived in trailers or caravans. The compound had a large cross which bled, a weeping statue and, best of all, the actual Ark of the Covenant, which was housed in the chapel (although it was invisible to everyone but Kamm). The compound was surrounded by a barbed wire fence, while another encircled the Pebble's house.

The activities of the Little Pebble came to the attention of the media in 1984. He was denounced by the Bishop of Wollongong, William Murray, who stressed that his ceremonies were not condoned by the Church. The Little Pebble had a meeting with Murray in 1986, during which he declared that Wollongong would soon be destroyed in an earthquake which only seven clergy would survive. "And you won't be one of them," he told the Bishop.

Dire prophecies have been the Pebble's stock-in-trade from the beginning. The Apocalypse was imminent. Sydney was going to be levelled by six atomic bombs. Russia

would invade America. San Francisco and Los Angeles would be hit by earthquakes and slide into the sea. In 1986, he told veteran journo Jim Oram that Perth was "like Sodom" and would soon be hit by an earthquake and a tidal wave. "It could be within the next month or the next two years," he said. Later, he predicted that the Sydney Olympics in 2000 would be cancelled because of a natural disaster.

Kamm has always liked publicity. In 1985, a photograph was released to the media showing the Little Pebble meeting Pope John Paul II. According to Kamm's account, after slipping a note to the Pope during an open-air mass, he was rung by a papal secretary who arranged a meeting between the two religious leaders. During this he told the Pope that the Blessed Mother had sent him, to which the Pope replied, "I know." The truth was a little

more mundane — the photo had been taken when Kamm attended a mass open to the public. It did the trick however, convincing many Catholics that the Little Pebble's activities had papal approval.

By 1988, William Kamm had cause to look at what he had created and feel pleased. Hundreds of people were turning up at his Nowra mission for the 'Atonement' days held on the thirteenth of each month, during which, dressed in his customary brown sackcloth, he relayed Mary's messages, while pilgrims drank the water from a sacred spring. He travelled the world regularly, visiting other sites of Marian devotion, and aligned himself with other seers (Kamm said he was one of 120 in contact with the Virgin). And the money was rolling in. The Pebble doesn't muck about here. His motto is "Give all, receive all", and he expects his followers to donate everything they have. So, things were looking good all round. Surely then, time to loosen up a bit, to enjoy some rewards for all the hard work?

He was in Poland, travelling with a Polish priest, Father Gebicki, who had joined him at the beginning of 1988, when he met a teenage girl named Bozena Golebiowska, and was given some startling news by the girl's spiritual adviser, a priest named Jankowski. According to Jankowski, Mary had entered Bozena's body, at the same time, and "in the most incomprehensible manner", that Jesus Christ had entered the body of the Little Pebble. The only thing for it, said the priest, was to arrange a "mystical marriage ceremony" between the two of them. (This sounds a bit like mystical incest to me, but that shows how much I know.) The ceremony was duly performed in Jankowski's parish church, with Father Gebicki doing the honours. Bozena declared that they would spend their wedding night in the same room, though in separate beds. The Pebble later confessed to Gebicki that when he got to the room there was only one bed in it. When Bozena approached him to consummate the marriage, however, he had realised it was "the work of the devil", and spent most of the night in the toilet.

If there's some doubt whether this mystical marriage was consummated, there's none concerning the one that followed it. In March 1991, the Pebble told several of his followers that his wife Anne (whom he had married in 1983, and with whom he had four children) was going to die in April that year. Luckily there was a 17-year-old girl named Bettina Lammerman, who lived in Germany. She had been praying to marry the Pebble since she was 14, he explained, and Mary thought it was an excellent idea that she should take the place of the unfortunate, if still living, Anne. Kamm flew to Germany the following month to collect Bettina. Somehow all of this was kept from Anne, who was under the impression her husband was bringing a nanny back from Germany. Soon after Bettina moved into their house she realised the truth and left, taking the children. All of this frolicsome and decidedly un-Marian behaviour was too much for Father Gebicki, who left the group and wrote a 66-page 'confession' detailing his experiences with the Pebble, which he gave to the Bishop of Wollongong, and which was later released to the media. Kamm fathered another four children with Bettina, whose

mother also joined his Nowra community.

All was quiet for a while on the Pebble front until reports began to appear in mid-1997 that the group was stockpiling arms for a coming confrontation with the army. According to 'Peter', a 26-year-old former member interviewed by the Melbourne *Herald Sun*, Kamm predicted that the arrival of the Hale-Bopp comet would bring the 'first chastisement', followed by two holy wars during which the army would try to take the group's children. Peter, who had been living at the Pebble's Victorian headquarters in Tyaak near Singleton, had gone out and bought a 150-pound crossbow. And it wasn't just weapons that the Pebble was stockpiling.

"As June 1 [when Hale-Bopp was due to appear] came closer, everyone was talking more and more about death, and I was spending thousands of dollars on food and stupid things like scanners, walkie-talkies, dozens of crucifixes, rooms full of statues and cards.

"Things just weren't adding up and I started to wonder if William was telling the truth."

Peter had left the group soon after the 'first chastisement' failed to take place. As for the Pebble, he seemed genuinely surprised when it didn't happen. As usual when one of his prophecies fails, Kamm used the excuse that our conception of time is different to the Almighty's.

The Pebble meets the Pope

"In God's eyes, when he speaks about time/day it has a much different meaning from our day.

"It's like the old prophets who were told something that's going to occur, but didn't occur. But did that make the prophets wrong?

"That Hale-Bopp event will still happen."

The Little Pebble made a memorable appearance on the *60 Minutes* programme in November 1997. When asked by reporter Jeff McMullen if he had told Mary about the film crew's visit, the Pebble replied he had, and that not only was she pleased about it, but "she came down with the Baby Jesus, and the Baby Jesus left our Mother and came over to all of you and kissed you on the forehead". (Not the sort of welcome Australian TV reporters are used to receiving.) Asked what Mary looked like, he pointed to a traditional painting of her, sacred heart ablaze.

He took McMullen on a tour of the Nowra

property, showing him a large rock, brought there from Jerusalem by two angels, which he said he will one day strike to bring forth a holy spring, and their extensive stores of food. The Pebble said he owned two shops and properties in three states, and estimated his net worth to be $4.5 million (which sounded like an understatement). He denied that he was stockpiling guns or that he encouraged his followers to join the army or police to gain weapons training, as had been alleged, although he admitted having a 'papal guard' called the Warriors of St Michael, who were licensed to carry guns. Throughout the interview he remained softly spoken and unassuming, the very model of, well, an ex-bank clerk.

Perhaps he was conserving his strength for the prodigious effort that he would soon be called on to perform — the repopulation of the world after Armageddon, no less. To help him (and his 'Holy Seed') in this task, he was seeking applications for a proposed harem of 12 queens and 72 princesses. Kamm explained that their pregnancies would not be effected sexually, but instead through a holy embrace during which he would impart his 'Holy Shining Thing'. (This was a phial of luminous liquid which Jesus had placed in Kamm "where the 'seed' must come forth".) He groomed his prospective queens assiduously with letters (both from himself and Mary). In one letter to a 15-year-old girl (who, like other children in his community, knew nothing about sex) he wrote, "As you are a virgin, we will make love slowly until your virgina [sic] gets used to my body penetration."

Among the former members interviewed on *60 Minutes* was a girl named Christine

Donohue who, at age 16 and having lived in the cult for eight years, was invited by the Pebble to become a princess. Whether the relationship was spiritual or physical was up to her. For some reason, she declined both offers.

In June 2002, the Bishop of Wollongong, Peter Ingham, issued a decree backed by the Vatican which banned the Little Pebble's order and repudiated his "absurd pretentions". Kamm announced that he was suing the Wollongong diocese for $300 million in damages, but as it turned out, the Bishop's decree was the least of his worries. Two months later, police and detectives from the Child Protection Enforcement Agency raided his property and seized documents and weapons. Kamm, then aged 52, was charged with sexually assaulting two female followers aged 14 and 15 whom he had selected to be queens. One of the girls had become pregnant.

The two cases were tried separately. In the first trial, which took place in 2005, Kamm faced four charges of aggravated indecent assault and aggravated sexual intercourse against the then 15-year-old. Letters written by him to the girl were read out in court. In one of them, he wrote "You have such a sexy body. I believe I should wait till at least the end of next year to conceive a child… that does not mean we can't make love." In a second letter he wrote, "I hope you have your running shoes on, once I catch you that is. I love your sexy mouth and smile." Even Kamm's defence lawyer was forced to admit that they were "the outpourings of a deluded and overly sexual individual". The girl testified that, having grown up in a Catholic family, she had received no sex education, and when Kamm suggested they sleep together, had not known what it meant. Kamm was found guilty and sentenced to a minimum of three-and-a-half years in jail.

The second girl told her story at a hearing in April 2007. The first time that Kamm had tried to have sex with her, he had taken her to a hotel in Figtree, but she resisted him. On the drive back to the order's compound, she said, "he was angry and said he was very disappointed in me and that I shouldn't have made him waste his money for nothing". Later, her mother told her it would be okay if she 'went' with Kamm because it was God's will. On one occasion, the girl said, Kamm had put her in a room in a motel, while another queen was put in an interconnecting room. She said that one of the rules of being a queen was that she could never be alone with a man other than Kamm.

In August 2007, a further seven-and-a-half years were added to his sentence. While in prison, he occupied himself making ceramics, fighting for prisoner rights, and being as unrepentant about his crimes as possible. He became eligible for parole in April 2013, but was not released until November 2014. After emerging from Long Bay Jail, he was walking through Sydney's Central Business District, hand in hand with an unnamed female companion, when a reporter approached and asked him if he had reformed. "Reformed?" he replied. "As much as possible."

The Order of St Charbel still exists, and the Little Pebble is still its leader, but under the terms of his parole he must wear an electronic tracking device, and is not allowed to go anywhere near it.

Bill Lilley, the Gatton murderer, or maybe not

GATTON MAN

A classic murder mystery matures like fine wine. As the years go by, theories multiply and the likelihood of revealing a murderer dwindles, unsolved murders acquire a rich patina of myth — the monstrous edifice of speculation erected upon the bare facts of the Jack the Ripper murders being the most obvious example. As the events surrounding a murder are examined, turned around and pulled apart by crime connoisseurs, the line between fact and fiction blurs. At the same time, such murders take on nostalgia value, with the Ripper murders being every bit as evocative of the Victorian era as gaslight, hot toddies and Sherlock Holmes. Indeed, the fictional Holmes and the factual Ripper seem to have swapped places — hundreds of people write hopeful letters to Holmes every year (these letters dutifully answered by the Abbey insurance company, which currently occupies Holmes's Baker Street address), while whatever really happened in Whitechapel in 1888 has long since been eclipsed by innumerable fictions. In 1993, for example, came the news that the diary of Jack the Ripper had been found beneath the floorboards of a Victorian mansion. Jack's real name, it was alleged, was James Maybrick, a man who already occupied space in true crime books by virtue of having been poisoned by his wife. While it took in a few people who should have known better, the diary was soon shown to be a forgery. More recently, in 2014, businessman Russell Edwards published *Naming Jack the Ripper*, in which he claimed to have established (via DNA testing of a blood-stained shawl) that the Ripper was a Polish hairdresser named Aaron Kosminsky. Whenever such claims are made, Ripperologists the world over, each with a pet suspect to defend — the Whitechapel barber, the demented schoolmaster, the member of royalty — all hold their collective breath, knowing full well that a solution for the most intractable mystery can always turn up in an entirely unsuspected manner.

In his 1994 book *Gatton Man*, Merv Lilley served up a similarly unexpected solution to one of Australia's most enduring mysteries — the Gatton murders of 1898. Notorious for its — unusual at the time — sexual savagery, the case possessed several puzzling features which have made it a perfect field for speculation over the years. The basic facts: On Boxing Day, 1898, Michael Murphy (28), his sisters Nora (27) and Ellen (18), set off from their farm in Tent Hill, Queensland, for a dance at the nearby town of Gatton. Arriving and finding that the dance had been cancelled, they immediately turned back, but never made it home. The following morning their brother-in-law, William McNeil, was dispatched from the Murphy farmhouse to search for the trio. Riding along the road to Gatton he came to some sliprails, the entrance to a paddock, and recognised tracks leading into it as belonging to the Murphys' sulky. Almost a kilometre from the sliprails he found the bodies of Michael, Nora and Ellen. Their skulls had been smashed in, and Michael had also been shot. Both sisters, whose hands had been bound behind their backs, had been raped. Their horse had been shot and lay still tethered to the sulky. Curiously, although the condition of the bodies indicated the victims had put up a considerable struggle, the surrounding ground bore no traces of disturbance, no footprints. Indeed, nothing of definite value as evidence was ever found in the paddock.

The discovery of the murders caused a national sensation. The police mounted a huge investigation but made two key errors. Firstly, they failed to seal off the murder scene, which meant that every man and his dog from miles around came to have a gape and trample over the site, obliterating whatever evidence might have been there. Secondly, they focused their initial suspicions on an undoubtedly psychotic American tramp named Richard Burgess who was roaming the area at the time, terrorising the populace. Several witnesses identified Burgess as the heavily built man, dressed in dark clothing with a hat pulled down over his face, seen loitering near the sliprails around the time of the murders. But Burgess's alibi, which put him some 30 miles (50 km) from Gatton on Boxing Day evening, was eventually confirmed.

Among those who had seen the man at the sliprails were a widow named Carroll and her 13-year-old son John. As they were passing him the boy said to his mother, "That is Clarke's man." He was referring to one Thomas Day, a man who had recently arrived in Gatton and found employment with the butcher, Arthur Clarke, carting meat into town. This Day is an enigmatic figure. Aged about 20 at the time, he was taciturn and unsociable, and quickly earned the dislike of Clarke and his wife. He liked reading, and his employer once found him engrossed in *Rienzi*, a historical novel by Bulwer-Lytton — fairly heavy stuff for a butcher's boy. Clarke suspected Day, who was near the scene of the crime on the night, and noting that one of his jumpers was stained with blood, advised him not to wash it as the police would want to question him about it. Day washed it anyway. He was interviewed by the police shortly after the murders but their suspicions were firmly on Burgess at the time, the blood stain was put down to his work, and they let him slip away. He left Gatton a few days later, went to Brisbane where he joined the army, then deserted. Nothing more is known about him, although an unconfirmed report from the 1920s claimed he died in the Boer War.

As time passed and no solutions to the Gatton murders were forthcoming, rumour and speculation moved in to fill the vacuum. It was the 'Dingo Baby' case of its day. Most suspicions centred on the Murphy family, who were alleged to have been strangely complacent about the murders (in fact, their fundamentalist religious beliefs seem to have induced a sense of fatalism in them). There were dark mutterings about incest. Michael

Murphy, it was said, had gone to the paddock to have sex with his sisters, and their father had found this out and killed them. In the more baroque versions of the story, he had cut off the horse's penis and inserted it into one of the girls.

Enter almost a century later Merv Lilley with *Gatton Man*, in which he claims that his father, Bill Lilley, was Thomas Day. The younger Lilley, a former cane-cutter, wharfie and union hard man among other things, was the husband of the writer Dorothy Hewett, who died in 2002 (incidentally, they played a vagrant couple in the terrific, underrated 1972 film of Patrick White's *The Night, The Prowler*). *Gatton Man* is a very odd book, written in an idiosyncratic, sometimes poetic, sometimes incoherent style which the publishers commendably decided not to clean up. It tells the story of Lilley's childhood in rural Queensland, growing up in the shadow of his ghastly father, referred to in the book as 'W.J.', 'the old fella', or with a Godlike, capitalised 'He'. Bill Lilley was a man who reacted violently at the slightest provocation, who spent his life abusing his wife, sons and daughters, who, in his twilight years, raped his six-year-old granddaughter in a paddock. His idea of fun was to castrate the nearest dog.

When Merv Lilley was 21, his father accidentally started a bushfire which he blamed on Merv. It was then that Merv's mother, fearing that Bill Lilley was going to tell the local people this lie, and wishing to give her son some ammunition against his father, told him that Bill Lilley was the Gatton murderer. Merv Lilley never spoke about it with his mother again, and never confronted his father about it.

The evidence that Bill Lilley was Thomas Day and by extension the killer is, it must be said, circumstantial. He could well have been in the area at the time, and his viciousness of character certainly makes him a worthy candidate. The man at the sliprails was seen to walk with a peculiar sideways gait which Bill Lilley also possessed (and his son inherited). He was in South Africa during the Boer War, which ties in with the unconfirmed report. He always slept with his trousers on, which Thomas Day was observed to do. Thin stuff maybe, but Merv Lilley writes with a conviction of his father's guilt which is almost religious. Clearly the violence in his father remains a profound mystery to him. He's spent his life trying to figure it out. Perhaps by fingering his father as one of Australia's most notorious killers, he wishes to get us all involved in the mystery, to share the blame around.

One day, Merv Lilley writes, the signature of Thomas Day may be located in army records and the handwriting compared to his father's. Until such a thing happens, the Gatton murders will remain unsolved. But if Bill Lilley was indeed the killer, this can't have been the end of the story. The Gatton murders were the sort of crescendo of violence that an ambitious murderer spends years building up to. It is inconceivable that a 20-year-old man could have committed them and left it at that. Bill Lilley worked as a travelling salesman, absent from his family for months at a time peddling tea. He had a lot of ground to cover and a lot of time on his hands.

ARTHUR CRAVAN
POETRY AND BOXING

rthur Cravan was my kind of artist. Possibly the only modernist poet ever to enter the ring with a former world heavyweight champion (Jack Johnson in Barcelona, 1916), the explosive Cravan was born Fabian Avenarius Lloyd in Lausanne, Switzerland, on 22 May 1887. He was the son of Otho Holland Lloyd and his wife Clara 'Nelly' Hutchinson, who were British, and the nephew of Oscar Wilde (the latter having married Otho's sister Constance). When Fabian and his brother, also named Otho, were young, their parents divorced and Nelly married a Swiss doctor named Henre Grandjean, after which Fabian did not see his father. He was educated in Switzerland and England, but after being expelled from a boarding school, went roaming around the world. His life during these years presents itself to us now as a series of vivid snapshots: here he is sleeping under London Bridge, carrying four prostitutes on his shoulders in Berlin, riding freight trains and picking oranges in California, chopping wood in the Australian outback.

In 1909, he hit Paris like some sort of living embodiment of a futurist painting. Over six feet tall, muscular and impulsive, he settled in Montparnasse and determined to make a name for himself in two pursuits — poetry and boxing. In the latter, he had some success, even attaining briefly the title of Light Heavyweight Champion of France (although that was because his opponent had failed to show up). He was now going by the name Arthur Cravan. The surname derived from the French village of Cravant, the birthplace of his girlfriend Renée Bouchet, whom he married during his stay in Paris.

The self-styled "poet with the shortest haircut in the world" became a familiar figure in the streets, selling a self-published review of poetry and abuse, *Maintenant* ('Now'), from a push-cart. He plastered the Boulevard San Michel with posters advertising his review, which he wrote entirely himself under a host of pseudonyms, and it was required reading for Paris's artists and literati, whether they approved of it or not. Cravan's energetic, scattergun writing style matched his exploits in the ring. His reason for writing? "To infuriate!" His greatest achievement in this line was his review of the 1912 L'Exposition des Indépendents, which was so ferocious that he was charged with libel and spent eight days in prison, while Guillaume Apollinaire, incensed by Cravan's remarks about a self-portrait by his partner Marie Laurencin (he had basically suggested she looked in need of a good hard shag), challenged him to a duel.

Cravan's drinking buddies included the writer Blaise Cendrars and the artist Robert Delaunay. They liked to go about in outrageous outfits, with dinner jackets half red and half green, and mismatched shoes. Another Cravan fashion statement was a black shirt with holes cut into it which revealed obscene words written on his skin.

Craven mastered the art of public provocations. He gave impressive demonstrations of tango dancing, boasted of having robbed a jewellery store in Switzerland, and gained the admiration of future Dadaists (the word had not yet been coined) like Marcel Duchamp for his spectacularly violent literary lectures, punctuated with pistol shots. He once announced a performance in which he would down a bottle of absinthe, strip to a jockstrap, then kill himself. When a sizeable audience turned up to see this, he abused them roundly for wanting to make death a spectacle. His friend Francis Picabia once remarked, "Cravan never tried to shock others: he tried to shock himself, which is a much harder thing to do."

"I will state once and for all," Cravan wrote, "I will not be civilised."

He published five issues of *Maintenant* between 1911 and 1915. His greatest coup was the article 'Oscar Wilde Lives', which appeared in the third issue in 1913. In this, Cravan recalled the visitor who arrived at his doorstep one rainy night six months earlier. A huge man with white hair and a white beard, he introduced himself as Sebastian Melmoth (a name Wilde used after his release from prison). Cravan recognised his long-lost uncle, who as far as the world knew died in disgrace in 1900, and was overjoyed. ("I wanted to fall on him and clasp his neck, to embrace him like a mistress, give him to eat and to drink, put him to bed, dress him, become his procurer, in short, to draw all my money from the bank and fill his pockets.") Wilde heaved his bulk into an armchair and Cravan was so impressed with his size (just as those who met Cravan were impressed with *his* size) that he was reminded of an elephant, or a hippopotamus. He imagined Wilde "among the riotous green of Africa, amid the music of flies, creating mountains of excrement".

The long-lost relatives proceeded to get drunk together. Cravan told Wilde about *Maintenant* and offered to publish any of his recent writings, or if he wasn't interested in that, send him on a lecture tour, or failing that, put him in a pantomime with chorus girls. Wilde politely ignored these suggestions, and instead wanted to know how Cravan's mother Nelly was. The question produced in Cravan "a bizarre physical effect because, had they not half informed me of my mysterious birth, several times very vaguely intimating that Oscar Wilde might be my father?" After more drinks, Cravan hurled vile abuse at Wilde, who merely laughed. Cravan wanted to go out bar-hopping in Montmartre, but Wilde demurred and slipped out the door. Giving his nephew a final embrace, he asked him to say nothing of their encounter for six months, called him a "terrible boy", then disappeared into the night.

Somehow, rather wonderfully, a few people took this absurd and dreamlike piece to be an example of journalism, and the *New York Times* dispatched its Paris correspondent to

investigate further. On 9 November 2013, it reported that he had been unable to find anyone who had seen Wilde dead, while one of Wilde's friends, Charles Sibleigh, thought Cravan just might be telling the truth. Cravan was said to be offering a $5,000 wager that, should Wilde's tomb be opened, another body would be found in it.

Fearing conscription when the war broke out, Cravan travelled through Europe on false passports, leaving each country as it declared war. He went from Budapest to Belgrade, then to Russia, then via the Black Sea to Constantinople, and on to Athens where he fought a bout with Georges Calafatis, the Greek Olympic boxing champion. After returning to France he swam from Hendaye to Fuenterrabila in Spain, then made his way to Barcelona where he hooked up with other displaced writers and artists like Picabia. It

was here that he cooked up the idea of a bout with Jack Johnson, who had lost his world heavyweight champion title in Cuba the year before. (Cravan had earlier met him in Paris, and been very impressed with his laugh.) The fight, which was well publicised, took place on 23 April 1916. Cravan was roaring drunk when he entered the ring, and Johnson knocked him out in the sixth round.

Cravan used his purse from the fight to buy a ticket on a steamship bound for America. Another passenger was Trotsky, who was impressed enough by him to record their meeting in his autobiography (noting that Cravan preferred "crashing Yankee jaws in a noble sport to letting some German stab him in the midriff"). Arriving in New York in January 1917, the boxing poet was welcomed with open arms by the local avant-garde, who at that time included Marcel Duchamp, Picabia and Man Ray. He created a famous stir with a lecture he gave at the opening of the American Independents' Exhibition. Duchamp and Picabia took him out drinking before it, so he was well oiled by the time he arrived — late — at the venue. Climbing onto the platform where he was to speak about 'The Independent Artists of France and America' to an audience largely composed of society matrons, he keeled over suddenly so that his head hit the table with an almighty crack. Recovering, he began to remove his clothes and shout obscenities before being dragged away by police. "What a wonderful lecture," said Duchamp.

The following day, the modernist artist and poet Mina Loy met Cravan at the home of the art collectors Walter and Louise Arensberg.

Mina had heard about him from some of the former Parisians now in New York, and seen photographs of him in a magazine. This had left her intrigued, but her first impressions of him were unfavourable. He was lethargic and taciturn, and when he did speak it was mostly to utter swear words in French. But on subsequent evenings at the Arensbergs', they could be seen curled up together on a chair, reading the same book.

Cravan had no regular work and no home. He slept in the homes of friends when he could, in a shed above Pennsylvania Station or on a bench in Central Park. Mina eventually took pity on him and invited him back to her tiny apartment, which he seemed to fill entirely. They gradually became close, then inseparable. The Dadaists joked that she had done the impossible and tamed Arthur Cravan.

When America entered the war, Cravan, again afraid of being drafted, left New York and hitchhiked north with a companion. They reached Nova Scotia, but were prevented from sailing to Newfoundland, as they had planned. Instead, they went to Mexico by boat.

In Mexico City, Cravan hooked up with a ragbag community of American draft-dodgers, anarchists, socialists and other ne'er-do-wells known to the locals as 'slackers' (!). He bombarded Mina with letters, saying that he missed her desperately, offering to marry her, begging for a lock of her hair. ("Better yet, come with all of your hair.") She gave in, and travelled by train to Mexico. When

she arrived, Cravan was teaching boxing at a school of physical culture. They were married, and moved into a tiny room in a tenement, but then he was knocked out in the second

round of a bout with a boxer known as the Black Diamond, and lost his job as a result. They survived on the money he could scrape together giving boxing demonstrations, but often went without food. Things got so bad Cravan proposed suicide. "How can we kill ourselves," Mina asked, "when we haven't finished talking to each other?"

When Mina fell pregnant in mid-1918, they realised they had to get out of Mexico, but as usual his papers weren't in order. With Cravan struck down by a stomach ailment, Mina wrote to his mother and stepfather in Switzerland, asking them to send his birth certificate, but received no reply. They travelled to Oaxaca, where Cravan had recovered enough to box again (and apparently won a bout or two), then took a train to the coastal town of Salina Cruz. The plan was for Mina to travel to Buenos Aires on a Japanese hospital ship, while Cravan would follow in a boat. He managed to raise the funds to buy a dilapidated boat, and as he busied himself plugging the hole in its side, she sewed a sail.

There are many different versions of the event which brought Cravan's career to a suitably enigmatic end — his disappearance. In one of them, he was keen to test the boat and set sail into the Gulf of Tehauntepec, with Mina waving goodbye from the pier. But in fact, Mina almost certainly left Santa Cruz before he did. According to her understanding of events, which she outlined in a letter to her family, Cravan had pooled his resources with three companions. He planned to sail

the boat to Puerto Angel, where he would sell it and buy a larger boat. He would then return to Santa Cruz, pick up his companions, and make the longer voyage to Buenos Aires. He set off for Puerto Angel one day in mid-October 1918, a trip which would have taken four days, but there is no evidence he made it there.

Of course there were rumours about the fate of such a larger than life character. Some claimed his corpse was found in the jungle; others said he had gone to live on an island. In the early 1920s, a mysterious figure calling himself 'Dorian Hope' appeared in Paris peddling forged Oscar Wilde manuscripts (very high quality ones, too), and some were convinced it was Cravan. But I find it hard to believe he could have kept a low profile in any city, let alone Paris.

Mina Loy, who gave birth to a girl she named Fabienne in April 1919, spent years searching for Cravan. She never recovered from the loss, and never had a serious relationship again. Asked by a magazine years later what the happiest time of her life had been, she replied, "Every moment I spent with Arthur Cravan."

NOTES AND SOURCES

THE STORY OF DONALD CROWHURST

The definitive account remains *The Strange Voyage of Donald Crowhurst* by Nicholas Tomalin and Ron Hall (Hodder & Stoughton: London, 1970). The authors were *Sunday Times* journalists who reported on the race, and afterwards were able to examine Crowhurst's boat and its contents and speak to all the major players. Their examination and interpretation of the often chaotic writings Crowhurst left behind is little short of brilliant.

Teignmouth Electron by the British artist Tacita Dean (Book Works: London, 1999) is a haunting book of essays and photographs of Crowhurst's trimaran on its final resting place, Cayman Brac in Jamaica. Each year, a little bit more of it disappears.

Deep Water (2006) is a documentary about Crowhurst by Louise Osmond and Jerry Rothwell which makes good use of the film footage he took during his voyage.

ROSALEEN NORTON

Barnes, Dave, 'I am a Witch!', *Australasian Post*, 20 December 1956.

—, 'Confessions of a Witch', *Australasian Post*, 15 June 1967.

Drury, Neville, *Pan's Daughter*, Collins Australia: Sydney, 1988.

—, *The Witch of Kings Cross* (a revised version of *Pan's Daughter*), Kingsclear Books: Sydney, 2002.

—, *Dark Spirits*, Salamander and Sons: Brisbane, 2012.

Kramer, Eileen, *Walkabout Dancer*, Trafford Publishing: Victoria (British Columbia), 2008.

Norton, Rosaleen, *Three Macabre Stories* (edited by Keith Richmond), The Tietan Press: York Beach, 2010.

Salter, David, 'The strange case of Sir Eugene and the witch', *Good Weekend*, 3 July 1999.

'Satanists in Weird King's Cross Ritual', *The Daily Mirror*, 25 September 1955.

'She Hates Figleaf Morality', *People*, 29 March 1950.

Zohar, Atilla (James Holledge), *Kings Cross Black Magic*, Horwitz: Sydney, 1965.

Richard Moir's memoir *Rosaleen Norton* was published in an undated limited edition of 250 copies.

Thanks to Ian Hartley, Wendy Borchers, Tony Moore and Sunil Badami for help with research

HARRY CROSBY

Conover, Anne, *Caresse Crosby*, Capra Press: Santa Barbera, 1989.

Crosby, Caresse, *The Passionate Years*, The Dial Press: New York, 1953.

Wolff, Geoffrey, *Black Sun: the Brief Transit and Violent Eclipse of Harry Crosby*, Hamish Hamilton: London, 1977.

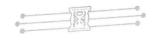

WILLIAM CHIDLEY

Chidley, William, *The Answer, or the World as Joy*, Sydney D. Smith: Sydney, 1915.

—, *The Confessions of William James Chidley* (edited by S. McInerney), University of Queensland Press: St Lucia, 1977.

Hornadge, Bill, *Chidley's Answer to the Sex Problem*, Review Publications: Dubbo, 1971.

No Room for Dreamers by George Hutchinson (Currency Press: Sydney, 1981) is a play about Chidley.

TALES OF THE HOLLOW EARTH

Bernard, Raymond, *The Hollow Earth*, Health Research: Mokelumne Hill, 1963.

Godwin, Joscelyn, *Arctos, the Polar Myth*, Phanes Press: Grand Rapids, 1993.

Kafton-Minkel, Walter, *Subterranean Worlds*, Loompanics Limited: Port Townsend, 1989.

Michel, John, *Eccentric Lives and Peculiar Notions*, Thames & Hudson: London, 1984.

Ossendowski, Ferdinand, *Beasts, Men and Gods*, Cornstalk Publishing: Sydney, 1926.

Smith, Warren, *This Hollow Earth*, Sphere Books: London, 1977.

Can You Speak Venusian? by Patrick Moore (Star Books: London, 1976) has a chapter on the hollow earth. This lovely little book by the late lamented British TV astronomer was my introduction to the subject, and to the wider world of the 'independent thinkers', as Moore called them.

Excerpts from Byrd's 'secret log' were reprinted in *Exposure* magazine, June–July 1996.

Will Storr spoke to Rodney Cluff for his article 'Hollow Earth conspiracy: the hole truth' (the *Guardian*, 13 July 2014). Cluff's website can be found at www.ourhollowearth.com

LESBIAN VAMPIRES

Barber, Paul, *Vampires, Burial and Death*, Yale University Press: New Haven, 1988.

Dresser, Norine, *American Vampires*, Vintage Books: New York, 1990.

Hicks, Ron, *The Vampire Killer*, Bantam: Sydney, 1992.

—, *The Vampire Killer* (second edition), Huon Media Enterprises, 2009.

Morrisey, Belinda, *When Women Kill: Questions of Agency and Subjectivity*, Routledge: London, 2003.

Parnell, Sean, 'Tracey Wigginton, due for

release after 22 years' jail, seriously ill', the *Australian*, 22 December, 2011.

'The little girl who grew into a monster', *New Idea*, 11 May 1991.

Thompson, Tuck, and Brittany Vonow, 'Taxpayers foot bill for lesbian vampire killer Tracey Wigginton', the *Courier Mail*, 14 January 2012.

'Trial told of blood drinking frenzy', *Sydney Morning Herald*, 1 February 1991.

'Vampire killer set out to scare', *Sydney Morning Herald*, 2 February 1991.

'Wife of vampire murder victim harassed', *Sydney Morning Herald*, 8 January 1991.

'Woman gets life term for vampire murder', *Sydney Morning Herald*, 16 February 1991.

THE FAMILY WAY

Campbell, James, 'Payout for The Family sect victims', *Sunday Herald Sun*, 16 August 2009.

Elisa, David, 'Freed… the children a guru kept locked away in the bush', *Sydney Morning Herald*, 17 August 1997.

Gora, Bronwyn, 'Sect child Sarah defeats the demons', *Sunday Telegraph*, 7 May 1995.

Gunn, Michelle, 'Sect children in world of their own', *Sydney Morning Herald*, 1 January 1994.

Haigh, Gideon, 'Child of the Damned', the *Australian*, 29–30 April 1995.

Hamilton-Byrne, Sara, *Unseen, Unheard, Unknown*, Penguin: Melbourne, 1995.

Johnston, Chris, 'Battle for control as cult leader deteriorates', *The Age*, 22 June 2013.

—, 'The Family's "living god" fades to grey, estate remains', *The Age*, 17 May 2014.

Madden, James, 'Child of The Family sect sues its leader', *The Australian*, 26 July 2004.

Moore/Hamilton-Byrne, Dr Sarah, 'Why I see Anne' (blog post), www.drsarahmoore.blogspot.com.au/2009/08/why-i-see-anne-by-dr-sarah.html

Pavoir, Andiee, 'Delivered from Evil', *Who Weekly*, 10 July 1995.

THE NIGHTMARE OF WILLIAM LINDSAY GRESHAM

Books by William Lindsay Gresham:

Nightmare Alley, Rinehart: New York, 1946.

Limbo Tower, Rinehart: New York, 1949.

Monster Midway, Rinehart: New York, 1953.

Houdini: The Man Who Walked Through Walls, Holt: New York, 1959.

The Book of Strength, John Day Company: New York, 1961.

A sample of Gresham's magazine work:

'Deep Lies the Treasure', *Saturday Evening Post*, 16 July 1949.

'Violence is the Job', *Blue Book*, November 1949.

'The Beast Can Think', *Blue Book*, January 1950.

'The Prince of Bindlestiffs', *Blue Book*, December 1950.

'Lost in the Caverns', *Saturday Evening Post*, 10 February 1951.

'No Holds Barred', *Saturday Evening Post*, 10 March 1951.

'Hell Driver', *True*, March 1953.

'The Star Gypsies', *Fantasy and Science Fiction*, June 1953.

'The Dream Dust Factory', *Fantasy and Science Fiction*, December 1953.

'Target: Time', *Fantastic*, June 1954.

'How to Keep from Feeling Tired', *Bluebook*, May 1956.

'Don't Believe a Word She Says', *Ellery Queen's Mystery Magazine*, August 1956.

'Secrets of the Sideshow Supermen', *True*, August, 1956.

'Mad Dog', *Saga*, March 1957.

'King of the Spook Workers', *Argosy*, July, 1957.

'Labor of Hercules', *The Gent*, February 1959.

'Battle of the Petersburg Crater', *Saga*, June 1959.

'Cole Younger', *Saga*, June 1959.

'Von Richtofen, the Last Knight of Battle', *Saga*, September 1959.

'The Passing of the Parlor House', *The Dude* No 7.

'Room for One More', *The Dude*, November 1960.

'The Pirate King of the Caribbean', *Saga*, March 1961.

'Sherman's March to the Sea', *Saga*, April 1961.

'King of the Flying Trapeze', *Saga*, June 1961.

A series of essays Gresham wrote for *Presbyterian Life* in 1950 were the closest he came to an autobiography. They were reprinted as 'From Communism to Christianity' in *They Found the Way* (edited by David Wesley Sloper, The Westminster Press: Philadelphia, 1951).

Dorsett, Lyle, *A Love Observed*, Harold Shaw Publishers: Wheaton, 1998.

Gresham, Douglas, *Lenten Lands*, Collins: London, 1989.

Polidoro, Massimo, 'Blind Alley: The Sad and "Geeky" Life of William Lindsay Gresham', *Skeptical Inquirer*, Vol 27 No 4, July/August 2003.

Sibley, Brian, *Shadowlands*, Hodder & Stoughton: London, 1998.

Wald, Adam M., *Exiles from the Future*, University of North Carolina Press: Chapel Hill, 2002.

Wilson, A.N., *C.S. Lewis: A Biography*, Flamingo: London, 1990.

Wood, Bret, *Introduction to Nightmare Alley*, Centipede Press: Lakewood, 2013.

In 2006, after the original version of this article appeared in *Bizarrism* No 8, I was contacted by the Rev. Perry C. Bramlett from Kentucky. Perry had founded the C. S. Lewis for the Local Church — Interstate Ministries, a travelling ministry based on the life and work of C.S. Lewis. Perry's interest in Lewis and Joy Davidman had led him to Gresham, and since 2004 he had been researching the first full-length biography of him. We began a long correspondence. Perry was incredibly generous with sharing the fruits of his research, sending me copies of obscure articles, some of the letters he had received from people who knew Gresham, and one of Gresham's own letters. I was able to reciprocate by sending him some Gresham pieces he didn't have. In the last email I received from Perry, in June 2012, he said that the biography was almost complete, but he had discovered some unpleasant information about Joy Davidman and her dealings with Gresham and Lewis, and was struggling with the ethics of how, or whether, to publish this.

Revising my Gresham article for this book, I was about to email Perry, but did a Google search first see if anything was happening with his biography. Sadly, this brought up an obituary — Perry had passed away on 29 November 2013, aged 68. It mentioned that he had been writing the Gresham biography, and said it was expected to be published in 2014. I do hope it sees the light of day.

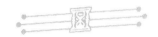

OFF WITH THE MASTERS

Roe, Jill, *Beyond Belief: Theosophy in Australia 1879–1939*, NSW University Press: Kensington, 1986.

Symonds, John, *In the Astral Light*, Panther: London, 1965.

Washington, Peter, *Madame Blavatsky's Baboon*, Secker & Warburg: London, 1993.

Webb, James, *The Occult Underground*, Open Court: Illinois, 1990.

—, *The Occult Establishment*, Open Court: Illinois, 1991.

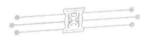

A CONVERSATION WITH MR PONNUSWAMY

'Curry on Campaigning', *People*, 27 March 1990.

Dunne, Stephen, 'Currying Favour, an Interview with Ponnuswamy', *Plexus*, April 1990.

VOUTOROONIE!

'Glad to be Gaillard', *NME*, 21 October 1989.
'The Slim-Slam Man', *Fanfare* No 3, Spring 1980.
'Voutie O Roonie O Scoodiliroosimoe', *NME*, 19 January 1985.

Sleeve notes to the albums *Opera in Vout* (Verve), *McVouty Slim and Bam, Son of McVoutie, The Voutest!* (Hepcat), *Chicken Rhythm* (Storyville).

At the time of writing, the first hour of *Slim Gaillard's Civilisation* is on YouTube.

OF DEROS AND TEROS

Nadis, Fred, *The Man from Mars: Ray Palmer's Amazing Pulp Journey*, Tarcher/Penguin: New York, 2013,

Skinner, Doug, 'Subterranean Wonderworld: The Forgotten Art of Richard Shaver', *The Anomalist: 3*, Winter 1995–66.

Toronto, Richard, *War Over Lemuria: Richard Shaver, Ray Palmer and the Strangest Chapter of 1940s Science Fiction*, McFarland: Jefferson, 2013.

Shaver told the story of Max and the Great Northern Empire Builder in 'The Masked World' which appeared in *The Hidden World*, Summer 1961.

The Shaver Mystery and the Hidden World by Timothy Green Beckley (Health Research: Mokolumne Hill, 1985) reprints a number of important Shaver texts, including one version of his autobiography (from which I have quoted the passages about Nydia).

THE SICK WORLD OF SIGMUND FREUD

Psychoanalysis is one of the most intriguing subjects I've ever researched, and I was lost in the world of Freud for months. Guiding me through the psychoanalytical maze were some terrific books. *Why Freud Was Wrong* by Richard Webster (Fontana Press: London, 1996) remains thoroughly readable and scrupulously fair to Freud throughout its 800+ pages. Also useful were *The Freudian Fallacy* by E.M. Thornton (Paladin: London, 1986) and *The Decline and Fall of the Freudian Empire* by Hans Eysenck (Viking: New York, 1985). *Freudian Fraud* by E. Fuller Torrey (HarperCollins: New York, 1992) looks at the malign influence Freud has had on American culture. For an evocative account of the medical climate surrounding the development of Freud's theories, see *The Birth of Neurosis* by George Frederick Drinka (Simon and Schuster: New York, 1984).

Although I think he's wrong about Freud and the Seduction Theory, Jeffrey Moussaieff Masson's books are well worth reading, particularly *The Assault on Truth* (Farrar Straus Giroux: New York, 1984) and *Final Analysis* (Harper Perennial: New York, 1991). *In the Freud Archives* by Janet Malcolm (Papermac: London, revised edition 1997) is an account of Masson's dust-up with the Freud establishment — and subsequent feud with Malcolm.

The Wolf-Man, 60 Years Later by Karin Obholzer (Continuum: New York, 1982) is a fascinating account of what it was like to be treated by Freud.

Among the works of Freud which I read — and greatly enjoyed, for regardless of anything else he was a very entertaining writer — the most important were his early collaboration with Joseph Breuer, *Studies on Hysteria* (Penguin: Harmondsworth, 1974); *Case Histories II (The Rat Man, Schreber, The Wolf Man, a Case of Female Homosexuality)* (Penguin: London, 1991); *The Psychopathology of Everyday Life* (Penguin: Harmondsworth, 1982); and *The Interpretation of Dreams* (Modern Library: New York, 1950).

After I finished this article, I was intrigued to read (in the December 1997 issue of *Fortean Times*) of a paper written by Dr Michael Richardson demolishing Ernst Haeckel's 'biogenetic law'. Haeckel's drawings of fish, cows, salamanders and human beings, showing how they all start as the same simple shape, still appear in medical textbooks. Richardson compared these drawings with photos of real embryos, and found they look no more alike than do the fully grown versions. His findings were disputed in Germany, where Haeckel is a scientific hero.

FOMENKO!

Gregory, Jason, 'Tarzan to jog the rest of his days', the *Courier Mail*, 24 August 2003.

Macmillan, Sally, 'Alive and well: Our very own Tarzan', the *Sunday Telegraph*, 7 July 1996.

May, David, 'Caught! POST's camera snaps the Mad Russian in his Cairns jungle lair…', *Australasian Post*, 24 February 1990.

Perkins, Kevin, *Bristow: Last of the Hard Men*, Bonmoat: Sydney, 2003.

Robson, Frank, 'The Outsider', *The Good Weekend*, 21 November 1998.

—, 'The Real life Tarzan of Australia's deep north', the *Sun-Herald*, 3 April 2011.

'"Tarzan" Fomenko tells his Story', *The Sun-Herald*, 14 February 1960.

Woodford, Peter, 'After 30 years Tarzan found', the *Sunday Telegraph*, 15 December 1985.

DON'T BUY THIS MAGAZINE!

Tom Brinkmann tells the story of Myron Fass and *Official UFO* in *Bad Mags 2* (Headpress: London, 2009). He also devoted the third issue of his excellent zine *Off the Rack* (Winter 2012/2013) to the illustrious magazine career of Jeff Goodman, which encompassed *Oui*, *High Society*, lots of rock and cinema one-shots and the incredible adult comic *Gasm*.

KELVER HARTLEY

Hartley, Kelver, *Eerie Tales*, Boombana Publications: Mt Nebo, 2001.

—, *The Haunting of Dr McCuaig*, Boombana Publications: Mt Nebo, 1998.

I first read about Hartley in the article 'Millionaire Professor who lived in a $25 room' by Richard Glover in the *Sydney Morning Herald*, 23 October 1989. This has been reprinted in *Kelver Hartley: A Memoir* (The Hartley Bequest Program: Newcastle, 1995).

The Hartley Bequest Program has also published *Kelver Hartley (a life in progress)*, a play by Foveaux Kennedy (Boombana Publications: Mt Nebo, 2004), and *A Toast to Professor Appleton*, two stories about him by a former student, Marion Halligan (Boombana Publications: Mt Nebo, 2007).

THE LIFE AND DEATH OF A LOBSTER BOY

'Gibtown, USA', *Sydney Morning Herald*, 7 January 1995.

Mannix, Daniel P., *Freaks: We Who Are Not As Others*, RE/Search Publications: San Francisco, 1990.

Rosen, Fred, *Lobster Boy*, Pinnacle: New York, 1995.

'Squalid End for the Lobster Boy', *Sydney Morning Herald*, 11 September 1994.

I wondered after I wrote this article whether I'd been too hard on Grady Stiles. Certainly his carny pals always had a good word for him (but then I suppose they would). You'll just have to make up your own mind.

BOVVER!

For background information on National Action and Bovver's role in it, see David Greason's memoir *I Was a Teenage Fascist* (McPhee Gribble: Melbourne, 1994).

'The life and death of a Nazi', *Telegraph Mirror*, 13 October 1992, gives an account of Bovver's childhood.

THE INTERGALACTIC ADVENTURES OF KIRK ALLEN

Elms, Alan C., 'Behind the Jet-Propelled Couch', *New York Review of Science Fiction*, May 2002.

Lindner, Robert, *The Fifty-Minute Hour*, Rinehart: New York, 1955.

Nicholls, Peter, *The Encyclopedia of Science Fiction*, Granada: London, 1981.

TICHBORNE-MANIA!

Annear, Robyn, *The Man Who Lost Himself*, Text: Melbourne, 2002.

McWilliam, Rohan, *The Tichborne Claimant*, Hambledon Continuum: London, 2007.

Roe, Michael, *Kenealy and the Tichborne Cause*, Melbourne University Press: Melbourne, 1974.

Woodruff, Douglas, *The Tichborne Claimant*, Hollis & Carter: London, 1957.

It was Edward Wybergh Docker who argued that the Claimant was the real thing in *Furphies* (Hampton Press: Hampton, 2000).

The quote from the trial regarding Roger Tichborne's education comes from 'The Great Impostor', *Australia's Heritage*, part 45, 1971. This beautifully illustrated partwork was my introduction to many bizarre facets of Australian history. (I was once intrigued to see a TV segment on the Tasmanian mass murderer Martin Bryant, which showed a neat pile of *Australia's Heritage* in a corner of his otherwise almost bare cell.)

The revelation that Darren Tichborne was an imposter (real name Darren Ryan) comes from the blog of anarchist Ian Bone: www.ianbone.wordpress.com/2007/07/31/the-tichborne-claimant-round-2/

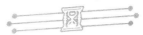

THE JOE MEEK EXPERIENCE

Repsch, John, *The Legendary Joe Meek*, Woodford House: London, 1989.

Anton LaVey's comments on 'Telstar' are from an interview published in *Rolling Stone* in September 1991.

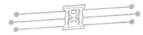

BELLERIVE THE POET

The Book of Bellerive, edited by Douglas Stewart (Jacaranda Press: Brisbane, 1961) is a marvellous collection of Tishler's poetry.

More information on Tishler may be found in *The Passionate Bibliophile: The Story of Walter Stone* by Jean Stone (Angus & Robertson: Sydney, 1988).

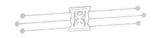

THE WONDERFUL WORLD OF MORMONS

Burrell, Maurice C., *Wide of the Truth*, Marshall, Morgan & Scott: London, 1972.

Earley, Pete, *Prophet of Death*, Avon: New York, 1993.

Hoekema, A.A., *The Four Major Cults*, Paternoster Press: Exeter, 1963.

Naifech, Steven, and Gregory White Smith, *The Mormon Murders*, Onyx: New York, 1998.

Sasse, Cynthia Salter and Peggy Murphy Wilder, *The Kirtland Massacre*, Zebra: New York, 1991.

Tucker, Ruth A., *Another Gospel*, Zondervan: Grand Rapids, 1989.

Weyerman, Deborah, *Answer Them Nothing: Bringing Down the Polygamous Empire of Warren Jeffs*, Chicago Review Press, 2011.

A CONVERSATION WITH SIR WAYNE

Slessor, Kenneth and Robert Walker, *Life at The Cross*, Rigby: Sydney, 1965.

Thorpe, Billy, *Sex and Thugs and Rock'n'Roll*, Macmillan: Sydney, 1996.

The Pink Pussycat by former stripper Lee Meredith (Gold Star Publications: Sydney, 1972) is a rather good little potboiler.

Interview with Sir Wayne Martin conducted on 28 March 1997.

MARY'S VOICEBOX

Boreham, Susan and Rosa Maiolo, 'Prophet & Loss', *Sydney Morning Herald*, 24 December 1993.

Carty, Lisa, 'The man who says he'll be the next pope denies nine sex charges', *Illawarra Mercury*, 3 September 2002.

—, 'Order of Saint Charbel Little Pebble sex charges', *Illawarra Mercury*, 2 April 2003.

Coffey, Michell, 'Sect Probe', *Herald Sun*, 9 July 1997.

Cornford, Philip, 'A man of visions', *Sydney Morning Herald*, 22–23 June 2002.

'Cult leader gets extra four years', *Sydney Morning Herald*, 24 August 2007.

Field, Alec, 'Virgin Mary's Mouthpiece', *Sunday Telegraph*, 16 December 1984.

Harris, Sarah, 'A vision not so splendid', *Sunday Telegraph*, 17 August 1997.

King, David, 'Little Pebble guilty of abusing girl', the *Australian*, 9–10 July 2005.

Lamont, Leonie, 'Little Pebble in court on sex assault charges', *Sydney Morning Herald*, 15 June 2005.

Oram, James, 'Apocalypse Now, says the Pebble', *Sunday Telegraph*, 5 April 1986.

Shadbolt, Peter, 'Cult leader denies sex with

teens', the *Australian*, 7–8 August 2004.
Smethurst, Sue, 'Young mum seduced by
bizarre cult', *New Idea*, 13 May 2000.
'The Little Pebble in big trouble after police raid
sect farm', *Illawarra Mercury*, 9 August 2002.

The only book about the Little Pebble is
Graeme Webber's *A Wolf Among the Sheep*
(Keystone Press: Tomerong, 2008). Webber
was a journalist who reported on the Pebble,
and decided to investigate further. He had
the cooperation of many former followers of
the Pebble, and quotes from a wide range of
documents, including Kamm's barely literate
and extremely incriminating letters to his
'queens' and 'princesses'.

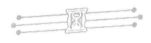

GATTON MAN

Barrowclough, Nikki, 'The Killing of a
Mystery', *Good Weekend*, 29 October 1994.
Gibney, James and Desmond, *The Gatton
Mystery*, Angus & Robertson: Sydney, 1977.
Lilley, Merv, *Gatton Man*, McPhee Gribble:
Ringwood, 1994.

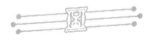

ARTHUR CRAVAN

Arthur Cravan: Poète et Boxeur, Galerie 1900
2000: Paris, 1992.
Burke, Carolyn, *Becoming Modern: The Life of
Mina Loy*, Farrar, Strauss and Giroux: New
York 1996.
Nicholl, Charles, *Traces Remain*, Allen Lane:
London, 2011.
Rosemont, Franklin, 'All Things, All Men
and All Animals', in *Free Spirits: Annals of
the Insurgent Imagination*, City Lights: San
Francisco, 1982.
Watson, Steven, *Strange Bedfellows: The First
American Avante-Garde*, Abbeville Press:
New York, 1991.

4 Dada Suicides (Atlas: London, 1995)
reprints a nice selection of Cravan's works,
including 'Oscar Wilde Lives!'. Most of
Cravan's literary works remain frustratingly
untranslated into English, and there is as yet
no complete translation of *Maintenant*.

Cravan vs. Cravan (2002) is a superb
documentary by the Spanish filmmaker Isaki
Lacuesta. It chronicles an investigation into
the poet-boxer's life by a writer-boxer, Frank
Nicotra. It's a mine of information about
Cravan which is otherwise undocumented (in
English language sources at least), and features
all the remaining film footage of Cravan,
including him training in the run-up to the
Jack Johnson fight. It's available on DVD with
English subtitles, and I advise you to order it
right now.

A HEADPRESS BOOK
First published by Headpress in 2016

[email] headoffice@headpress.com
[web] www.worldheadpress.com

BIZARRISM VOLUME 1
The Revised and Expanded Edition

Text copyright © Chris Mikul
Illustrations © Glenn Smith
This volume copyright © Headpress 2016
Cover design & book layout: Mark Critchell <mark.critchell@googlemail.com>
Archive images are from the collection of the author.
Headpress diaspora: David Kerekes, Thomas McGrath, Caleb, David, Giuseppe

The moral rights of the author have been asserted.

A CIP catalogue record for this book is available from the British Library

978-1-909394-32-2   ISBN PAPERBACK
978-1-909394-33-9   ISBN EBOOK
NO-ISBN HARDBACK

WWW.WORLDHEADPRESS.COM
the gospel according to unpopular culture
Special editions of this and other books are available exclusively from Headpress

CPSIA information can be obtained
at www.ICGtesting.com
Printed in the USA
FSOW02n0230271116
27746FS